Dr Max Skittle is a practising GP.
We can't tell you any more
than that . . .

THE SECRET DOCTOR

What really goes on inside your GP's surgery

Dr Max Skittle

First published in the UK by 535
An imprint of Bonnier Books UK
4th Floor, Victoria House
Bloomsbury Square
London
WC1B 4DA
Owned by Bonnier Books
Sveavägen 56, Stockholm, Sweden

facebook.com/blinkpublishing
twitter.com/blinkpublishing

Hardback – 978–1–788703–30–7
Paperback – 978–1–788704–52–6
Ebook – 978–1–788703–31–4

A CIP catalogue of this book is available from the British Library.

Printed and bound by Clays Ltd, Elcograf S.p.A

1 3 5 7 9 10 8 6 4 2

First published as *The Secret GP*, by 535 in hardback in 2020.
This edition published as *The Secret Doctor*, by Blink Publishing in paperback in 2021.

Blink Publishing is an imprint of Bonnier Books UK
www.bonnierbooks.co.uk

For my family

And to everyone sitting in a waiting room:
Sorry, we're probably running late . . .

Prologue
What Exactly is a GP?

A General Practitioner (GP) is a medical doctor who treats acute and chronic illness, and provides preventative care and health education to patients.

A bit on the dry side, Wikipedia, but yeah, alright. Still, let's add a little more sauce to the job, shall we? Here's what I think . . .

Being a GP is about compressing life into ten minutes. Six hundred seconds. You've got to be prepared to manage the physical, mental, social, and spiritual health of the person sitting in front of you in all its glorious, confusing, and terrifying totality. Cradle to grave. No room for error. It's about looking through the window of that person's life and trying to make it better somehow. To make it healthier. Happier. Longer. Embedded within a community, the job asks you to be detective, mediator, doctor, and counsellor, unearthing why that person feels the way they do. Yet the surprising thing about such a life – *my life* – as a GP is that the hardest part is everything *in-between* the medicine. It's the anger, the sadness, the frustration, the love, the joy, the tragedy, the fear, the compassion, the hate, and the loss. You go on a journey with that patient. Life in ten minutes. *Tick. Tock.* And yet, strange as it may sound, sometimes they don't even realise you're there, like some tacit travelling companion. Hidden away in a pathology result processed. A phone call to a specialist. A clinical letter read and filed. Names without faces. And then, at the end of every day, you go home, having collected up the emotions and concerns of society, and try to live your own life. Unencumbered.

Unsurprisingly, this means learning to compartmentalise the job from your own life is a mandatory requirement. One that is, in reality, always out of reach. You have the privilege to see the light and dark of life. And all those endless shades in-between. Which is where *life really happens.* Where the stories are told. Like a chameleon, it's about always adapting to that person in front of you. Working out how to meet their needs. Their wants. Their expectations. And when they leave, you then have to work to digest the truth that it's you who has ultimate responsibility. You manage their risk: your diagnosis, your decision, your treatment. Get it wrong, and they suffer. Not you. Plus, you'll probably get sued. Yet with all this omnipotent worry and stress for company, my life as a GP is fundamentally, truly, and resoundingly, fucking brilliant. It's why I chose to be a GP. For the people. To help. And I wouldn't dream of doing any other job.

This book is about why. This is my story.

Introduction

Monday, 4th June 2018

My name is Max Skittle and I'm a 32-year-old GP. It's 7:45am on a Monday morning in June 2018 and this, as it so happens, is the perfect day to start the story of my life as a GP. Right now, I'm sitting at my desk in the inner-city GP surgery where I've worked since qualifying as a GP three years ago, so you're joining me at what is the relatively fresh and exciting early stage of my career. Yet right now that's by the by – as all I can do is stare. Stare down at my violated crotch, not quite believing my appalling luck.

Stained crusted white this morning, courtesy of what at the time seemed like an innocent spoonful of whole-fat Greek yoghurt. With five woefully insufficient minutes before my clinic's due to start, I make a tragic decision to pat down the area with tap water. Four minutes until clinic starts . . . Now I look like I've got something wholly incriminating on my trousers – and tried to hide the evidence – or I've simply pissed myself. Life's pendulum swings. Deliberating, I try to refocus. It will be a good day today. It *must* be a good day – I'm definitely due one after all. A rational thought until my eyes absorb this morning's clinic list. Between the unrecognised names are some well-known regulars. A few of them I'm looking forward to seeing. Others . . . well, less so. I stare into nothing.

Three minutes until clinic starts . . . My trousers still aren't dry. Sadly, like some uninvited yin to its yang,

I notice the pot plant my wife, Alice, got me for my clinic room *is* though. Not an altogether positive message to my punters: here's your doctor, he can't keep a £5.99 supermarket pot plant alive, but he'll have a crack at you. Leaning back in my broken three-and-a-half-wheeled chair, I swivel unevenly around, taking in three deep breaths before bringing myself level again. I straighten the keyboard and align my pen parallel to it. One minute before clinic starts . . . I hover the mouse arrow over the bell icon, ready to call in my first patient.

Still damp, I smile. My heart beats a little faster. I love it, I really do. I love this job and wouldn't, despite my daily moans, want to do anything else. Which is precisely why I've written this book.

Think of it as an angry and confused extension of that love.

So, yes, welcome. This is my book about life. To be precise, I'll be throwing out a clinical dragnet to compile some of the messiest, most bewildering, most humbling, and funniest stories of the lives that cross the threshold of my GP consulting room over the next year or so. All the patients, and the stories that come from my encounters with them, will be genuine. And, I'd be surprised if any Hollywood effects will be needed to sex them up. The rich texture of life – *of our lives* – assures me this won't be necessary. Naturally, all the names, dates, ages, ethnicities, even genders, will be changed. That way you can only giggle, cry, jaw-drop or frown at them as you read this book rather than in person. The latter, we can all agree, would be more than just a little playground cruelty. Oh, and if you think I've written about you, respectfully, you're mistaken. If the facts do happen to align with you, it's merely coincidence. Trust me on that. Any and all identifying features have been changed or removed. I say that confidently as, despite writing this book, patient confidentiality is a principle that I don't fuck around with. Plus, I don't want to get fired. Or struck off by the General Medical Council (GMC). My wife would unquestionably kill me (very slowly, I expect). Especially as we've a baby on the way.

*

The first thing to know about me as a GP is that I'm human too. I don't mean that on some New Age, hemp-loving, hessian-wearing, sentimental level. I simply mean that I'm not some giant absorbable sponge, sitting in clinic day after day, here simply to soak up all the spectral outpourings of emotion that patients unload. Instead, just like you, I judge, I dislike, I disapprove, and I anger. And yes, on the flip side, I laugh, I cry, I smile, and I like. And because I'm human like you, there are times when it's bloody hard (impossible even) as a GP to stay being a nice person. Because being a GP is difficult. Being anything in the NHS is difficult, tiredness and overworking bringing out any human's worst side. Myself very much included. Which is why I'm dropping an early spoiler alert: There is absolutely no doubt that this job has changed me as a person. It's pushed what was a moderately dark sense of humour even darker. Pitch black at times. And it's pushed what was a reservedly crude sense of humour into being now overtly crude. All of which I suspect after three years in the job are competing coping mechanisms and collateral damage in equal measure, as I try to do the best job I can for the person in front of me – while staying sane. And I really am trying to achieve both.

Long story short, I'm issuing a pre-emptive apology to you all (and well, yes, sorry, Mum, for all the swearing) as I know I won't be everyone's cup of tea and may offend at times in this book. But look, it's just how I cope. We all have our ways, don't we? And with this in mind, no matter the mental armour I think I may have, I still get up each day knowing the daily fight that lies ahead of me to keep these emotions in professional check. The veneer of professionalism isn't scratch-proof after all. I'm no baking tin. Last week was a prime example. There was a day I wanted to cry at what I'd heard. A day I wanted to physically harm someone once I learned from the family social worker what they'd done to their own child. A day when I felt such unfiltered joy that I embraced someone in cancer remission. And a day when I wanted to quit this job, there and then, as I drowned in the annually increasing unparalleled demand. This is the unpredictable and discerningly addictive ebb and flow of my clinics. Of life as a GP. *My life.* Every single day without fail.

Now I want to tell you a secret. When a GP tells you they don't mind if you tell them your fourth and, you really do promise this time, last problem, they are totally fucking lying to your face. You are in fact wreaking carnage on the rest of their day, ending hopes and dreams of ever chewing their lunch sitting down or going to the toilet without making it into a time trial event. Who, *just* you? No, that would be a little dramatic for even the most emotionally delicate of GPs. But, when half a clinic of patients does this (and they do), that is what happens. Yet still they warmly open their arms wide at the prospect of receiving this fourth problem. Why? Because they're sitting in front of you, telling you as their unanonymised *selves.* Transparent? Honest? Come on. No, their punches are being pulled. Their true feelings about the situation sugar-coated. And this key fact, this truth, brings me to what I want to tell you next: my name isn't Max Skittle. My name is completely irrelevant. What *is* relevant is that I speak to you from this book with a full, visceral, unfiltered, and brutal honesty. Something I intend to do. And while we're at it, just to throw a cat amongst the pigeons, what makes you think I'm even male? Short for Max*ine* perhaps . . .

Before we dive deeper into the world of being a doctor in general practice, I thought it might be useful to briefly paint a picture of me outside of work. I'm six foot three inches. Good-looking. Funny (but you'll know that already). Body of a Greek God. Well, all in the next life, perhaps. The reality is that I reach just about five foot ten on a warm day (in thick-soled trainers) and last saw the inside of a gym at school. Somehow, despite this, there is Alice, my kind, funny, beautiful, feisty (she's a redhead, obviously), and intelligent wife. We met through university friends, rescuing me from a life of online dating and misunderstood inappropriate emoji use. Together, we've lived in the same poky flat in the heart of a busy and unrelentingly noisy city for the last four years. Our home also serves as her office, where she works as a rather in-demand freelance graphic designer. To me, she is nothing short of amazing for letting me be her husband and I love her as much – if not more – than I did the day we married six years ago. She keeps me in check, being the only one who can successfully get through to me when I'm being a dick. Which is often. And she's twenty-seven weeks pregnant. Growing a bump – *our bump*.

Parenthood looms. What an emotional melting pot that one is. Like many couples and individuals, this wasn't an easy journey for us. Alice and I have trodden some dark days, weeks, and months before this point. And yes, although we could have done without the traumas, it sealed our love and commitment to each other in a way that words on this page will never do justice. Every day, I wake up appreciating just how lucky I am. No apologies for the gush here: fact is fact, I don't want for more. Though if England were to win the Rugby World Cup a few more times in my lifetime, that'd be very much welcomed – unlike your fourth patient problem. And although I may think (and want) my personal life to be unmistakably distinct from my working life, I'm sure, like yours, that's just not the truth of it. In fact, Alice and the bump have a huge influence on what sort of GP my patients meet. If the bump, for example, has spent the night being a total dick, keeping Alice up (and therefore me, in some macabre, unenthused form of nocturnal marital moral support), with backache and a bladder squashed to the size of an immature chickpea, I'll be short and sharp with my patients. Yes, I'm blaming an unborn human. I never said I was an angel. And, for what it's worth, I regret it immediately when I realise I've done it. If, on the other hand, Alice and I have spent the day before painting the nursery for the bump, daydreaming about the adventures ahead, then I'll be on cloud nine – and may even listen to your fifth problem then. Family . . . Both armour and Achilles heel. Work and life as one.

Right, I want to talk to you about windows. The bread and butter of it all, they are what being a GP is principally about. And it's what makes working as a doctor in general practice one of the best jobs in the world. You see, every time a patient comes to see me, they're holding up a window into their lives. I then have the responsibility, and the privilege, to peer into it and help make it better. No other profession holds on to such total, encompassing, and lifelong views. Yet these windows aren't all the same. They come in four distinctly different styles. The most common is your clean, crisp, clear window, through which you as the patient point to something for me to look at. For example, your painful knee which you twisted while running. Easy. The second is less clear: it's your grubby window. Here, you want me to help you with something that neither of us can immediately see the cause of. Take a symptom such as feeling tired all of the time. We both need to squint and strain through the gaps in the dirt on your window, perhaps throw some spit and give it a rub using our shirtsleeves so we can help clear the view together. Only then can we look into your life and work out what might be causing your tiredness. Your third type of window is the one you hold up to show me something over *there* (your agenda). In fact, I'm more interested in what's over *here* (my agenda). This might come, for example, from a routine NHS health check which shows you have chronically high blood sugar levels. You wanted the blood test as you were worried about your cholesterol level – and you weren't expecting me to now have my nose pressed to your window, snooping around to find out how on earth you've ended with a blood test result suggesting you're at high risk of developing type 2 diabetes mellitus. An important discovery since my job's not just about diagnosing, it's about helping to prevent disease too. Finally, there's your fourth window. This is the one that someone else holds up for you. Often, it's because they're worried about something in your life. An all-too-familiar example is concern over an ageing parent's memory, or their inability to cope day-to-day due to increasing frailty. All fascinating windows to be shown. And that's why, whatever the window held up in front of me, I'll always see it as a privilege to be entrusted with the responsibility to help you. Deep . . .

While looking through all your windows is great, the reality is that my ability to do this is rapidly changing. This is thanks to the seismic political, economic, and structural changes reverberating throughout the National Health Service (NHS) – and into general practice. Well, I say *changes.* Actually, I mean it's being gagged, beaten, and tossed into an abandoned, flooded quarry. NHS GP surgeries, including the one I work for, are buckling under the strain of a demand for services far outstripping our ability to supply them. And that's the same if it's the little rural surgery looking after 1,500 patients or the large city surgery (or group of surgeries) looking after 60,000-plus patients. Waiting times for appointments are growing unacceptably long, patient dissatisfaction is now an expectant part of my day, and herds of seasoned and skilled GPs are quitting early, citing stress and burnout. In my three years since qualifying as a GP, I've seen all of this grow painfully louder. And while the newspapers may opt to vilify those GPs who leave, I in fact congratulate them all for lasting as long as they bloody well have. They did their time. Rest easy now, comrades.

We know full well that it's all too simple and painless to judge someone until you've walked their walk and worn their shoes. I trust I'm still early (and naive) enough in my career to go home each day to Alice and the bump and leave the stress that comes from hoping you haven't missed *that* cancer at the door. In thirty years, maybe my perspective will have changed. Evolved, having grown tired and weathered with age, I'll be the one waiting for my P45 and nursing a bottle of Scotch. Being a responsible party for another person's health is both a privilege and a curse. To see a patient get better, that's the best drug in the world. You just don't ever want to be on the losing side – breaking that trust a patient puts in you – by getting it wrong.

That, I hope, serves as a quick snapshot of me as a person, why I love this job, and how those in control of the NHS are spoiling the party for us all, patients and healthcare staff alike. To finish, I thought it might be handy to shed some light on my thought processes when you, as the patient, walk into my GP consulting room. That way, as you move through this book, you'll have a sense of how easy or hard that may be. Before this though, let's take a look at how a week looks at my GP surgery. A typical day runs from 8:15am until 6:15pm. I say 'typical' but the truth is that I'm in work earlier and leaving later, trying to keep on top of all the work generated from patient consultations. Full-on *Titanic* mode these days.

The bird's-eye view of my typical day is this: I've one morning clinic lasting about four hours and an afternoon clinic lasting another four hours. In between these clinics (and why you can almost never get an appointment over lunchtime) there's time allocated for me to attend at least one emergency home visit, a few trees' worth of clinical letters to read from medical specialists, community teams, and social workers; phone calls to make, and blood test results to check (along with all the other pathology results like vaginal swabs, skin scrapings, and ultrasound scans), which may or may not require me to call the patient to discuss if abnormal. Yet, to be honest, most results end up getting checked at the end of the day after 6:15pm, as I'll usually be running late – like every other GP in the world.

A clinic typically consists of around twenty ten-minute face-to-face appointments and five seven-minute phone call appointments. Each day, that's roughly forty patients seen, ten patients called and one patient visited. Conservatively. So, in a four-day-clinic week (more about that fifth day later), I see one hundred and sixty patients, call forty, and visit four. That's of course unless it's the walk-in clinic day (where you don't need an appointment to be seen, you can just turn up and wait), which runs once a week. In this case, a million people turn up and fuck up my day entirely by sheer volume alone. Still, I don't blame them – it can be a nightmare trying to get an appointment with a GP – making the walk-in is a sure-fire route to one. And if any of you are very sharp on the maths, you'll work out that yes, I do only work a four-day week as a GP – five consecutive days of seeing patients is simply too much to take on. It's important to know too that all GPs will work different hours. This ranges from some working one day a week up to the very rare few working five days a week. Many supplement their income with other work (bulking it up to a five-day working week, I guess), such as working for primary care governance groups who help develop healthcare services in the local area. Basically, few GPs will sit seeing patients five days a week. Trust me, that would be a killer not only for the GP but equally not great for the patient, seeing an exhausted and burnt-out GP. Everyone deserves a sharp, focused GP.

Now, the consultation. It all kicks off when I press the call bell and draw an expectant breath. It's also when the ten-minute hypothetical timer begins. This presents the first challenge: to get the patient into the bloody room. Something that can take up five minutes in itself. From the eldery or injured on crutches, to the wheelchairs, to the twin prams with terrible steering, to those who simply don't see or hear their name come up in the waiting room because they're engrossed on their phone. I meet them in my room and introduce myself as Max Skittle – though never Dr Skittle – all far too formal a title for me (and personally, I think it sets an unnecessary hierarchy between me and the patient). Once in, I take a focused history (what's the problem today?) and review their clinical notes on the computer system to see what their past medical problems are, what drugs they're taking, and so on.

Next, I'll examine them, take their observations if needed (including heart rate, blood pressure, temperature, respiratory rate, and blood oxygen levels), try to make a diagnosis, a management plan that they don't hate, type up the notes to a standard that will make sense to anyone else who reads them, and then – because it gets me out of the chair – show them to my door, gently pushing them out like a model boat onto a millpond (with a gale force nine wind behind it). And exhale . . .

While the automatic, subconscious part of my brain guides me through these steps, the conscious part aims to decide what the investigations, treatment, and follow-up should be – all by the third minute of the consultation. Translated, at that point I've ideally worked out how to get the patient out of my room on time and not die in the process (or be closer to death). I now have seven minutes to make that dream a reality. Of course, as I expect you'll see throughout this book, reality always spices up this challenge once you factor in your psychotic patients, your five-issue patients, your non-English-speaking patients, or – my personal favourite – the patient who can't even find your room. All within ten minutes, back-to-back.

What's not to love?

That's enough explanation for now. Let's kick this Monday off, shall we? *Click! Ding!* Trousers still damp, I rise to meet the first patient of the day . . .

Hello there, I'm Max Skittle. How can I help?

JUNE 2018

Monday, 4th June

I must confess I'd never actually heard of a butt truncheon. Yet thanks to Leigh's enthusiastically vibrant description of his nocturnal adventures the night before with new Grindr pal, Steven, a mental image soon took shape. Quite a start to the week. It was only 8:30am and any thoughts of a quick mid-morning poo were soon put on hold as my anus tightened. Typing into Leigh's clinical notes, I worked hard to appear deep in diagnostic thought about his concerns today – whether a vigorous butt-truncheoning could burst his bowel – all while I struggled to work out if truncheon was spelled ending *–eon* or *–un* (it's good to be accurate in clinical notes as you never know when that lawsuit is coming). Naturally, it felt inappropriate to ask Leigh, though I was convinced that he must know – he'd ordered one after all. Punting for *–eon*, I addressed his question: hypothetically, yes, of course it could. I mean, any foreign body up your arse has the potential to rip through your strong but thin 2mm bowel wall. Then again, since Leigh's only symptom today was indigestion, I had serious doubts that the truncheon would have travelled the thirty feet of his gastrointestinal tract, from anus to the neck of his stomach, to cause this – no matter how enthusiastic Steven might be. I watched the worry lift from his face as I explained this (especially given the lack of any other symptoms and normal examination). I can't help but be impressed by his total lack of embarrassment. Good for him. Life's for living. Usually I'd wrap up this kind of consultation with a sketch of the gastrointestinal tract to illustrate my points but since I wasn't sure how to draw a butt truncheon without it looking like some kind of Viking weaponry, I decided against this and saved face from my total lack of worldly knowledge.

Tuesday, 5th June

I knew the duty doctor had totally fucked me over as I stood inside Anton's ground-floor flat. 'Just a quick home visit,' they said. Like hell it is. Home visits, by the way, are typically for elderly housebound patients who can't get into the GP surgery for their health issue. Today, though, Anton needed a visit to check on him since our community mental health team couldn't get hold of him. Well, I had. He'd let me in – and now he didn't want to let me out. He said he was protecting me. As I stood there, I couldn't help but think, *seatbelts protect me, mate, not you.* To make matters worse, he was big, like tank-big, largely thanks to his cocktail of antipsychotics (which clearly weren't working right now) and the tsunami of empty takeaway boxes that I was now standing in. My new shirtless friend, Anton, was sadly experiencing an acute psychotic episode.

As I stood there, a) wondering if a butt truncheon would have been handy (as a weapon, mind you) in this particular escalating scenario, and b) trying to digest *what* he was protecting me from – the three Orcs (yep, the big ugly fuckers from *Lord of the Rings*) waiting for him outside to kill us – I couldn't help but wonder how the hell he could afford an 82-inch smart TV. Plus, why on earth is every patient I ever visit at lunchtime watching *Loose Women*? As Anton tells me how impressed he is that I even managed to get past the Orcs in the first place (I find myself giving a modest nod of acknowledgement to this praise), I see it as my window of opportunity to get him onside.

After twenty minutes of negotiation and explanation that he's not well, that the Orcs are not real despite what his mind's telling him, and that he needs more support (all while trying not to be distracted by the debate of the day on *Loose Women*), Anton agrees to let me call the community mental health rapid response team in to help him. They're coming today. The mood lightens. I no longer feel as though I'm about to become a hostage to Anton and his terrible TV choices. Plus, I really need lunch. Finally, Anton steps to one side and the door – and sunlight – dazzle into view. Leaving, I'm enveloped by a bear hug from the man-mountain as he thanks me for listening and believing in him. As the air leaves my lungs with the squeeze and my mouth fills with sweaty chest hair, I realise that everyone just wants a little love, don't they?

Thursday, 7th June

After my near-death experience with Anton I'm relieved to find that I don't have a home visit today. Home visits often make or break my day. Get one and lunch becomes an exercise in partially chewed food and caffeine inhalation timed in-between afternoon calls so that the final swallow comes the breath before *'Hello, it's Max Skittle calling'*. No home visit, and I can sit down (even wash my hands) and eat lunch like an actual human being, all while recharging my batteries for the afternoon clinic.

An aside, how I've actually come to *gain* weight over the last three years – since I rarely get to eat lunch – is beyond me. When I first started out as a GP, I didn't actually need this *recharge* – I was an excited puppy, nipping at the heels of patients, desperate to get them into my consultation room and fix them. Yet here we are, a paltry three years in, with my proverbial tyres already showing a little wear. Now, given that Mrs Tally was first on my call list today, I need this break. Stuff of nightmares doesn't begin to describe her. At seventy-three years old and housebound, she's managed to rotate through more care agencies than cats have lives in as little as two years. There are literally none now who will work with her. A feat that would deserve a medal of recognition if it wasn't so bloody annoying. I mean, it takes serious skill to be able to do that since these hardworking, underpaid, and (very often) underappreciated carers typically can tolerate a lot of abuse. Mrs Tally, however, has a unique blend of overt condescension, patronisation, and ignorance that allows her to be fully blinded to her ways. For instance, phone call appointments are meant to be seven minutes long. I've never got Mrs Tally below fifteen minutes. I dream of having the spine to just hang up on her one day but deep down, I'm a soft touch and it'll never happen.

Today's call goes the same way as all her weekly calls to me: the carers are totally incompetent and none of them speak English properly. During these calls I can usually reply to a few emails as ultimately, I'm her GP, not her social worker. She has one of those. In fact, she's had a lot of those – they all quit her case after a while. Like Everest before Hillary and Tenzing, she's inconquerable. I end the call the same way

I always do, asking if there are any actual medical problems (there never are, today is no different), before telling her to keep going and to hang in there (which she always giggles at). Then I email the social worker (as I *always* do) to let her know Mrs Tally *still* isn't happy with the care and can they look into it.

My work here is done.

Friday, 8th June

I've an enormous Friday feeling. It's 1pm and I'm on a half-day today. One last patient to see and then I'm back home to Alice and the bump. I truly am motoring. Clinical paperwork, done. Emails, read (and selectively ignored). Blood results, checked and actioned. I look at my jobs list and even that's clear. In this moment, I feel like a capable GP. I close my eyes and hold on to it all for a few golden seconds, packing it away safely in my memory bank for a rainy day.

With the wind in my clinical sails, I greet Duncan, a nasally well-endowed 23-year-old. As he places a matchbox next to my keyboard, a small alarm bell rings (a sort of evolved GP Spider-Man sense of the Peter Parker variety) that this is a bit weird. From then on it all happens in slow motion. I sit there, listening to Duncan, but already mentally checking out and on my way home to watch *Love Island* on catch-up with Alice, as he tells me he thinks he's got bed bugs, but wasn't sure. I nod – again in slow motion – still listening, but not quite putting together the shit-storm coalescing in front of my eyes. Before my brain catches up with Duncan's explanation of how, since he wasn't sure, he thought he'd bring one in that he caught, he slides open the matchbox. If

I inhaled any faster, the now-liberated bed bug would've been up my nose in a heartbeat.

Despite every fibre of my being wanting to tell Duncan he's a fucking idiot, I shut the box, quickly print out a patient information leaflet on bed bug eradication and delicately instruct him to burn the box and its contents and never to bring a suspected bed bug into my clinic room again. Ever. I think I've hurt his feelings so I finish off by commending him for catching the little bugger. I'm in two minds whether to tell Alice when I get home – may find myself sleeping in the spare room . . .

Saturday, 9th June

Woke up itching (not in the spare room). Thanks, Duncan!

Monday, 11th June

The week was always going to start well. I knew that ever since the email flew into my inbox last Tuesday, telling us all practice staff had a mandatory Basic Life Support (BLS, for short) training afternoon today. GP surgeries all run these types of training courses for staff throughout the year and they're a great way to help us bond as a team (key for a slick patient journey in the surgery) while brushing up on skills or learning new ones.

As I settled into the cornermost secluded chair, with the rest of my GP surgery team including the three nurses, one pharmacist, ten doctors, six reception staff, one practice manager, and four administrators (all definitely needed to look after our 14,000 registered patients), I prepared myself for a chilled three-hour refresher. Unfortunately, Kev, our BLS instructor, then pitched up. Legs about four feet apart (clearly to allow room for his subjectively massive balls), arms crossed, with *Always Faithful* tattooed in large italics on his musclebound forearm, he stamped his size-13 military-grade hiking boots to get our attention. Red flag right there. We're in the city, a flat one at that. Hiking boots aren't a requirement. Now, I don't want to sound ungrateful. This bloke is clearly doing a really great job and we should all be able to perform BLS on a family member, friend, or a stranger if push comes to shove (it really does save lives). I was, however, totally blinded by the fact that this guy thinks he's turned up to a dick-measuring competition, holstering an anaconda. Immediately he picked out the doctors (I tried to slide my chair back behind Sally, one of our receptionists, but was rumbled). He fired out a GCSE-level question about the heart and blood circulation to me. I got it right, thank God (though it pissed me off that I *wanted* to get it right). Did I subconsciously want to impress? I'll process that in the bath tonight.

With the pop quiz over, our boy, Kev, continued his war on my will to live by regaling us with stories of his BLS heroics. It's too much. Right now, I'd rather face a clinic full of the best of the best heartsink patients (those who make me want to rip out my heart and put it in a microwave with some metal cutlery), Mrs Tally included. Alice always tells me I struggle to hide my expressions (I wonder if the bump will inherit my *fuck-off* face?) and for this reason, I decide tactically to focus on his gesturing hands rather than be in his eyeline, revealing my true feelings. The collateral damage was that his big mitts kept floating in front of his subjectively massive balls. I draw breath. *Just survive*, I think, *survive.* Amazingly, every time I thought Kev couldn't get worse, he managed to. The final straw (and I mean I very nearly reached for the scissors) was when he tried to tell us all that when out on *civvy street* (again, we're not in the military here, mate) if we see an incident, we should go up to the police or paramedics involved and quietly whisper, *'I'm healthcare, mate'. Someone get this bloke a taxi!*

Longest three hours of my life.

Tuesday, 12th June

The week isn't panning out well. I'm sitting here in work, trying to figure out how to reassure Alice after there was another mugging a road over from our flat (triggering yet more conversations about whether we can afford to move somewhere safer and bigger than the shoebox flat we live in) and now I've learned that Mrs Collins has breast cancer.

Fuck!

Five months ago, I saw her after she found a lump in her breast while in the shower. I examined her and explained that she needed to be seen in two weeks by the local breast team (any suspected cancer is referred on a very successful two-week wait cancer pathway on the NHS, hence the two-week time frame). Sadly, she then decided that work was more important than the appointment. I suspect this was a catastrophic mix of her diligence and pressure from work not to take time off at short notice.

Three times.

Three times she didn't attend her appointments.

Every time I re-referred her to the specialist and every time I pleaded with her to go, stressing how important it was to exclude cancer. Fourth time around, she goes. That's when they discover the cancer. I'm totally gutted for her. I know she thought she was doing the right thing and needed to work but you can't work if you're dead, Mrs Collins. Sitting in my consultation room with her now, I'm overwhelmed by an accidental sense of solidarity. She's hugely likeable (unlike some of my patients) with a charming, soft Scottish accent. She doesn't deserve to be in this position (then again, nobody does, cancer is cruel).

She's attending her son's university graduation next week, for God's sake!

After a few tears and discussion about the chemotherapy plan from the specialist, we hug as she leaves. I don't hug all my patients (I'm not sure what the official [snore] GP rules are on this) but it felt right. On my way home, I get to thinking again about how this job is extraordinarily bigger than just dishing out a few drugs here and there. It really is a privilege to look through these unfiltered windows into other people's lives. Just a bit shit that sometimes I've got to get out a hammer, smash the window in, and trash their house with bad news like today. But maybe I'd rather that than have them live without knowing before it's too late.

I'm hopeful for Mrs Collins despite the delay in diagnosis. And I bet with the important things in her life now sharply reframed and refocused (cancer can do that), she'll see her son's graduation with a technicolor vibrancy like never before.

I wonder if I should get Alice some pepper spray . . . Cheaper than buying a new house.

Thursday, 14th June

I'm not too sure how to formulate my reply. Benny sits looking at me.

Blank.

Just waiting for me to serve up a fantastical medical answer to his utterly ridiculous problem. I pause and look out the window. This is going to be an interesting consult. I have ten minutes to help Benny here work out the meaning of life. Yes, that's his problem. He looks normal. Which makes his question even weirder. I mean, it's near-impossible to get a GP appointment nowadays, yet he fought through the masses to secure one. And for this?

I try to dig under his perceptibly unflappable veneer. Is this a joke? Am I on some shit TV show that punks GPs? Maybe the *Loose Women* panel are wreaking their vengeance? Nothing. He gives me nothing. No mental health issues. Well in himself. No weird religious beliefs. I punt for drugs. He's seventeen years old, he must do some weed at least. Nope. Right, well that's all I've got.

I'm fucked.

You see the thing with medical training (especially GP training) is that nobody teaches you how to deal with all the weird stuff that you see every day (which, I might add, never gets old), lurking amongst the routine coughs and colds, sore ears, and ankle sprains. I look out the window again for a second, serving the dual purpose of buying me more time and hiding my smile at the thought of telling Alice about this later. In the end, I go for glory with what may be an unexpected answer. I straighten up from a *who-the-hell-knows-mate?* posture and inform Benny there's no one answer to this. That life will mean different things, at different times, in different places, to different people. Then I strike out with a final cliché, telling him (with classic GP weaponry, the *head tilt*), *'It's all a journey, mate.'*

He leaves more confused than when he entered.

Well, Benny, that's life.

Friday, 15th June

Six-year-old Charlie is currently spinning around in *my* chair with *my* stethoscope swinging around her neck, having a grand old time – despite being about to take her four-year-old brother's eye out with the sharp end of *my* tendon hammer (like a tent peg, but for testing tendon reflexes at joints). She's also one of my favourite patients partly because she never makes me feel useless and partly because she actually asks her mum to come and see me (ashamedly, yes, I'm saying it's sort of an ego rub that I might be seen as the *cool* doctor, even if it's in the eyes of a six-year-old).

Today she's here with Mum because she's got a sore throat. In fact, thanks to my apparently magical medical powers (as if I'm going to argue with Charlie on this point), I diagnose her with acute bacterial tonsillitis – an infection of the tonsils which sit at the back of her throat. She ticks all of the Centor criteria – a set of criteria used to estimate the probability of this being a streptococcal throat infection: no cough, a fever, pus on her now-colossal tonsils, and golf-ball sized cervical lymph nodes in the front of her neck. It's a slam-dunk diagnosis, and an easy one at that. Her prize? Ten days of antibiotics and a shit load of ice cream (I always prescribe this as kids go mad at the notion of *enforced* ice-cream consumption).

Charlie spins faster and faster as I explain to Mum the management plan. I've always found kids so great to see in clinic. Not only can they be total medical marvels by actually being really quite sick yet still looking pretty perky, but they allow me to be a kid myself for ten minutes. I'm thirty-two years old going on nine, for sure. Alice would argue five. Charlie shrieks with delight as we nail the double jumping high five and I give her a Minions sticker for being a mini-legend once again. I only realise once they've gone just how much of a mess they've made in my consulting room. *Will the bump be like that one day?* As for the mess, well, I don't care. That consult was pure joy. And despite some days these being few and far between, when they do come, they feel amazing. On to the weekend!

Sunday, 17th June

Went for a walk in the park today with Alice and the bump. It's always amusing when you stroll past a patient. Take Mr Stone, for example, out for his Sunday jog. It was only last Thursday that I had my lubricated index finger firmly up his arse, checking his prostate. We share a glance and a nod as he pants breathlessly past me.

Shared trauma, bonding every time.

Monday, 18th June

He's dying. I know it, his wife knows it. Sadly, Mr Cline doesn't. As I'm standing over his bed in this, his beautiful family home, lovingly decorated with photos of family and friends, holidays and celebrations, I get a rising urge of wanting to rush home to hug and kiss Alice and the bump. I offer a sympathetic smile to his wife but all I see is pain and heartbreak.

Before today, I hadn't met Mr Cline. I never knew he was treading this path to death, courtesy of the advanced prostate cancer that spread to his bones earlier this year. But his family certainly did, and I've no doubt that it hurts every single one of them, cutting into their very cores. A story, I expect, many families will know in one form or another. Now sitting on his bed, I try to guide Mr Cline to the same bookmarked page everyone else is on – the one that says the end of his life is near. Prompt after prompt, he doesn't bite. I'm desperate for him to tell me that he knows he's dying so that I don't have to. His wife now cries quietly in the corner, gulping for air between tears. A flash of guilt comes over me at my own self-pity as I check my watch and flinch that this is yet another home visit that'll leave me running late for my afternoon clinic. I hate myself when these selfish thoughts creep in.

We all sit in silence for nearly five minutes – not easy, trust me. All too often we're desperate to fill these voids. Silence breeds uncertainty. Uncertainty breeds fear. It's just human nature . . . unless you're a psychopath. In which case, you probably love it.

It's time. I invite Mr Cline to let me summarise his condition and prognosis. He accepts and so, with that, I fire the warning shot and tell him it's not good news. The look he gives me tells me he knows this. Of course he does, he just can't accept the thoughts in his head. So, I give him mine instead, providing sound, reality, and validation to his: I tell him he's dying. I say we should prepare for this. And prepare sooner, not later. His wife, who has been his rock, shatters into a symphony of sobs. My thoughts flash to my own family again and I hold them tight in my mind. No matter the shit days as a GP, this job never fails to gift reflective perspective on my own life. I'm thankful for that. It's the indirect and unexpected reward of the job that they don't tell you about when you apply to train as a GP – and they really, really should.

Silence falls for the second time. I break the news for a second time and explain that I want to refer him to the local hospice to holistically support his end-of-life needs. He nods as a man who knows that the sands of time are slipping away. It's a nod that makes me want to cry. I hold back. After all, it would be an action entirely unhelpful since what the family really need to see right now is calm, composure, and control from those trying to help them.

I return to the afternoon clinic now running forty minutes late. Today, in Death's spotlight, it doesn't really matter.

Tuesday, 19th June

Accidentally hit the panic button in my consulting room today. A skill, given that you have to hit it twice to activate it. Poor Mrs Chatterjee nearly had a heart attack when five colleagues stormed into my room like it was the O.K. Corral – she was only there for a mole check.

Thursday, 21st June

Well, this is certainly different. Ciara sits in front of me, with her friend whose name I've already forgotten. She's only sixteen years old but already looks like she's seen a lot of life.

Multiple holes in both ears and her nose with all kinds of sparkle poking out, fetching tattoo on her neck, and a face that just says, well, *hostile.* She tells me she thinks she's pregnant. My heart sinks. In the next breath, she tells me she had a negative pregnancy test last week. My heart lifts. There's hope after all. Especially since the new over-the-counter pregnancy tests are pretty accurate, even at the earliest of stages.

We look at each other for a second in a sort of *'and?'* moment. We've stalled. She stares at me blankly. I don't have time for a non-pregnant girl who thinks she's pregnant and so I default to reboot this, a now-limping consultation. So I start again and ask what I can help Ciara with, if she's already had a negative test. Reassurance, that's what she wants. This is a girl who is putting on her big girl pants in front of her mate but is actually quietly shitting herself. I don't like to judge but knowing the area I work in, I can't help but worry she's gang-affiliated. I ask about the boy (or man) involved with this *non-pregnancy* pregnancy. He's the same age. *Thank God.* I immediately happily tick off not having to make a safeguarding referral. But, she shares, he is in jail at the moment. Just wonderful. Her likelihood of being gang-affiliated just shot through the surgery roof.

After some more history, I finally get the bigger picture. She's in a relationship with this, well, inmate, last had unprotected sex with him a month ago (before he was nicked by the police) and since then has had a period – and negative pregnancy test. Twice (now that I've just done another one for her). Now unless she's the next Virgin Mary, she's clearly not pregnant. I pitch a quick GCSE-level science lesson about how babies are made in the hope that it will a) stop any future unplanned pregnancy, and b) help her pass her GCSE biology. She leaves content in the knowledge that she's not pregnant (this month) and with as much contraception advice material that I can print out and fill her child-like outstretched arms with. I then fire an email off to social services to flag her risk.

Her friend never looked up from her phone once. Classic.

Friday, 22nd June

So apparently, according to my latest NHS Friends and Family feedback, 10 per cent of the 2,417 patients I saw and who responded would NEVER recommend me as a GP. NEVER. That's 241 (*and a half?*) patients. Are you kidding me? I can't be that bad, surely? Oh, and by the way, I wasn't simply checking for some self-imposed ego rub. Rather, I'm nervously conscious of the fact that I'll be having an annual performance appraisal with work near the end of this year. That means I need to make sure there wasn't too much mud-slinging my way from the punters, which requires me to go on some sort of hearts and minds campaign. Anyway, I've started to compile a mental list. Mrs Tally is definitely one of them, as I never actually do anything for her. Probably Benny too as I've no doubt he went home and realised my meaning-of-life answer was a bit shit. Yes, Mr Stone too. I mean, you really can't rate your GP as *excellent* after a rectal exam, can you? *Can you, Mr Stone?* I think I'm going to try a little psychological warfare and stick up a poster on my consultation room door, thanking the other 2,000 patients for my positive feedback. That'll flush out the guilty parties.

Monday, 25th June

Apparently, I'm not allowed to flush out the guilty parties with a poster. My surgery practice manager, Jasper, has told me this would be passive aggressive. No doubt that'll now come up in this year's appraisal. All very hard to take when coming from a grown man who signs his emails off with a smiley face emoji.

Tuesday, 26th June

Mr Toska is sixty-two years old – and a total rock'n'roller. As he swaggers in, smelling of expensive aftershave, sex, and stale cigar smoke, I immediately remember why I like him – he reminds me of some guy straight off an aftershave ad campaign on television. Here for the results of his recent NHS general health check, he wants me to tell him that he's not likely to have a massive heart attack and drop dead. *Sorry, mate, you're in for some disappointing news.* Mr Toska smokes like a chimney, drinks like a (big) fish, has high blood pressure and thinks exercise is for the snowdrop (I think he means *snowflake*) generation. When you add in his high cholesterol – despite protesting he eats healthily, which is clearly an exuberant fabrication of the truth in light of his clinical obesity – his risk of cardiovascular disease (for example, a heart attack or a stroke) is positively celestial.

I explain all this and tell him he should consider changing his lifestyle and commencing a cholesterol-lowering statin (although that particular advice will all change in the next ten years, I'm sure) if he wants to live longer. Mr Toska looks at me like I just flicked his wang and tells me he doesn't want to do any of that stuff – he has a great life. Oh, and by the way, he wants some Viagra as he's got a new girlfriend – who's forty-three years old and I quote, *'has a high sex drive'*. I daren't probe further, despite my morbid curiosity (which you can't help but develop with the job). Anyway, now he's definitely going to have a heart attack. Despite my concerns and forceful advice, he leaves no different to when he came, seemingly about to shag his way into an early grave. Like I said, total rock'n'roller.

Wednesday, 27th June

Today's my turn to be the duty doctor at the GP surgery again. All the GPs rotate to do this role three or four times a month and to be fair, it's actually quite a nice break from the monotony that can creep into routine clinics day after day. Being duty doctor means that rather than having a set morning and afternoon clinic where patients can book an appointment to see me, my day, from 8am until 6:30pm, is completely unbooked. Instead, I come in to my desk, sit down, hold my breath. And wait. Then, by 8:01am, I'll already have a list of jobs as long as my arm. This can vary from dealing with any acutely unwell patients who call up on the day or walk into the surgery needing urgent clinical reviews (but not sick enough to go straight to an A&E department to wait for seven hours to be seen), or dealing with any urgent prescription requests to managing *seriously* abnormal patient blood results that then need contacting (to check they're not dead).

Then there are the social issues. Interestingly, this takes up a large portion of my day as the duty doctor – calls from family members often in crisis about their ageing parents but who can't contact social services because social services are busy calling us for medical details about *other* families in crisis. Which is why, amongst today's loveable chaos, when Mr and Mrs Patel walk into my room just before 11am, they are a very welcome break indeed. New to the GP surgery, they're both in their sixties, still utterly full of life, and here today only because Mr Patel's run out of his blood pressure medications. It's a bit of a weak reason to be placed on the duty doctor review list but I don't care as I like them already. Bizarrely, there's often this inverse correlation in my GP consultations: unlikeable patients can actually handicap my ability to think straight clinically because I'm so preoccupied with with how openly hostile they're being. Yet when I get a pleasant and engaging patient, no matter if they've a straightforward or a complex issue, I'll always be drawn to address it as thoroughly and directly as I can. Don't get me wrong, I realise people can be, let's say, prickly with me for all kinds of reasons – fear, anxiety, and frustration probably being the top three. I get that. And so I'll always try to get to the bottom of their current hostile status (though sometimes it really is just their baseline personality).

I examine Mr Patel's cardiovascular system, which includes listening to the four chambers of his heart with my stethoscope, and measure his blood pressure and heart rate. All perfect. I re-prescribe the 10 milligrams (mg) of amlodipine, his once-daily blood pressure medication, arrange follow-up, and we finish with five minutes of chatting about their recent travels to Ireland. I tell them about Alice and the bump and close by saying if they've any concerns to come and see me anytime. Mr and Mrs Patel might be brand-spanking new patients to the surgery but they've already made it into my top-five list of favourite patients. Don't worry, Benny, with questions like *what's the meaning of life?*, I sincerely doubt you'll ever leave my top spot. And with no more reason to keep them here, I show them out reluctantly. They leave in a flurry of laughter. What lovely people!

Thursday, 28th June

I think I might be honourably gang-affiliated. As I'm out today with Alice and the bump, we see a cluster of dodgy-looking youths hanging out by the door of the corner shop I'm about to pop into. Alice wants me to buy us two lollies. *Lollies* . . . Talk about putting a giant fucking target on my head. Tough guys don't lick lollies, Alice. I straighten up, making myself as big as possible (knowing full well that'll do sod all when I get stabbed anyway), and stride past them into the shop. I choose the two toughest-looking lollies (Magnums, obviously), pay, and brace myself for the conflict ahead as they block the door. Then it gets weird. They make an opening and then one of them turns to me, casually extending a fist (I think for me to *pump*, maybe?) and says, '*Alright, Dr Skit? Av' a good 'un, yeah?'* Dr Skit. Yeah, I like it. I pump back (correctly, I think) and with my streetest of street voice that makes me sound like I've smashed a bottle of Scotch and smoked a whole pack of cigars the night before, casually reply, *'Cheers, you boys have a good 'un too'* – before adding shamefully – *'and stay safe, yeah?'*

Where the hell that last part came from, I'll never know. The new emerging parent in me, perhaps? Do I now feel paternally responsible for all children and not just the bump? In any case, after racking my brain, it turns out he's one of my gang-affiliated teenage patients, who I'd seen a few months ago and helped out with a few issues. Alice watched the whole thing with her mouth hanging open before calling me a twat for sounding like a headmaster. And there was me thinking she'd be impressed – I guess I'm still no Mr Toska.

Friday, 29th June

Mr Patel's dead. He had a massive heart attack yesterday. I got the message as I arrived into work this morning. I'm rocked both with devastation for Mrs Patel and overwhelming guilt (and I won't lie, fear) that I missed something. Was his death my fault? When a patient dies, whether a GP admits it or not, there's always a part of them that'll replay their involvement in their care over and over to see if they made a mistake. I'm no different.

Already feeling like I just want to pack up, go home, and open a bottle of whisky, the day wasn't going to get any better. Mid-clinic now, and already running late through sheer brain fog, I'm pacing the corridor towards reception to get an urgent letter faxed off when I'm faced with Mrs Patel standing at the other end. A car crash in tragically slow motion. I soften my stride, arriving in front of her with a slow stop, extend a hand, and try to give my condolences. Naturally, she ignores all of this. In front of a full waiting-room audience, she tells me in a voice that I'll always only ever remember as pure heartbreak that *I* missed something; that it *was* my fault her husband is dead. My face goes flush. My heart rate changes gear, thumping out of my chest.

I open my mouth to say something but nothing comes out. No words will make this better. Crushing.

Internally, I grab on to a glimmer of positivity. The last time somebody accused me of killing (yes, *killing*) their family member, they tried to attack me with a fire extinguisher on the hospital ward I was working on. Mrs Patel's hands are empty. The silver lining fades away as I realise in reality, her words are doing far more damage than any fire extinguisher ever could. One more time I try to extend a hand to the now-widowed Mrs Patel but it's rightly pushed away. Defeated, I pass the fax (now damp from my sweating hand) to Rita, our senior receptionist, who was by now standing behind me to see if she could help diffuse the situation. The waiting room remains deftly silent (apart from Mr Swift, one of our more challenging local patients with more than just a splash of an anger issue, who's shouting for us all to *shut the fuck up*).

I leave offering my last unsolicited and unwanted condolence to Mrs Patel, who by now is in Rita's arms, crying. As I walk away, I feel a sea of waiting-room heads turn in unison to watch my retreat from reception. A *left stage* exit for the villain of this act. What a show they got! Doubtless, they'll be talking about how I missed a patient's heart attack for the rest of the week. Sitting back at my desk, I stare into nothing. Time ticks over. I blink. My mind feels numb. I just want to cry, I need to cry. To release some of this damaged emotion from me. I recheck his clinical notes again to see if I missed anything, did anything wrong. The fact that I don't think I did is irrelevant and I just end up hating myself for checking, slowly strangling the confidence I had in myself as a GP. Maybe I should see *my* GP if this doesn't get better? Counselling to talk through life issues and worries is for GPs too after all. It doesn't matter now. For Mrs Patel, she's lost her beloved husband and rightly or wrongly, I will always be the one she blames. The tears will have to wait. Despite all this, I still have patients waiting to be seen.

Friday, 29th June (2:18am)

I just can't stop thinking about Mr and Mrs Patel.

JULY 2018

Monday, 2nd July

I needed a pick-me-up after last week. Thankfully, Mr Devlin is just the ticket after an otherwise dry start to this morning's clinic. He sits down on the uncomfortably cheap plastic chair in my room (deliberate, so nobody outstays their welcome) with the same subjective massive ball syndrome that Kev, our enigmatic BLS instructor, had. Legs cast apart, shoulder-width. His seven-year-old son, Sam, skips in behind, looking, well, clearly, absolutely fine. I glance at my computer screen again: yep, this appointment is definitely for Sam. I nod at them, both signal and invitation for Mr Devlin to clear the clouds of my doubt and drop Sam's clinical dilemma in my lap. And what a bombshell it is.

'Sam's willy's on the small side.'

I blink. Then I wait for the inevitable *'and . . .'* to come but of course it never does. I root around in the back of my brain to see what neutral, inoffensive, and balanced response I can throw out to manage the genital crisis unfolding before me. Another subtle glance back to the screen. I realise this is yet another family that's come from yet another practice that's closed in a nearby town. Somebody, please plug the holes in this sinking NHS ship, we're going down faster than Leo and Kate. And it all means that the demand on our surgery grows, faster and faster. The weight of which I've definitely begun to feel over the last six months. It's frustrating.

I refocus and muster a lacklustre *'right'*, allowing enough pause for Mr Devlin to gather up the hint I've just handed him, shove it in his mouth, and digest the fact that there clearly needs to be more to this if he wants to get my true attention. So, he does his best: *'And that, you know, doesn't really run in the family'.* Spectacular effort! What I'd pay to follow this guy around for twenty-four hours and see what other gems he comes up with. Sam, by the way, is totally oblivious to what's going on. Busy instead, furiously colouring in the Princess Elsa drawings I have out for kids. The Transformers colouring-in sheets lay idle, no doubt something else that'll be keeping Mr Devlin up long into the night.

And so I'm invited to look at this anomalous micropenis falling far from his family's giant cock tree. I involuntarily choose not to speak for an uncomfortable amount of time, my brain processing the bullshit coming out of this man's mouth. I explain an examination won't be necessary – he is, after all, seven years old with no *actual* symptoms. More to the point, he doesn't need to have an issue made out of no issue. I give Mr Devlin a quick biology lesson about puberty and the changes Sam will go through and tell him that yes, in time, his penis will grow along with the rest of him. A sentence, I might add, that medical school neither teaches nor prepares you to say.

'So, isn't there anything you can do?' Seriously. This concerned father looks on expectantly. I give a firm 'no'. With that, I stand – international code for *we're done here.* With more questions than answers, I expect, they leave. I smile at Sam, carefree and unaware that I've just had to treat

his dad's ridiculous anxieties, as he carries his coloured-in Princess Elsa picture, happily swinging from his hand.

Tuesday, 3rd July

We're all in yet another surgery team meeting. Take me out back and shoot me. To make matters worse, Alice was up and down all night to the toilet, courtesy of the bump endlessly ricocheting off her miniature squashed bladder, so I'm more than a little sleep deprived. As I visualise both metaphorical gun and bullet, Jasper, our GP practice manager, explains passionately that today we're discussing all the significant events of the last month. These are events where there was potential, near, or actual harm to a patient through the actions of any staff member at the surgery (mainly the doctors, just to kill off any remaining confidence you might have in us). It's a monthly event.

Slumped in my chair, dark circles dancing under my eyes, I sigh. Judging by my exponentially climbing rates of exhaustion, I expect I'll have more than a few to discuss at next month's meeting. I make a mental note to turn up early to that one and bring some *you can't handle the truth! A Few Good Men* lawyer-style rebuttals with me. Thankfully, as I scan the printed list of significant events for dissection and discussion (otherwise known as *finger pointing*), I don't see my name attached to any of them. Small victories. Or should that be mercies? In any case, I opt to embrace the absence of the unwelcome spotlight and sit back with my proverbial popcorn to watch the show. You see today, Nigel is here. Nigel is one of the GP partners. A GP partner is typically someone who is not only one of the senior GPs at the surgery but also owns a percentage of the GP surgery as a business (and thus has a share of any profits left over at the end of each financial year). Along with the practice manager, they are ultimately responsible for the decisions as to how the surgery can serve the needs of the community around it and how to make a profit. And Nigel can also be a bit of a knob. He has a way of taking anything and making it both condescending and boring in equal measure. What an egregious couple he and Mrs Tally would make.

Truth be told, I didn't realise how much of this skill he had until I spent some time being the target of criticism in meetings like this over the last three years. Take today, for example: one of my colleagues had sent a patient referral for physiotherapy a little later than they should. This loosely translates to 'she forgot'. Nigel took what should have been a simple, *OK, here's the learning point, get referrals off within forty-eight hours of seeing the patient* type of debrief and instead became a *Harry Potter* Dementor. Now if you don't know what Dementors are, they're these deathly creatures (which I was sure were fictional, until I met Nigel) that float around and consume happiness, creating an atmosphere of misery and despair. Quite literally, they drain the life out of you. That's Nigel. What a skillset. I bet he doesn't have that on his LinkedIn profile. It's also a shame because the beauty of working in a GP surgery is that success in treating patients comes from success in working as a team, from the receptionist who books your appointment based on the specialist clinical letter received from the hospital which the administrator has received and uploaded to your clinical notes, to the GP who then sees you to discuss this letter and arrange some blood tests, to the nurse who then finally takes the blood. Negativity is the enemy of this success. Unhappy staff equals unhappy teamworking.

By the end of the meeting, which like all other meetings here, has fantastically overrun, we trudge out of the room like inmates heading back to their cells. My poor colleague, and Nigel's victim for today, works hard to hide the tell-tale glaze in her eyes. But we all know she's going to cry tonight. A lot. *Well done, Nigel.* I catch her eye and give her a supportive and over-the-top eye-roll. A small gesture that we're all in it together. Teamwork makes the dream work, after all. Even teams with Nigels in them.

Wednesday, 4th July

Well, this *is* odd. No dramas. No weirdos. No speechlessness. Just lovely, normal, grateful patients. All. Day. Long. As I turn my computer off, I can only hope that tomorrow is more interesting.

Thursday, 5th July

And it certainly is. I'm standing in front of Patsy. Patsy is sixty-three years old and has the biggest smile I have ever seen. She also suffers the most significant morbid obesity I have ever seen – in fact, the last recorded weight we have for her was from seven years ago when she topped the scales at 151.9 kilograms. And I instantly love her. Patsy tells me, outstretched and relaxed on her bed (also her home, bath, dining room, and perhaps most depressingly, only view), that she's been on a diet. Her eyes light up with infectious joy. *'Fantastic!'* I say with a bewildered smile, covertly scanning her, trying to figure out *where exactly* she's lost the weight. Patsy must be a mind reader too. See, she's so great! She holds up her arms, explaining, *'my bingo wings are less flappy.'* Bingo wings, by the way, are the fat that can hang from the backs of your upper arms.

I wonder if Alice would mind if I brought Patsy home to live with us. I effortlessly congratulate her on her amazing success, smile etched on both face and heart, lifting with every positive word leaving her lips. Pity it had to end. My heart sinks like a stone as she explains the reason she needed this home visit: an itchy vagina. So many questions flood my mind. At the front of the queue though – and I mean this seriously – how she can even tell, given the several large abdominal folds that lap over her pelvic area? It could be that the itching is coming from somewhere other than her vagina. In fact, I'm expecting to find some intertrigo, an inflammatory skin condition caused by sweating (large skin folds will do that).

My mind leaps back to *The Great British Bake Off* and Patisserie Week when they fold the pastry, over and over again. After *Escape to the Country* and *Countryfile*, it's Alice and mine's next favourite show. As I place my medical bag down on the carpet, I finger my jacket pockets to locate my clinical gloves. Just lining. Seems they're still safely sitting above the washbasin in my consultation room. I cry a little inside. Taking a deep breath, and making a mental note never to tell Alice about this when I get home tonight and stroke the side of her face, I begin to lift up the folds. They peel apart, revealing treacle-like residue.

I look up and smile at Patsy, who observes with enthused curiosity. Three folds in, I find the intertrigo I suspected.

Thank fuck. One more layer and we would have been in vaginal territory. An undiscovered world I don't wish to explore without gloves. Or, actually, *with* gloves. Prescription and medical advice issued, I sit and talk with Patsy for another twenty-five minutes. She's adorable. It upsets me to think she's in this position. Nobody plans this as their life. As we talk more, it's impressionable how her loneliness is reflected by the obvious joy she has in having some conversation. She tells me her carers aren't big conversationalists. So, I make a resolution: Patsy, let's see if we can't make your life just a little bit better. When I get back to the surgery, I send off several referrals for therapy assessments, social service *re*assessments, and get the details of some befriending organisations. All in the hope that we can keep this wonderful woman smiling.

Sunday, 8th July

Acknowledge my toes? I add an extra squeeze to my eyes, drown out the external noise (namely the sound of Alice, singing Elton John's 'Rocket Man' in the bathtub, butchering it in the process), and think more about how the hell to do this right. The mindfulness app, now in full swing, stretches my amateur ability a step further. *Now scan up and acknowledge your knees.* I don't think I've said hello to my toes yet? I thought body scanning was meant to relax, destress, and refresh. As I lie on the sofa in just my boxers, waiting for Alice's bathwater, all I am is confused. Thankfully, fate intervenes. My battery dies and with it, my first mindfulness experience.

If I want to destress from work, the latest growing feeling of the last six months, there must be an easier way. My thoughts digress from relaxing and I try to rationalise my stress. Is it too much work? Are my patients becoming too complex for the time I have with them? Is it my frustration at the NHS system for being so slow? Is it that I can never keep Alice's pot plants alive? I shake my head and work to block them out – it's a Sunday, for fuck's sake. With a second-hand bath abandoned, an hour later I return from a peaceful run along the canals. Seems there *is* an easier way. And it didn't need an app telling me to chat to my toes. For the rest of the afternoon my mind is filled with nothing but that of my little family-in-waiting. Work, a million miles away. If only for a short, blissful time.

Tuesday, 10th July

Yesterday opened my eyes to a reality that things are seriously changing here. I saw five newly registered patients yesterday and had to wonder what the hell their last practice (now closed, thankfully) were even doing with them. They marched in, one by one, over my morning clinic, totally oblivious to the unmitigated clinical wreckages they were in; from a patient with chronic heart failure not given nearly enough furosemide, a medication to help keep the fluid off their lungs (and so presented to me, essentially drowning), to a chronic pain patient who seems to have been allowed to roam the opiate drug pick'n'mix stand with a no-scoop limit. The outcome? Yesterday was painful. I came home in such a spectacularly bad mood, that any trophy husband prizes up for grabs last night definitely went begging.

You see, if there's one thing I truly loathe in general practice, it's laziness in GPs. We get to sit here in a position of authority, with the access, and knowledge to help make someone's life better and healthier. To skirt over the more cerebrally demanding issues that a person brings to you or to just give 50 per cent effort, well, it makes you a twat. And that's why Daniel, a squat little 22-year-old Geordie now sitting in front of me at the end of today's clinic, was just what this doctor ordered. He thinks he fancies his first cousin, Steve.

'What do you like about Steve?' (Naturally, my first question.)

Turns out, Steve is not only a walking Adonis but clever and funny too. Nice, a triple threat. I get it. Understandably, Daniel hasn't mentioned this to his family or, to my more pronounced relief, specifically his aunt and uncle. The joy of being a GP is that one minute you're sending someone to the local A&E department as they drown in their own lung fluid (like yesterday) and the next you're offering (albeit, pretty creepy) relationship advice. In this case, I opt to bypass the standard question of *'And how do you think I can help?'* because seriously, come on! Instead, I skip to my DIY pub advice.

Step one is to give him a little reassurance that it's normal (*it's really not*) to have feelings that we sometimes find hard to process and understand. That way, Daniel, doesn't go away thinking he's too weird (*he is a little*). Step two is to get him to reflect on the reality of the situation, principally that he and Steve will never be a couple and the implications on their wider family is that this will likely cause more harm than good (*categorically, no good can come of this*). Finally, step three is to explore whether there are any other Steve-like guys he knows that are, perhaps, not a blood relative. A wave of relief. Seems there is. Plus, he's on a dating app that uses your geolocation to find dates (*again, pretty creepy, but maybe I'm just old school*). And so, after much discussion, we agree that to get over his feelings towards Steve, Daniel needs to focus on dating. Yet again, another life conundrum they don't teach you in medical school. Still, job done and now home time for a dinner date to my favourite local Italian restaurant with Alice and the bump.

Wednesday, 11th July

Saw one of the surgery GPs waiting for the lift on our surgery ground floor. To get to our lunchtime meeting, which is on the first floor. For a society in which obesity and physical *in*activity is now perilously close to being completely normalised, what can I say? Role model!

Thursday, 12th July

Today's phone call signals terminal news: a syringe driver has been started for Mr Cline, my patient from last month with prostate cancer. It's a small infusion pump which, via a needle inserted under the skin, slowly administers one or more medicines to combat ailments such as pain, nausea, distress or anxiety. Really only prescribed by the hospice specialist palliative care team, it means that Mr Cline's not only nearing the end of his life but is likely now standing at the door marked 'Exit'. A concessionary nod to Death, that Mr Cline is now too weak to consume tablets.

As I continue the call with Maude, the palliative care nurse, trying to digest the most indigestible of updates, I feel my head droop. My mood helplessly adjusts to match it. I exhale. Nothing really prepares a person for death. I lie in bed thinking about it sometimes. A morbid confession, perhaps. Then again, it's tricky not to after endlessly peering into the windows of patients – sorry, no wait, *people* – like Mr Cline. And his family. What of them? Desperately torn between wanting more time but equally, wanting to end the suffering, nobody ever wants to let go of Love. I think of my own emerging family. I think of who will leave this earth first, Alice or me? Either option generates a lump in my throat, knowing the pain will be felt in equal measure. Unless of course Alice gets fed up of me down the line and doesn't mind a few years without me (I'll ask her when I get home).

Thanking Maude for the information and knowing there's little else I can do now but wait, I end the call. It's hard to accept, but accept it I must. Yet, as is the life of a GP, I instantly get a new call come through. This time it's from Asif in reception, telling me a prescription for omeprazole, a type of heartburn medication, requires my *urgent* signature. I explain to him that such a prescription is *never* urgent.

Besides, I need a minute.

Friday, 13th July

I'm tired. That tiredness that makes you ache. Mentally. Physically. Emotionally. And now I've got to call Mrs Tally. *And*, it's Friday the 13th. An *unlucky* day doesn't do it justice.

Sunday, 15th July

Peaceful. Friendly. Clean. We're returning from an idyllic baby moon weekend in the Lake District. And as Alice, the bump, and I sit in the traffic jam leading us back into the city, I can't help but suddenly envy people living in the countryside. I've never had so much fresh air fill my lungs. It felt like some elixir to a long life. It was essentially our last weekend away together before the baby comes – and our lives therefore forever changed. Call it overly cautious but we're basically going full-on nesting mode for the next however many weeks until the bump comes. I sigh quietly (Alice is asleep next to me) as the individual flashes of car brake lights around me seem to angrily push all that peace, friendliness, and cleanliness further away from our immediate realities. I try to think of the positives to city life: great culture, always things to do. After that I give up. I'm sure I'm just tired, I'll think of more in the morning . . .

Monday, 16th July

Mr Cline died over the weekend. I'm happy for him. This was a good death: his family (including the dog) were all at his bedside, and I'm told he slipped away, holding his wife's hand. The reality is that he probably died before that moment, but it really doesn't matter. Those split-second instances are the timeless photographs that we all want to hold in our memory. And who could ask for more? I'd kill for a death like that when my time comes. To die with your loved ones around you is one thing, but to also do so at home, where life itself is celebrated in framed pictures, trinkets, and worn armchairs, all warmly protected by endless memories of parties, familiar smells, softly spoken words, and *I love you*'s echoing within its walls? Well, perfect.

Not for the first time in recent weeks, as I put down the phone to Maude, the palliative care nurse, I just want to speak to Alice and hear how she and the bump are doing. I love to think about them both, of course I do. Yet eating away at the back of my mind somewhere is the again-rising concern at my recent levels of emotion. I worry. I worry as I start to dial the next patient's phone number that this job might be scratching away my emotional resilience faster than I might have hoped.

Wednesday, 18th July

Well, fuck me, Benny's back. He's sitting in front of me, *Star Wars* Jedi T-shirt just about stretching to his plump little navel. I can't help but lean back in my chair and just stare in wide-eyed excitement. What gem has he got for me this time? Perhaps, and I truly *do* delight at the thought, he's got a follow-up question to last month's *Meaning of Life* enquiry. I reminisce. That was one hell of a consult. Secured him top spot as Best Patient. Of. All. Bloody. Time. Yet here I am, flopping forward in sheer disappointment. An ingrown toenail? Internally, I lament.

Really, Benny? Really? A toenail.

Not quite flopped back to a more neutral and professional position, I remain hunched over the desk, displaying my disappointment like a bereft peacock. After reassuring Benny I'll refer him to the chiropodist for his boring toe problem, I try to steer him in a more prosperous direction: *'So, how's, you know – LIFE?'* A gentle probe. I inhale. Pause, not daring to exhale.

Come on, Benny, you can do it.

He blinks a few times. I don't blink. The anticipation is too much.

'Good, thanks.'

Exhaling, I snap out of my trance, leaving his gaze and returning to his clinical consultation screen. Blank – waiting, wanting, needing, to be filled with a *Meaning of Life* question once more. Instead, I write about his gammy toe.

My God, you've let me down, Benny.

Thursday, 19th July

Alice isn't talking to me today. Turns out referring to her upcoming maternity leave as a 'year-long holiday' isn't very funny.

Friday, 20th July

I can see the sweat from here. Positively glistening under my room's artificial strip light, as she rubs her hands backwards and forwards metronomically over her jeans. She might only be twenty-three years old, but for Sadie it's clear that anxiety is choking the life from her. Like a maladjusted chameleon, this anxiety, both vicious and unsympathetic, evolves to any situation that she finds herself in, from travelling on the bus or being in a work meeting to going to a bar with some friends. Sadly, this isn't uncommon for those with her diagnosis of generalised anxiety disorder. Her jeans are now smudged with sweat.

Feeling this is going to be a consultation in which I need to tread lightly, I tilt my head barely a fraction and give her a smile. It's too late though: she catches me clocking the smudges. Physical signs of an all-too-hidden, intangible condition. Anxiety is cruel. Largely, because those unaffected can't see it. And when people can't see something, it can be a struggle not only to understand it but crucially, to sympathise with it. That's what makes the sufferer, well, just suffer even more. Isolated. Misunderstood. Self-critical.

Sadie looks as if she's about to cry. Given my last patient finished up the remaining tissue from my Tesco's Finest box, lamenting her late cat, I hope for her sake that Sadie pulls it back. So close. She doesn't. She opts to recruit her sleeve as a blotting pad for her eyes. And, not having an alternative, I collaborate by inaction. Through the tears, Sadie tells me her life is crumbling. She's now off work because of her anxiety. Her boyfriend apparently *doesn't understand*. Now, it's so bad that even leaving the house has become her Everest without supplemental oxygen.

Still I make a point here of congratulating her for *summiting it* today (pointing to our surroundings). Thanks to our unspeakably embarrassing and frustrating local NHS waiting times for psychological talking therapies for the next six months I'm pretty much the best Sadie is going to get. I joke that I'm cheaper than a private therapist and we both laugh at the situation, finally breaking the deadlock of tears. She and I both know that I'm no therapist. For starters, I don't have a shiny fountain pen to suck on and look thoughtful with, or a living pot plant (*sorry, Alice, it happened again, my love*). What I can be, though, is an ear to listen, a sounding board for the thoughts crashing round in her head. Someone impartial, and I would always hope, understanding. When you add that to all the advice she already has about the value of exercise, the benefits of breathing techniques, and all the self-help material slopping around online – plus of course the anti-anxiety medication that she started last month – I tell her that her ability to tackle this anxiety will only grow in strength. And the mountain *will* get smaller each day, every breath richer in oxygen. I'll support her, best I can. Because the truth is that's all I can do when my hands are otherwise clinically tied, mental health services supply endlessly swallowed up by demand. And of course, yes, that means, I do worry that one day suicide may be seen as the only option for people like Sadie, suffering with their mental health. I just pray it's a day never realised. No matter how bad it may seem.

She leaves once again, ironically without actually that much new. But she thanks me and tells me that she feels better just having this chat. I guess that's because sometimes the conversation *is* the medicine. Sadie leaves with an appointment to see me in two weeks' time, and a resuscitated hope that she can beat this. And she will.

Tuesday, 24th July

Impressive. I've not seen someone quite this whipped for a while. Jeremy's a 42-year-old sinewy little man. He sits opposite me, head down, proverbial tail between his legs, every inch the naughty schoolboy.

'Well, go on then! Tell the doctor about your knee, Jeremy!' Orders barked from his girlfriend – and apparent handler – Chloe. Jeremy is shrinking before my very eyes, her thumb of dominance pressing down upon him with exhausting pressure. Turns out he's had knee pain for six weeks but hasn't done anything about it. If I was about to ask Jeremy for some

more information about it, I needn't have worried. His handler, Chloe, has taken over his speaking role. She is, based on her current performance of belittling Jeremy, my actual patient, deeply unlikeable. And because of this, I make a power play, telling her I want to hear from only Jeremy.

'After all, you don't know what his knee feels like, do you?' I smile as I finish, subtly passive aggressive. She sits back, face chewed up by its own scowl. Jeremy looks terrified. Guilt floods me as I realise I've just provoked the beast. That it will be him, not me, suffering the consequences later. *Poor bastard.* Jeremy explains more about his knee pain, which hurts at the front, just over the kneecap, coming on after a recent carpentry job he'd done. Kneeling in front of him, I examine it: tender and swollen over the kneecap. I diagnose prepatellar bursitis (inflammation of a pillow-like pad called a bursa, which helps reduce friction around the kneecap). It'll clear up with some non-steroidal anti-inflammatory medication, ice, and a break from kneeling for a couple of weeks.

'Are you going to remember all of this, Jeremy?' The chair creeks as Chloe leans forward and barks some more. *'Write it down!'* He nods. A whimper escapes his mouth. I can't help but be embarrassed for him. With the prescription printed, I get up to shake Jeremy's hand. As I do so, I can't help but look in his eyes: abject resignation, that's what I see. He knows he's dominated by her and he's ashamed. *'Come and see me any time,'* I add in the vain hope that one day he'll come alone and I can understand what the *fuck* he's doing with her.

I don't shake Chloe's hand.

Wednesday, 25th July

Managed to irreparably damage my credibility as a GP today. Was overheard by one of my more high-society patients discussing the upcoming *Love Island* TV show final with Ginny, our teenage receptionist. That's the kind of shit that sticks. As I walk back to my room, cheap instant coffee in hand, I conclude that I'll have to do some proper grafting if I'm ever going to get that patient back onside.

Love Island fans will get the joke here . . .

Friday, 27th July

As far as funny-looking lesions go, it's a pretty funny-looking one. With the examination lamp targeted on Mr Speller's torso, I peer in at it. Close. Nose almost touching his chest hair close. He sits there silently as I go about my examination. I've definitely no idea what this is. There's an air of awkwardness about him. I can feel his body tensing as he sits on the examination couch, shirt neatly folded next to him (my personal red flag for *weird* – who folds their shirt up *this* neatly when having an examination?). I suspect he hasn't been examined like this before. He's only thirty-six years old so I don't have the heart to tell him that in another thirty years doubtless there'll be some digitally endowed doctor with their index finger up his anus checking his prostate. That all means today should really be a walk in the park.

I stare some more. The lesion is odd. We've been treating it with a combined anti-fungal and steroid cream for six weeks (usually more than enough time) on the basis that it's probably a fungal skin infection called tinea corporis (also known as *ringworm*) yet it's still there, red and as angry as ever. Bigger, in fact.

Moving away from the lesion, I look up at Mr Speller, but of course he's not looking at me, he's looking dead ahead. He's really not enjoying this at all. I cough to get his attention. He looks at me.

'Right, let's take a skin scraping and see what the lab can show us about this little fella!'

He frowns at my choice of descriptor before reluctantly nodding at my suggestion. As I sit back at the computer to quickly print off the request form, Mr Speller starts to get dressed.

Really, pal? How does he think I'm going to be getting this scraping? *Through* his clothing?

I explain that the skin scraping will be done right now . . . with his shirt off. He nods again, even less enthusiastically this time before reverting to his thousand-yard stare. So I wheel my chair in front of him and sit down, scalpel and sample paper (to catch the skin scrapings) in hand. I look up and smile. Of course, he's not looking at me – I should've learned by now. I gently guide the scalpel back and forth over the lesion, sending a little dermatological cascade of dry, red flakes onto the sample paper. After one more pass of the scalpel I think I'm done.

'All finished, Mr Speller,' I announce.

It's at that point, it goes tits up. I spin around, sample paper in hand. Still open. Straight into the path of the freestanding fan. Set to high speed. I watch in slow motion as Mr Speller's skin scrapings effortlessly blow all over me. *Fuck.* My mouth is open. I pause motionless, unsure what to do. *Fuck.* Somehow Mr Speller hasn't noticed my minor technical hitch. Finally, that thousand-yard stare's come in handy. I have two options here: I could be honest and tell him what's just happened or I could say a tiny white lie and explain that I think we need just a little more sample. A white lie never really hurt anyone (though everything's scalable, I guess – look at President Clinton and Monica Lewinsky).

Self-justification made, I retake the sample on the basis of needing more. Again, Mr Speller's thousand-yard stare never breaks. As he gets dressed, he never looks at me, never asks me when he'll get the results, or even drops in some easy small talk about the weather. Unsurprising then that once dressed, he bolts from the room. His notes typed and with a plan to follow up with him once the results are back, I remember my shirt. *God!* And my mouth. I look down at my shirt and make a mental note to wash it on a high heat. And brush my teeth when I get home. Immediately. And definitely before kissing Alice.

Sunday, 29th July

Not in a good mood this weekend. Our city's finest youth decided last night that our road would be the perfect setting to launch multiple fireworks – horizontally. After making sure that the front of our house doesn't have any disused rockets sticking out of it, I then discover that our car has once again been keyed – this time on the bonnet. *Brilliant.* The car now looks like a shit version of Etch A Sketch. Without the erase function.

I bet they don't get this in the countryside.

Monday, 30th July

I guess this is what white-noise torture techniques are like. Mr Peck lists the fifth reason he's here. The fact he's doing it with a smile, as if doing the NHS some kind of favour by saving up all his problems for one consultation, is particularly irritating. Ordinarily, I would have shown him my iron fists but today, refreshed by a rare night of uninterrupted sleep (Alice and the bump are away visiting her parents on the South Coast, so it's not like sleeping with an epileptic walrus), I've slipped on the velvet gloves.

With so many issues, I choose to type his clinical notes *as* I listen, giving occasional feigned nods of interest, agreement, and collaborating concern. As an aside, I usually type the clinical notes after the patient has left my room. That way, you summarise the key points rather than do a *War and Peace* number on their consultation record. However, Mr Peck's body language is too comfortable. It says, *I'm here to stay.* I mean, he's taken his coat off, for God's sake! Red flag. We just can't have that.

Having addressed four out of the five problems, namely (1) a blood pressure check (*boring, but important*), (2) a blood form for his kidney function annual check (*more boring*), (3) does he need antibiotics for his cold? (*absolutely not unless he wants to contribute to global antibiotic resistance*), and (4) does the cut on his finger from a carpentry injury last week look infected? (*nope*), we move on to his fifth and final issue: his moob issue. I stop typing and look up.

Not so boring.

Seems he's been hiding his concerns for a while but since he got himself a new girlfriend, he thought he'd better check after she made a joke about it. Apparently, and I really do try not to smile, *his* are bigger than *hers.* Guiding him to the examination couch, I have a gander at the offending pair. I smile reassuringly: he's definitely got moobs. After sitting him back down, I explain he has a condition called gynaecomastia (normal breast tissue in men that's developed a little more than usual).

He stares in shock.

'So, I've got boobs?'

I thought he was about to ask me if he needed a bra (to which I'm not actually sure of the answer), but thankfully he just opts for asking *why?* In fairness, I don't have time for another full GCSE science lesson, but the handout I gently place in his hand explains about the hormone imbalances which can occur between testosterone and oestrogen. Besides, I'm pretty sure there's nothing more sinister going on.

Forlorn, Mr Peck looks at me.

'Is there any surgery?'

I jovially explain that won't be necessary. Weight loss. That's his answer. And that can be helped straight away by not smashing a bottle and a half of red wine a night with his new girlfriend. He nods in sobering resolution. We agree to do some blood tests just to make sure there's nothing else pathologically fruity going on. But like the philosophy of Occam's razor, *if you hear hooves, think horses – not zebras,* common things occur commonly. Armed with his handout, blood test form, and philosophical quote, Mr Peck exits.

All in twelve minutes.

I'm back on form. *Wow, the power of sleep!*

Tuesday, 31st July

Boy, am I glad I asked 5-year-old Hattie's mother what her job was as I finished up reassuring her that Hattie's external ear infection (called otitis externa) will clear up with some simple ear drops. Nothing like a clinical negligence lawyer as a patient's mother to sharpen your note keeping!

AUGUST 2018

Wednesday, 1st August

Now this *is* satisfying. Susan, a 62-year-old retired geography teacher, rubs her left elbow and eulogises how desperate she is to know what's wrong with it. The tennis bag she has with her slips to the ground with a tinny thud from a tennis ball cylinder. This is one of those moments. A bit like when you're a teenager and have just negotiated the phone number (landline, back then) of the girl you've a massive crush on. You're bursting at the seams to blurt it out to your mates but you try, oh, how you try, to be as cool as you can. You see, the times in clinic when an on-the-spot diagnosis is made are much less common than you might think. That's partly because patients' problems are overall becoming more complicated. Why? Who knows. I expect though, that greater access to health information online is partly responsible. But most of the time it's all the random problems that we have to investigate and scratch our heads at, like that crippling simultaneous tingling of your right little finger and left ankle – but only after Wednesday's curry night. And I'm the fifth GP you've come to about it.

When it's a slam dunk like this, it's thoroughly enjoyable. Susan here is your classic tennis elbow patient – the active retiree, the empty nester. She continues to rub her elbow in tactile distress. I bide my time, chewing my pen thoughtfully, stopping only once I remember it's the one I found on the waiting-room floor. I cast my rod out and probe with a few more choice questions: *'So, it hurts when you unscrew a jar?'* She nods enthusiastically, taking the bait. I look intrigued. Now this is not, by the way, me simply being a narcissistic dick. This is me applying some positive reinforcement for my own job satisfaction. Something we all have to bank when it comes our way. I continue to internally revel and examine Susan's elbow with all the focus of a seasoned Matador. It's time. With an overdramatic pause, and a pensive nod to myself as if the answer's only just come to me, I lean in and deliver the diagnosis. She pauses, sits back, delighted.

We have a winner!

I work to maintain momentum and enthusiastically explain that she has an overuse injury of the extensor muscles in the forearm – which is why opening a jar or nailing a blistering forehand in tennis (hence its colloquial name, although medically known as *lateral epicondylitis*) can both cause and exacerbate the condition. Her response is golden and for split second, I think of Benny: this should have been his reaction when I gave him the answer to the meaning of life. As my ever-faithful printer of the last three years, Hewlett Packard B5L25A ('Hew'), whirs into action, I reassure Susan that it should settle after some rest, anti-inflammatory medication, and rehabilitation exercises. I smile and tell her she'll be back on her game in no time at all. She leaves, lightened as the weight of uncertainty is lifted. I sit back in reflective satisfaction. It might be an easy case to manage but they sure are lovely when they come around. It serves (no pun intended) to remind me too that one person's 'small issue' can be another's 'gigantic, all-consuming one'.

Thursday, 2nd August

It appears that Mr Thornton truly has every intention of doing what I think he's about to do. I swivel around on my chair, letting it drag caustically on the floor to catch his attention. Leaning over my shoulder, I clear my throat. Just as his hand is about to stroke the zipper, I explain that we have some very charming – more private – toilets just outside. And that he might perhaps find these a more suitable and relaxing spot (for the both of us) to provide me with the requested urine sample.

He stares are me, thumb and forefingers cradling his knock-off Levi's 501 jeans button. I stare back, defiant. *My house. My rules. Case made.* Yet Mr Thornton then does something that I wasn't quite expecting: he looks put out. He genuinely looks like I've disrupted what was going to be an entirely suitable action. And with a grunt of *'Alright then'*, he leaves to do what any other normal person would do and use a toilet. I sit in silence, not yet having fully unwound my body back to face the computer. *Is this guy serious?* Shaking my head in disbelief, I hold my breath, half-expecting him to come back in with the urine sample tube stuck on the end of his knob.

Friday, 3rd August

'Antibiotics?! Really?' I shake my head in disbelief. Alice and the bump are sitting next to me on the sofa. She is, however, comprehensively ignoring me, opting to perform a more sensible and grown-up evening activity rather than shout at *GPs: Behind Closed Doors* on TV. She's planning all the items

we'll need to take into hospital when the time comes for the bump to show their face. I peer over. Then immediately wish I hadn't. The list is massive! Also, I'm sure it contains everything in the house – we might as well have the baby at home. Less packing, better Wi-Fi.

I settle my head onto the back of the sofa and stare at the next consultation on the show. It's some old boy with a stiff and achy knee that he's had for years.

'It's arthritis, clearly!'

Alice glances at me before continuing to expertly ignore me in a manner that only comes from six years of practice. The GP on the show dishes out some pretty lazy management advice and I find myself grumbling in disapproval at what I'm watching. I will *not* be that GP, I will *not* be that lazy. Sure, I can dislike my patients at times (show me a GP who doesn't and I'll show you someone lying to your face). But that doesn't mean they're getting poor care. They get the same care as the patients I love to see. As I turn off the show, the television screen blinks into darkness. I turn to Alice. Now there's something – *someone* – I could watch for my whole life. Cringy, I know. And with that thought in mind, I lean over and ask her to tell me about this bloody list.

Monday, 6th August

The week hasn't gotten off to a flying start. In fact, this plane has no fuel, one engine is down with a bird strike and someone's having a fag in the toilets. I fake a smile at Mrs Delaware, now sitting down in front of me. Her 4-month-old baby girl, Angel (*of course*), complete with left- and right-ear piercings (*of course*), sits on her, using her like some human bouncy castle. She's scowling, like a pro. To complete the set, Mrs Delaware's 15-year-old daughter, Amber, slumps in the corner of my room, staring at her phone, unblinking.

Owing to its clear lack of efficacy, I decide to abandon smiling and work to get this consultation over as quickly as possible. Luck is on my side. Turns out Mrs Delaware only wants a repeat of her medications (Orlistat, to help her lose weight). We sit in silence, waiting painfully for the paper prescription, called an FP10, to print from 'Hew'. If only . . . If only I hadn't asked Mrs Delaware – *and* Amber – *'So who's mum to this little one?'* as they walked in and I waved at Angel.

Not my finest opening line to date.

Tuesday, 7th August

You've got to be fucking kidding me. Mr Richmond lies splayed out on my desk, panting like a dog. I sit, swivelling back and forth in my chair, looking on with a mixture of bemusement and irritation. I start with as open a question as I can muster: *'What seems to be the problem?'* I've a feeling quite a large net might need to be cast for this question. He lifts his head from my desk and – this is my favourite part – with his eyes *still* closed, delivers a verbal tsunami of utterly unrelatable symptoms. As he begins, I start typing them one by one but quickly stop. I let my fingers hover over the keyboard, turning to this man, this clinical melting pot of every sodding symptom under the sun.

Now unless Mr Richmond's entire body is about to spontaneously combust and evaporate into the ether, he's chatting shit. Aware too that he's my last patient of the day and I'm meeting Alice for the bump's 36-week antenatal appointment, I decide to take control. Slapping my blood pressure cuff on his left arm, I bark for him to sit up. He promptly responds to this sadomasochistic show of clinical dominance and before he can list any more symptoms to go along with shortness of breath, bilateral ear pain, nausea, urinary urgency, his left leg rash, and tight mouth skin (*I mean, seriously*), I've measured his temperature, heart rate, oxygen saturation, and capillary refill time.

As I enter these observations onto his clinical notes (*all normal, of course*), Mr Richmond slumps back down to desk level, his face now a sad bulldog pressed against a car window. *No, you fucking don't,* I think.

'Up you get!'

I position him on the examination couch and check his heart, lungs, abdomen, ears, and throat. All normal. *Well, I never.* I head him off at the pass as he attempts to lie down on the couch – I'm not being late for Alice's appointment, not for this. I war-room the scenario in my head: had he been successful in lying down, could I just turn the light out and leave? I stare at Mr Richmond, my patience now a melting ice puddle over a very deep, angry lake. I stare some more, daring him to dance over it.

'What is it you actually want?'

Interesting. He straightens up at this question: he wants a blood test. I jump into action, already priming the blood test request form as I ask him to explain more. Turns out he has this fixed belief that he's got something wrong with his blood. Bit of a weird one, but OK. Usually it's that they think they've got cancer. I stop typing the blood test request form and half-turn to begin explaining that this is essentially not the case but stop myself mid-chair spin and turn back. I don't speak again.

I love this tactic. Patients hate it – it makes them nervous of you as they just sit there. In a room. With a stranger. In silence. After 'Hew' (which I now realise really, *really* needs to be replaced) finally coughs out the printed blood form in barely legible ink toner, I explain this will give us *all* the answers we need. Like a phoenix from the ashes, Mr Richmond rises with newfound strength and shakes my hand. He sniffles a thank you. I tell him it's an absolute pleasure to help. A momentous lie in truth. Some GPs will hear this case and think I made the wrong call giving him a blood test. They can have their opinion. I will, however, respectfully disagree. You see, often these patients don't stop until they get what they need to put their mind at rest, even if it is rubbish. To deny them of that, well, all they'll do is see GP after GP, or even attend their A&E department time and time again, absorbing precious time and resources, until someone actually asks them what they really want. I'm cauterising a wound otherwise people like Mr Richmond will just bleed all over the NHS.

And we can't have that now, can we?

Thursday, 9th August

Rubbing my eyes, my mind still refuses to rouse. Numbed. Sedated by workload. It's 7:15pm and it's been a long, long day. I continue to file the last of the clinical letters for patients of a colleague, away on their holidays. Some yoga retreat . . . I think back to my mindful failure to acknowledge my toes last month and shudder at the idea of a week of that stuff. As I refocus on the clinical letter from a urology consultant about Jamie, one of the surgery's younger patients, defiantly static on the screen, I feel myself physically, consciously, drawing a long, slow breath.

Holding it, I scan the letter, digesting the investigations and diagnosis: testicular cancer. I exhale, dejected. The words are both unfair and violating. A staging computerised tomography (CT) scan is planned to check his cancer has not spread to other areas like the lymph glands in his abdomen or his lungs. Ultimately, Jamie will require surgery to remove the invaded testicle and adjuvant chemotherapy to help prevent the cancer from returning. He's only nineteen years old.

Sitting back, I file the letter in his clinical notes. Not for the first time, I hate myself for the self-pity transiently flooding me as I think of the time, how drained I feel, and how I'd murder a holiday right now. I stretch back, craning my neck to the ceiling. I know that I can get away with this now – letting work take over my evenings periodically – but when the bump arrives, I need (and want) to be home on time. It'll be all hands on deck. This will have to change.

My consulting-room phone announces itself. Unwelcome. It's reception. Ignoring it, I stare back at Jamie's notes. My stomach knots and I mentally clip Jamie over the back of the head. He'd seen our practice nurse, Irena, over five months ago and mentioned this lump. Quite rightly, Irena told him to see a GP urgently (*that week*) and have it assessed. Because Jamie was too embarrassed, he left it another four and a half months before seeing a colleague of mine. The clear, ordered black Times New Roman font in front of me from July's consultation says all it has to: *On examination: Large, firm craggy mass palpable on the right testes.* I haven't ever met Jamie but I know him. I've seen men like him more than once, all too embarrassed to get their balls out in time when they sense something's wrong. Thankfully, the tide is turning and an openness about these issues is emerging. I'm not particularly religious but I pray that Jamie's time lapse hasn't given time for his cancer to spread – and really fucked him.

I'm frustrated at him.

For him.

With my mind slowing by the minute and headache strengthening with equal velocity, I complete my final task: leaving a message for his regular GP to contact him when he's back next week. I don't even bother shutting the computer down. Again. I just get up, lock up, and leave.

Saturday, 11th August

I built a baby's cot today. Wait, *my* baby's cot. Mind-blown.

Sunday, 12th August

After breakfast in bed Alice informs me that I've put the sodding cot sides on backwards. She tells me gently though – and I love her for that.

Tuesday, 14th August

Ordinarily, I like jam jars, because I love the jam in them. But the jam jar that 71-year-old Gerald's just plonked down in front of me clearly hasn't fulfilled its destiny. And, as with a growing number of my new patients, I allow a silence to envelop us as I wait for Gerald to tell me what the hell is in it.

With a Scottish accent thick as you can get, he tells me that he pulled it out of his penis.

Like a magic trick?

The comment speeds from my brain to my mouth but I lock it down before released. I sit back and smile.

'That must have been a surprise?'

I like Gerald, he's blunt and unflappable. He tells me in vivid detail how he was *taking a leak* (his words, not mine) and suddenly there it was, floating around in the toilet. Gloving up, I raise the jar to inspect Gerald's specimen, a cross between those delicious red jelly snake sweets (I'm a big fan) always found in service stations and the redcurrant jelly for your lamb roast.

Gerald looks at the jar, then at me, then the jar, before finally back to me, asking, *'So, what came out me dick?'*

It's a blood clot.

I've known Gerald for a while. More than once he's had a camera put up his penis by the urology team to investigate macroscopic haematuria – medical speak for visibly bloody urine. There's nothing nasty going on. I also know that he's on an essential blood-thinning medication for his atrial fibrillation (AF), a type of irregular heart rhythm. It's essential because it stops him developing blood clots in his heart chambers, which can spill out and block a blood vessel in the brain or heart. Which essentially stops him from having a stroke, heart attack, or, well, dying. With his clinical observations stable, I reassure him that while certainly not that pleasant, there's nothing we need to be concerned about (unless of course another clot blocks his urethra – the tube through which urine passes from the bladder to the outside world – in which case, he'll know about it pretty quickly and be on the way to his local A&E department).

He twizzles the jar around and looks deep in thought – before checking that what I'm saying is that this is just clotted old blood. I nod in a sort of *well done, Gerald, you've been paying excellent attention today way.*

'Like Haggis?'

I feel sick. *Jesus, Gerald. You wouldn't, would you?* He clearly reads my face and reassures me, laughing his hearty, deep, guttural Scottish laugh, that it's not for him. The food returns to my stomach.

'I'll feed it to me dog.'

Showstopper, Gerald. Total showstopper.

As he leaves, I mourn the fact I'll probably never see jam in the same light again.

Wednesday, 15th August

Thank God I slept well because James, our practice administrator, told us all he's already called the police and locked the door. I knew today was going to be a lesson on the realities of obscure policy making and my GP surgery, like all those up and down the country, is packed with them. Thankfully, they usually live dormant, unglamorous lives in dust-covered folders or on computer shared-drives that nobody knows how the hell to access.

As I stand there in reception, a fresh lower vaginal swab sample swinging from my hand, the collective sense of confusion is palpable. James looks proud, accomplished even. He is in fact being stupid. As we stand in silence, the antennae of the waiting-room mob pricks up on hearing the word *police*, now a congregation of unwell meerkats, craning for gossip.

'There's a baby changing bag in the baby changing room. Unattended.'

Oh, James. One of the oldest members of the surgery team, he's not short on passion. He's also frustratingly obsessive over policy, my inbox regularly flooded with new, apparently *exciting* policy updates (there's no such thing, I concluded long ago). And of course, the most recent one is about terrorism. In particular, how to act when you suspect an *actual* or *potential* terror threat. James thinks there's a bomb in the bag. *Well, thank God he locked the baby changing room door! That'll contain the blast.* I decide I can't take it any longer and return to my clinic room to call the next patient.

By the end of the session, nothing's exploded. The police have been and gone. The changing bag was indeed just a changing bag. I go home at the end of the day, nervous that I think I left my pen on the radiator in the staff toilets.

God only knows what James will do.

Friday, 17th August

The queue moves at a painful pace. A line of hungry, socially awkward GPs, all waiting to collect their rations for lunch. I don't mind admitting, I'm far from enthusiastic about GP conferences. The fact that it's been twelve months since I last attended one is probably testimony to that. You see, the days where you could sign in at a conference in the morning and bugger off at lunchtime for a five-hour pub lunch are long gone. Nowadays the organisers don't give you the certificate of attendance unless you're there to sign out at the end of the day. So here I am, still here at lunchtime, shuffling along, having spent the morning trying to consume knowledge about the latest heart failure, migraine, and diabetes guidelines. All to make me a better GP. I say that, but most of the information is available online as well so this is more about a trip out of the surgery. Still, at nearly £250 for the day's educational experience, I expected better food. Finally arriving to the front of the service station, I stare down at anaemic meatballs and congealed pasta.

'Glad to see we're practising what we preach.'

The station attendant doesn't get the joke. Instead, she simply asks if I want broccoli. I'm in two minds. On one hand, it looks like that's the only marginally healthy food option I'm going to meet. Yet on the other, who the fuck pairs broccoli with meatballs and pasta? I accept, and so armed with the solitary source of dietary goodness, I find a place to sit. This in itself is a minefield. I survey the GP savanna, a room packed largely with people who don't know each other. In situations like this, it's important to take your time before making a decision. The fact that my fork can already stand upright in my block of pasta tells me I'm in no rush. Besides, a wrong seating choice here can ruin an entire lunch break. I rescan; the area to my left primarily dominated by the loners is already taken. They have characteristic behaviour: sitting with *at least* one chair between each other. A delicate GP ecosystem for them, and so to move in and sit down in a seat next to them, thereby bridging the gap so human contact *is* possible – well, a contentious act to say the least.

The next ecosystem I spot straight ahead, dominating the middle ground, is the senior GP set. Usually the senior GP *partner*-types I've mentioned before (see page 40). They sit side by side, confident, relaxed, and very much in control of their environment. You only go there if you're one of them. I'm definitely not and so I continue to scan. To my despair, the only other option is *band-camp* on my right. This ecosystem is for those GPs who want to make friends, but just may not be particularly good at it. And there's a seat spare at the end. I sigh. With my fork beginning to sag, and only ten minutes until the afternoon session on mental health starts, I go for it. I put on my best *no, no, don't talk to me* face and move to the free seat. Now the next part takes practice. *As* I sit down, I seamlessly slide my phone from my pocket and immediately begin looking at it with an intensity that says *this guy is closed to conversation.*

But Tilly didn't read it like that. Tilly is (probably) in her forties, and wearing hiking boots paired with *Mountain Wear rambling* trousers. Great! A discreet Google Maps check confirms we're at least fifty miles from the nearest mountains. Maybe it's better to be prepared? As she opens up a conversation with me, I fold like a house of cards and smile. It seems as much as I love to think I can be a dick to people in my head, it's so much harder in reality. Tilly's come up from London and she's tells me about GP life there. She also has food on her face that moves up and down every time she speaks. I stifle a smile. It's like it's waving at me. *How do I tell her?* In the end, I opt not to do so, feeling better in the knowledge that when it does eventually fall off, it'll land on durable clothing at least.

I nurse my block of pasta around the plate, moving as one, like the swell of the sea, all the while nodding at Tilly's polite conversation. My eyes keep casting off to the three GPs opposite me, all clearly new friends, but still talking to their shoes. I can't help but hope they at least give their patients some eye contact.

Spiteful Max. Stop!

Ding! Ding! The sound of rescue – the bell signalling the imminent start of the afternoon session. I smile one last time and rising, tell Tilly how lovely it was to chat and that maybe I'll catch her in the afternoon break to hear more about her trip to the Lakes (*I won't*). She looks pleased at our future arrangement, making me transiently loathe myself. Lunch goes in the bin. As I sit back down in the lecture hall, hungry, I feel myself physically sigh louder and more heartfelt than anticipated. Something's off – *I* feel off. I should be in a room of likeminded people – fellow GPs – feeling stimulated, excited, impassioned, yet all I feel is oddly disconnected from those emotions. I rub my eyes. Who knows, maybe it's just the general moaning that goes on in the NHS that's finally getting to me (and which is easily magnified at a GP conference)? Or, maybe it's just that I'm tired. In any case, I sink into my chair a little more and try to push it out of my mind.

Saturday, 18th August (03:47am)

I'm lying in bed next to Alice. Well, I *say* next to her. What I actually mean is that I'm hugging the cliff edge of my side of the bed, abutted by her pregnancy vision of the Berlin Wall. Nine pillows, architecturally placed to provide optimum support for the bump, now in a sizeable third trimester mass, as she lies on her side. I stare into the darkness and bite my bottom lip like some hormonal angst-ridden teenager. Why is it then, when all I should be thinking about is the bump's arrival and life after, that instead I'm replaying my reaction to yesterday's GP conference? For the first time (ever), am I nervous I've made the wrong career choice? It keeps me awake for the rest of the night.

That, and Alice's East Germany.

Monday, 20th August

Sick day. Man-flu. Hazard of the job.

Wednesday, 22nd August

Largely recovered from my man-flu, but with self-perpetuating questions about my career choice now turning over in my head, a fast spin to make Hotpoint proud, the phone call from Mrs Tally wasn't particularly welcome. She's been talking for a full fifteen minutes now, but like a prehistoric cellular organism adapting to its environment, so have I.

Speakerphone. Ingenious!

I've no idea why I hadn't thought of this before. By the end of her nineteen-minute monologue (*not quite your record, Mrs Tally*), I've managed to complete another patient's haematology (the medical specialty related to diseases of the blood) referral, reply to a social worker's email, text Alice to get her thoughts on whether I should retrain as an international spy, and review all of my pathology results. As for Mrs Tally, I learned once again that her carers still remain spectacularly shit and that this remains absolutely nothing to do with her. As ever, she thanks me for my time.

Alice texted back. Says I'm an idiot.

That'll be a no then.

Thursday, 23rd August

Is it possible to *kill* a job?

Friday, 24th August

I should probably explain yesterday: I cracked. In my defence, it was the perfect storm. It was like all the patients who possess the right blend of skills to each individually smash ten-inch nails into my mental health coffin booked into the same clinic – my Thursday afternoon clinic. From the patient who needed me to examine both his anus and his penis for two separate issues (despite unapologetically arriving fifteen minutes late) to the pain medication addict who tried to intimidate me into prescribing more of his prescribed highs, I really had it all. Layered on this, the bloody computer kept crashing and so I kept having to re-write my consultations. Oh, and I forgot to bring any lunch with me and had no time to go out and get some, partly because I'd left my wallet at home.

Even so, despite this rarest of rare phenomena, I still thought I'd manage to keep a lid on my emotions. Until my last patient arrived. All guns blazing doesn't quite do her justice. Bernadette storms in, bag furiously slammed on the table and tells me, before I've even opened my mouth, *'all you FUCKING GPs are in it together!'* I boil. Zero to one hundred degrees in a fraction of a second. I inhale through my nose. *'In what, exactly?'* I ask, trying to remain as calm as I can. Given her timing at the end of the clinic I've just had, she's fortunate to still be in the room.

She proceeds to roar at how I'll clearly think *she's on the sick* and so probably won't give her a sick note. Which actually is pretty fucking right if she keeps this up. Then I really pull the pin on this social hand grenade and ask why she's unable to work.

'Me FUCKING Stomach Pains!'

Spit lands on my chin, millimetres from my mouth. I swear my eyelid just twitched – the kind you see the unhinged loner experience in the movies just before they crack and kill everybody. *Wow! The emotions I'm feeling right now. Next level.* I don't think Bernadette here quite understands how GP consultations work, or basic manners for that matter. And given that I've allowed her ample time to pull it back from the brink, it's time for some pushback.

For re-education.

I move my chair in line with Bernadette's, so removing the desk as a barrier and making a clear signal of intent to get her attention. I tell her she needs to listen. The fifth time of saying this, she stops. Her entire body sits there, a coiled spring ready to just unfurl, sending her into orbit. I explain that I'll happily end this consultation right now if she doesn't stop shouting or demanding without explanation. This is not a one-stop *I want* shop. She threatens to complain. I hand her the complaint form, not quite letting go as I tell her, *'Or you can listen to me.'* She opens her mouth to speak. My raised hand stops her. *'Please, Bernadette, do yourself a favour,'* I say with a smile this time, *'and LISTEN. TO. ME.'* Flicking to school-teacher mode, I explain that you don't walk into my consultation room and behave like this. I tell her that I don't care what success rate she's had with that behaviour in the past, it's never going to work in my consultation room.

After a few minutes of back and forth, both room temperature and pressure start to become more compatible with life. Finally, I ask her to explain what her stomach issue is. She starts at speed again. Another hand raised, now the understood signal for *slow down.* She starts again, this time more slowly. Turns out it's not her stomach but her pelvis. It's definitely complicated but sounds like a chronic pelvic pain picture that the doctors haven't really figured out the cause of. I tell her it sounds shit for her. She nods, surprised a GP swears (*if only she knew*). Looking at her clinical history, I can see too that she's not had an easy time with her health over the years and while it's still unacceptable to lay siege to my room, I can see more why her approach is the way it is.

My brain is so tired, it's hard to think. I press on, sensing Bernadette has softened a little. In the end, we close the consultation infinitely better than when it started. I do give Bernadette her sick note, organise some further investigations including a transvaginal ultrasound scan, and plan to follow up with her and see if the new pain medication I started is helping. She leaves looking a little less like she wants to stab me.

I shut the door behind me, shaking with anger still. I look at my face in the mirror: I look awful. Exhausted. More than that, for the first time ever in a consultation, I'm visibly red from dissipating anger, the sweat on my hands slowly drying. *Thinking* and *doing* something in anger are usually miles apart. This time though, I know I *was* close to telling her to fuck right off. A slow drowning in patient demand.

Maybe I don't have the mental capacity for this job after all. Exhausted, I lie on the examination couch and stare at the ceiling. Worried. Nervous. I can't ever get that close again.

Monday, 27th August

Well, I never! The first Instant Message I had this morning was from Sally in reception. Blinking in black type font, it reads: *'Bernadette told us all that you are the best doctor she'd ever seen when she left yesterday.'* I can't help but smile at the irony. *'That £10 I slipped her worked then,'* I write back.

Sometimes you can never really guess what patients are thinking as they leave.

Wednesday, 29th August

Any GP who says they don't love a contraceptive pill-check consultation in their clinic is lying. As Katie sits there, having her blood pressure taken, telling me about her Business Management course at university, I know I can put my brain in a low gear. This is essentially a medication review. I feel myself relax, safe in the knowledge that I'm chaos-free for ten minutes.

As I slide the blood pressure cuff off and point Katie in the direction of the weighing scales, I ask her some routine pill-check questions. These include making sure she knows what to do if she forgets to take the pill, then has sex but doesn't want a Mothercare loyalty card in nine months' time.

It all takes less than five minutes. I feel myself get excited: this means five extra minutes to make a proper cup of tea, actually *sit down* on the toilet and enjoy the experience, or call Alice to check up on her and the bump. Now thirty-nine weeks pregnant, she's fit to burst, and to be honest, we're a bit bored of this stage now. As planned, just shy of that five-minute mark, Katie skips out with her anti-Mothercare contraception prescription and I skip off to the toilet. Sitting here in its solitude, I realise it's not even just about getting this time back. It's about respite.

Respite physically. Respite emotionally. Respite mentally.

If every clinic was like last Thursday's, rammed full of the most complex, demanding, and unrelenting patients, back-to-back every ten minutes over a three-hour clinic, I'd surely go up in flames. A simple pill-check like this – well, that's a fire-hose.

Friday, 31st August

So, life will change next week. Alice got the call this morning – she's being induced on Monday. Thank God I took next week as annual leave – we thought this might happen. I fight endless smiles as I sit on the bus home. But I give up. I can't, I'm so excited.

I'm going to be a dad.

SEPTEMBER 2018

Tuesday, 18th September

Fuck me, this is hard work.

Thursday, 20th September (02:54am)

William Arthur Skittle, 9lb 2 oz. Half me, half Alice. Now fifteen days old. No longer just *the bump*. I'm obsessed. His eyes. His feet. His hands. In the walled protection of his dinosaur changing mat, I watch them all. I'm consumed with love. Alice continues to blow my mind, first navigating the birth process like a Viking storming ashore – focused, aggressive, passionate, and since then, being the mother I knew she would – kind, loving, and gentle.

Drunk with love, that's the only way I can describe my feelings. But like I said, the other day, it's hard work. For starters, Alice and I haven't slept properly since he shot out with some forceps wrapped around his head. The cycle of feeding and nappy changes is endless. *'Not yet independent, are you, William?'*, I whisper.

I start to encase his bottom in yet another nappy – a fraction too slow. Shit everywhere. *Everywhere.* William stares up at me patiently under the glow of his night light, indifferent to it all – a signal that this doesn't become *his* problem for a few more years.

We start the cleaning process once more.

Thursday, 20th September (03:38am)

William clearly has a thing for this changing mat. Here again less than forty-five minutes later. In his defence, I think I forgot to poke his alarmingly tiny penis downwards on the last change, so he's probably sent pee up himself.

Sorry, pal, lesson learned. Though you try pointing a press stud in any sustainable direction.

Thursday, 20th September (06:47am)

The night over, I let myself quietly collapse into bed, catching the first signs of this morning's sunrise through the blinds as I do. *God, this mattress feels bloody good!* Alice has already drifted off next to me, having once again provided our insatiable boy with another milk binge. *Greedy fucker.* My eyes hurt now. I'm not sure if I slept. I don't think I did. *Maybe I'm asleep now and this is all a dream? It can't be. William's already crying again.* I say a few quiet words to the bed (principally, *don't go anywhere, please, I'll be back*) and, circumventing its frame, I collect up my 10lb sleep-crusher and cradle him. Once again a sense of exhausted euphoria floods me.

Friday, 21st September (11:58pm)

The sitting-room floorboards creak in protest as another night begins and I gently bounce from side to side. In one hand a whisky, in the other, the TV remote control. William nestles between the two, fast asleep in his carry harness. I kiss the top of his tiny bald head in celebration of our teamwork – he gets to sleep, and I get to watch all the TV shows that Alice hates to watch with me.

Ingenious. We should have had a baby years ago.

Saturday, 22nd September (04:12am)

Alice looks at me, perplexed. I continue to bounce in front of her with William fast asleep before whispering, *'I just need another twenty minutes.'* I explain the documentary – about a climber trying to be the first to free-climb this monster rock face, El-Capitan – that William and I are watching is reaching its climax. We'll be with her soon. She seems to enjoy reminding me that I go back to work next week, so this might not seem as much fun then. I smile in defiance. Then her silhouette about turns and pads off to the bedroom, shouting, *'Have fun in your boys' club!'* I think she was deliberately trying to sabotage my scheme by shouting.

Still, you hear that, William? We've got a club! How about that?

Saturday, 22nd September (2:49pm)

Woke up on the toilet. That's what exhaustion can do. Still, one to tick off the bucket list.

Monday, 24th September (04:01am)

We stand here, peering over his Moses basket. Really not sure what to make of it, I cock my head to get another angle. Yep, definitely a cross between a shit high-street facial and budget superhero mask. Alice nods, commenting too on the impressive uniformity of distribution. We look at each other and then burst out laughing.

William, you fucking legend! Somehow, while fast asleep, you've managed to vomit a perfect film of white backwards over your face, from your top lip to the top of your head. I mean, how? HOW? Two very surprised newborn eyes blink at us through the white, a silent mouth in accompaniment, too shocked to cry. I wipe the vomit away with my hand, gently using a thumb to clear his eyes. Then, William does something that makes us fall in love with him a little bit more: he releases a huge gummy smile. Like I say, our little legend.

Monday, 24th September (08:47am)

Google *how much caffeine can kill you?* and you get 173,000,000 hits. It's too much for me to take in right now, so I'll chance it and make another one. And it's needed, since today signals the end of my two weeks of paternity leave and the return to work. Tiredness is sadly no longer something to share quietly with Alice and William in the safety net of our home. Now it's on display to my patients. Caffeine therefore serves as an important lifeline to put forward some kind of public façade that I am indeed, ready to begin doctoring once more. Even if that's some way from the truth. And there's no getting away from it, they're certainly going to be getting a slightly more dishevelled version of the GP they met before William was born. At least for the short term. (I hope).

Since his birth, exhaustion's crept into every cell of my body. Mentally, well, I clearly have a 'baby brain', my mind primarily now a melting pot of knowledge on sterilising baby bottles, feeding regimens, navigating complex baby grows, changing nappies, and the best ways to clean up shit and/or vomit. Plus, let me put it bluntly, my thoughts and focus are entirely back home. Wondering what Alice and William are up to. Are they alright? Are they missing me as much as I'm missing them? Silly, I realise.

I'm sure all that medical knowledge is still in there but right now, it's like someone's locked it in the boot of a nondescript car in a cerebral multi-storey in my brain – and forgotten what level it's on. It'll come back to me, I hope. If it doesn't, we'll soon find out. As I take another long sip of black coffee, I can't help but wonder just how much becoming a parent will change me as a GP.

Well, I guess we'll find out.

Monday, 24th September (09:58am)

How have I only been at work for two hours? It feels like a lifetime. Petunia sits in front of me. I wonder if she can tell I've only had four hours' sleep since 11pm last night – I definitely can. Yep, she probably can too. I'm displaying that classic stifling yawn, something patients hate as they assume you're bored of them (*sometimes true*), rather than just tired (*always true since William's pitched up*). The fact it looks as if I've dressed in the dark (*I did*), not paying any attention to what I was wrapping around my body (*I wasn't*), is likely a big clue.

Despite all this, at least Petunia's interesting. Not clinically, as from her history it sounds like she's got a simple urinary tract infection (UTI). What *is* interesting though is her prolific use of the word *piss*. I've never seen it used, both as a verb and a noun, quite so enthusiastically. Of all the frequently used options available – to *urinate*, to *go to the toilet*, to *pass urine*, to *wee*, to *pee*, to *spend a penny*, to *take a leak*, to *whizz* – her default option is *piss*. As I test her urine (sorry, Petunia, *piss*) sample for evidence of infection, I ask her more about her symptoms. *Piss* continues to be brandished in every painfully shared sentence. I check her past medical history. Nope, this isn't a verbal tic. It is grating though, now eight minutes in.

Nails on a blackboard.

Yet I know this really shouldn't be bothering me. Everyone's different, and so chalk it down to lack of sleep. Or perhaps it's just the sheer repetition of the word (*any* word said enough times begins to sound odd, try it). I keep my head low as I wash my hands, cleansing myself of any of Petunia's *piss* and, with drawing breath, turn around. She sits, awaiting the verdict. I deliver the unexciting news: she does indeed have urinary tract infection. Yes, a *piss* infection. The good news is she'll be back to normal in no time after a short course of antibiotics.

Happy with the outcome, she looks up at me as I stand to get the door for her.

Yes, Petunia, this is now your cue: *piss off.*

Monday, 24th September 2019 (5:59pm)

I'm not sure what I did wrong to deserve such a treat as the last patient of the day. Mr O'Keefe is fifty-eight years old and your classic ex-financial services sector man, retired for the quieter life out of London following a messy divorce and a breakdown. And he's still very tightly wound. He's here for his 24-hour blood pressure recording results. Organised because Sarah, one of my colleagues, noted a high reading when he saw her in clinic last month.

It would have been great if Sarah had followed him up herself but the days of easily being able to regularly see *your* routinely GP on request are petering out (well, clubbed to death) due to the ongoing increase in demand. So it's more about taking an appointment when you can get it, sadly. And Mr O'Keefe got me. To be honest, it doesn't surprise me one bit that his blood pressure is raised. He hasn't stopped talking. And not just talking but, my God, talking with an urgency, frustration (mainly at the NHS, of course), and force that's quite something to marvel at. I sit there, perfectly still. Like I'm playing *What's the Time, Mr Wolf?* and don't want to get caught. I'll let him talk. Men like this rarely have an off button you can ask to press.

Control. Control. Control.

Maybe he should meet Mrs Tally, my 83-year-old, who tries to exert a similar control over which carers she gets? Mind you, maybe too much of an age gap? With Mr O'Keefe, I decide to type as he talks. Mainly since he's clearly going to have no bloody interest in what I have to say about his blood pressure. It seems he's booked this appointment to come and talk *at me.* How lovely of him. When finally he pauses for breath, red-faced, I turn and explain that, irrespective of his frustrations, he has high blood pressure. This is a fact that he cannot reason away. I pause. He remains red-faced. I continue. Explain this increases his risk of a catastrophic adverse health event like a heart attack or a stroke. He blinks, stunned. As if I've just confessed my undying love for him. And then, off he goes again, ranting about how he already has a low-salt diet, exercises with a personal trainer, and has started mindfulness.

I stop typing. *'Mindfulness?'* I try to ask without dumbfounded astonishment but definitely fail, as he ignores my question and continues to rant. There's no way this guy is ever going to achieve a state of mindfulness. Not with this rod up his arse, anyway. He's the guy who'll have a heart attack at the sheer frustration of trying to get the mindfulness app to download. I zone out for a little while longer, wondering what Alice and William are up to. Then I glance at the clock on my computer: right, he's had ten minutes of my time. We're achieving nothing here. I swing my chair around and give a professional smile. I explain that sometimes, despite a person's excellent efforts, blood pressure can still rise with age. In these cases, we still need to try to control it. With this for context, I ask him directly if he'd consider taking a daily medication to help control his blood pressure.

No, Max, of course he fucking wouldn't.

He starts to go off on one about how *all we GPs do is dish out drugs.* I stand up and extend a hand. I explain we're going around in circles and so should end things here. The Mr O'Keefes of this world, I expect, need a little hardball thrown in their direction if ever they're going to listen. I tell him it's nice to meet him (*it isn't*) and if he changes his mind about controlling his blood pressure and reducing his chances of death, to come and see me any time. He shakes my hand, equally unsure and unsettled by my approach – and leaves. I doubt I'll ever see him.

His health. His choice.

Tuesday, 25th September (11:32am)

I never appreciated that talking about sleep – when all you want to do, is sleep – would be so bloody painful. I suffer in silence. Jerry's sitting uncomfortably close. He's a *dragger*. That patient who comes in, and as they sit down, they drag their chair in close to yours. Uninvited. Unwelcome. With my personal space overrun, the inside of my head silently screams at him to fuck off. My mouth instead draws a welcoming smile. Our knees are inches apart. So close in fact that if they were lips, and we were maladjusted teenagers, well, someone would be going in for a kiss right now.

Jerry also has a large neck. A twenty-inch collar size, he tells me. I nod with interest, knowing full well this'll be part of the reason why his issues – poor sleep and snoring – are going to be tricky ones to overcome quickly. I sit, half-awake, half-asleep, and invite him to tell me more – anything really to allow me another minute to sit quietly. I ask him what collar size he is. Again. He looks puzzled. I apologise, though – I'll probably be asking him again in a couple of minutes. Jerry tells me his snoring is ruining his relationship with long-term girlfriend Ellie (who now makes him sleep in the spare room when the snoring gets really bad). It's also bankrupting his ability to get a good night's sleep and do his job at the local supermarket in the daytime (as he's so exhausted and sleepy – *I know the feeling, mate*). At least he doesn't drive. That saves me a trickier conversation.

As I listen, I subliminally *will* him to stop saying the word *sleep*. It's torture. I feel the awareness of my own body sneak off, neither with forewarning nor permission, and realise I'm on the cusp of nodding off. I lean forward and take a sip of coffee. Stone-cold. Who cares? Right now I'd lick coffee granules off the patient toilet seat in winter Norovirus season if you told me they were the last ones on earth. As I listen more, it turns out unfortunately Jerry's ticking every snore-promoting activity in the book. He drinks alcohol most nights. He sleeps on his back. He even takes sleeping tablets sometimes. And let's not forget that massive neck. I flick around my computer screen and show him an anatomical image of the human mouth and neck, explaining that as he sleeps, all these muscles and other soft tissues relax. As he then inhales air, the turbulence generated over these now jelly-like structures causes vibration. That's snoring. The booze, the sleeping tablets, the sleeping on his back, and the large neck (due to the weight of compression) all make snoring worse. As an added bonus, it sounds like when Jerry sleeps, he not only snores but has pauses in his breathing. These are called apnoeic episodes. That's why he quite literally snorts himself awake. His clever brain, keeping him alive by waking him to breathe.

I give him space to digest everything I say, turning back to the computer and typing up his clinical notes. Plus, if I start typing, I'm being active. If I'm active, I can't fall asleep (though I thought going to the toilet was an activity and that didn't work out so well the other day). He starts to ask more questions but my now palliative printer, 'Hew', beats him to the punch, spitting out a patient information leaflet (PIL) on snoring.

'Right, Jerry. Stop drinking every bloody night,' I say with *a sympathetic smile. 'Sleep on your side. Buy your girlfriend ear plugs. No more sleeping tablets.'* I pause, before adding, *'And strap a tennis ball to your back.'* Jerry looks up as I finish

delivering my cliff notes summary of snoring management. He tells me he doesn't like tennis. I smile, moving my knees even further away – my sign to him that this consultation is over – and reassure him that this non-interest in tennis shouldn't harm his prognosis.

Tuesday, 25th September (1:12pm)

I feel like I'm walking (well, lying) in the shoes of the thousands of patients I've guided to this examination couch over the last three years. I stare at my room's ceiling, examining it properly for what feels like the first time, and listen to my breathing, slow and deep. I realise how incongruent my mind is with my physical position – patients no longer dominating daily thought.

I have a son. An amazing wife. A little nuclear family.

I break out into a smile. Everything feels different. Life *feels* different, private and professional. The two really are inseparable. I close my eyes and am met with a sense of serenity, something that has been increasingly hard to find at work for a few months now. *Who would have thought a baby would have changed my life as a GP so quickly?*

Setting my phone alarm, I allow myself ten minutes of sleep.

Tuesday, 25th September (1:14pm)

Knew I should've taken the bloody room phone off the hook.

Wednesday, 26th September (1:17pm)

A 99-year-old vagina. As I stand at the bedside armed with the smallest speculum I could find, I explain to Elsie what's about to happen. She raises her eyebrows and tells me to *'do what I have to do'*. That's probably the right word for it, Elsie – *have*. Because, respectfully, it certainly isn't out of *want* that I'm doing this. Her carer, whose name I've been told twice – and forgotten twice – is the reason I'm here. Blood-stained discharge (thought to be from her vaginal canal) was seen when she changed Elsie's urinary continence pad this morning. Somehow the duty doctor at the surgery felt this was the perfect home visit case for me.

Lying on her neatly made bed, both knees bent, ankles apart, and her dignity covered by the most fantastic patchwork quilt I've ever seen, I make my descent. The key trick here is as you approach, not to breathe through your nose. To complicate matters, the light in here is awful. In position, I part both her labia (skin folds either side of the vagina) before advancing the KY Jelly lubricated speculum into her vaginal canal. I'm half-leaning on Elsie's bed, half off it. And with my head bent at ninety degrees, craning down the speculum, I try to visualise her cervix and the anatomy of her vaginal canal. It's pretty dark but I can't see anything immediately of concern. No blood. No discharge. No masses. I think about asking her carer to flash my iPhone light down there for me to get a better look but realise how that might come across. Plus, with both my hands busy, she'd have to rummage it out of my front trouser pocket. Just too many *Daily Mail* headlines there, I fear.

Reassured this is just a vagina consistent with an impressive ninety-nine years on earth, I remove the speculum and gently help Elsie get dressed and into a more comfortable position. She is utterly fantastic throughout the process, telling me afterwards, it *'just tickled a little'*. I seriously doubt that. I explain that I couldn't see anything worrying and we agree to watch and wait. No further investigation at this stage. Both of us are of the mindset that, at ninety-nine years young, some things should be left alone, undiscovered. What Elsie's saying here is that if there's, for example, a cancer, she doesn't need to know about it – not at her stage of life. I respect every word. At ninety-nine years, the cancer would outlive her (that is, more likely she'd die of a brief acute illness or old age).

She offers me a cup of tea and I duly oblige. We sit for ten minutes, talking about her life, her work during the war, her late husband, Stanley, whose photo she still kisses goodnight *every* night, and how she never got the chance to have children. As I sit beside her, I show her a picture of Alice and William. She beams with joy and gives me a hug, congratulating me. I radiate with new family pride and at the warmth of this woman. This is why I love being a GP, being *my* kind of GP. After all, how many jobs can start with a vaginal examination and end with seeing a glorious near-centurion-year-old woman light up as someone takes interest in her life? A life that clearly brought her so much joy.

I think of Alice and William on the walk back to the GP surgery, of our life ahead yet to be lived. Happy tears prick my eyes.

Wednesday, 26th September (10:50pm)

I place all four paediatric (children's) thermometers on the pharmacy counter. The cashier looks at me and asks which one I want. I smile, knowing how this is going to sound.

'All of them.'

My tone implies this is obvious. *Smart arse. The things we do for love.* As he rings the thermometers through the till, he earnestly advises me I should see my GP if I'm this worried about my son. I nod, keeping my head down as I get out my credit card, before telling him, *'I am a GP.'* His condescending smile is like dragging knuckles over gravel. I want to tell him that I'm *not* actually worried, but I hold back, fully aware of how unbelievably incongruent that is with my actions right now, standing in his late-night pharmacy.

Rewind one hour ago and I was sitting on the sofa, enjoying an episode of *Game of Thrones* with Alice. William was asleep in his Moses basket on the floor in front of us with this creepy glowing sheep that's meant to make sounds like the womb (to comfort William) next to him. *Can't wait for the batteries to die.* Alice then decided that William *looked warm.* From that point, my evening was over. Jon Snow's battle with the White Walkers – and my beer – would have to wait. It's true when you're in love, you do the things you wouldn't normally do. Which is why when Alice began to worry that William had a fever, I headed off to the local pharmacy, with a *'Sure, no problem, my love.'* My internal monologue more of the *are you fucking kidding me?* ilk.

On my return, I dramatically rip open the bag and let four thermometers scatter the kitchen table, inviting Alice to her pick of the spoils. She surveys her options. We have axillary (under the armpit), thermadot (for the forehead), infra-red (definitely the coolest), and tympanic (in the ear) thermometers. William just lies there, the picture of health. All four thermometers show that not only is he appearing like this, he's also got a completely normal temperature. It's too late now to pick up with Jon Snow, so I pack up our new stash of thermometers and head off to bed with Alice, ready for another night cycle of feed-sleep-shit.

Like I said, love.

Thursday, 27th September

This isn't love, this is cruelty. Jealousy. Cowardice. I've not met Natalia's husband but already I know I hate the fucker. With a female colleague, Sarah, also present, we gently examine and photograph her bruises. The room feels quiet. Cold. Awkward. I'm finding it hard to maintain a professional tone as Natalia tells me that *he* didn't mean to do it – this time. My stomach knots as she discloses only today what is apparently a three-year history of abuse. One we, at the surgery, had no idea about.

Inviting Natalia to sit down, I let Sarah go back to her own clinic now that the physical examination is over. Natalia is only twenty-eight years old. She came to the UK on her husband's VISA. He knows this apparently and it's one of the main reasons she's stayed with him – fear of being forced to leave and losing her son, Ethan, only six years old. I tell her she's been incredibly brave coming here and that she should be proud of taking this step. The consultation runs well past the twenty-minute mark. Nearer thirty now. No matter, this woman needs time and support in a way that a routine blood pressure check, sore ear, or a renewal of a sick note do not – so it's my decision to overrun. We might all have ten-minute appointment slots, but the reality is one size doesn't fit all.

Natalia doesn't want to go to the police. I quietly sigh. It turns out despite being a total prick, her husband is apparently a good father. The vision of a man who physically beats his wife but can still be a good father cannot materialise in my mind. She's in denial. Completely understandable. She can't see the unfiltered truth that sits outside her own created fictional perspective designed for the sole purpose of protecting her son and his opportunities in the UK, I expect. I know there's an uncomfortable conversation ahead. I ask again about Ethan. My heart sinks as the words leave her mouth and puncture the air. Yes, he has seen his mum get beaten by her dad. I think of William. I think of Alice. I've seen my fair share of abuse presentations when working in A&E departments but there's something detached, even surreal about such a violent discussion in this, such a calm setting. In an A&E department there's that congruent sense of urgency and acuteness. You can lose that in a GP surgery setting, everything slowing down.

Natalia doesn't seem to think Ethan understands much of what's going on. At six, I disagree – I'm sure he knows enough. Gently, I pull my chair in closer and fire a softly-spoken warning shot that I've something difficult to explain: I need to inform Children's Social Services. Natalia's reaction is volatile. Unsurprising. She stands up and with her hands to her temples, revealing the fingermarks of abuse around her upper arms, starts telling me that I can't do this, that she'll lose Ethan, and that he (her prick of a husband) will find out. Sadly, this isn't negotiable. I have a professional responsibility, I explain, to her but also a legal responsibility to Ethan as a child involved. He cannot be exposed to this. The brutality of the truth is that Natalia *can* choose to remain, *can* choose not to report him to the police. Ethan *cannot.* He simply doesn't have the capacity, at six years of age, to make that choice.

Natalia stands over me, staring. Betrayed. I don't get up to challenge her. Instead, I let her dominate me and say nothing. After what seems like a measurably uncomfortable period, Natalia sits back down and faces me. It reminds me that at some point I've become comfortable with uncomfortable situations and if you want to have a long shelf-life as a GP, I think it's essential. It's wearing on the soul otherwise. The natural instinct at this point is for me to say I'm sorry. Because I want to. Because I'm human. But that would also suggest that I'm taking an action to cause harm. And I'm not: I want to prevent harm. It's a really complicated issue but in this case it's the only action to take. It's also the right thing to tell her with an unvarnished truth. A sugar-coated shit is still a shit. And people just chew it, confused at the disparity between taste and look.

I'm feeling as though Natalia is coming down from her unimaginable set of emotions. I also expect that she's frightened. Terrified. With a calm now coming over our consultation, I ask if she would see a woman I know from a local domestic violence charity that supports women in her position. Having worked with her before, I know that she doesn't mind me telling others that she was once in Natalia's position – a victim of abuse – and now works to help others. A motivational fuel like no other, I expect. Natalia nods quietly. I build the bridge back up. I explain that this charity worker can meet Natalia anywhere she wants, including here at the GP surgery, embedded within a normal consultation. Nobody needs to know. She can communicate through me to this charity worker and so her husband would not only have no idea but also have no right to ask about a confidential GP appointment.

The prick.

She agrees. I lean back slowly. Exhausted, but relieved for her. She's taken another step. We discuss some more issues for a further ten minutes, from what to do in a domestic crisis situation and what will happen with Children's Social Services – Natalia now slightly more understanding of this action and I reassure her they'll be equally discreet and supportive – to how to contact other support services. I also book her back in to see me again soon. With all that done, she leaves for home.

Back to her abuser.

I close the door after her and collapse in my seat, completely and utterly drained of emotion.

Friday, 28th September

'*It's Peppa Pig or nothing,*' I explain firmly. Isabelle sits there, arms crossed, tiny legs swinging from the chair, twig-like and not yet anywhere close to reaching the ground. Little in stature, large in personality. I let out a theatrical sigh, throw my hands in the air, and promise her by next time I'll have some more *Frozen* stickers for her. Her mum looks on, bemused at the ongoing, protracted negotiations now easily in their fifth minute. She juggles her car keys, a gentle but indisputable signal that she wants me to hurry this up. I exchange a nod of receipt and turning my attention back to Isabelle, can see that I'm in for a battle – her arms now folded even tighter. I lean in to her.

'Did you know that apparently, Elsa loves Peppa Pig?'

She might be six but she throws me a look that says she's no chump. It was worth a try. *Fuck it.* I send an URGENT Instant Message to all the clinical staff in the GP surgery that day, asking, *'DOES ANYONE HAVE* FROZEN *STICKERS? NEED ASAP. CHEERS, MAX'.* Various GPs reply with varying levels of banter, all equally unhelpful. *Twats.* Finally, one of the practice nurses, Pat, replies: she has some.

I bounce from my chair, telling Isabelle to wait one more second. Then I sprint down the stairs two at a time, towards the nurses' room by reception, grab the generously donated stickers, and sprint back up to my room. I deliver the stickers to Isabelle. She peers at them. Studies them. I think I even see some scrutinising. At last, she points.

'That one,' she commands.

I carefully peel it off and after being directed as to the *precise* location, stick the Elsa sticker onto her jumper. She nods. A silent approval. With that, she hops off the chair, landing with a slap of her tiny shoes, shouts *'Thanks!'* and walks out with Mum. I stand there, still clutching the sheet of *Frozen* stickers – now minus one Princess Elsa – that I've just worked so hard to get. I sit down to type up her consultation notes, having to take a moment, after sticker-gate, to remember why Isabelle was even here today. Many consultations are like that though, memorable for everything other than the medicine. That's the beauty of the job. In Isabelle's case, she might well have been here for a simple cough (part of a viral illness, I concluded) but her first consultation with me will always be remembered for stickers.

Just stickers.

Saturday, 29th September (4:13pm)

Moths to a flame. That's the only way to describe the scene unfolding this weekend. Standing in the gardens of this incredible castle, wedding guests – some of whom I know but many of whom I've no idea who they are, migrate towards William. Some approach on a direct line, others take a more subtle, indirect, almost accidental approach. And he's not even doing that much – just sitting there in his carry harness, strapped to me like some sort of small, squashed, boring mole, head slumped against the white of my shirt.

I suppose he does have the novelty factor of being one of the younger wedding guests here by quite some margin. More importantly, he famously slept through the church service. A novelty given that the other four babies didn't (they all had massive meltdowns, much to my delight). The trick? Alice and I basically decided to fill him up with as much milk as we could – thereby knocking him out. Fool-proof! I must remember to share this, an accidently discovered top tip, with any parents of babies I see in clinic in the next few weeks. I smile at the thought. I mean, who would have thought becoming a parent would have paid itself forward into work so early on?

As I continue to rotate William around the gardens, the migration continues. And though not wanting to stereotype, there's definitely more women than men approaching him. If I wasn't happily married, William, you'd be an unbelievable wingman, my son. Even better than the dog I borrowed that weekend (*pre-Alice, I might add*). I take a sip of champagne and try to wash away this stream of consciousness, now getting uncomfortably weird. As for the men coming over . . . well, it's fair to say most are being dragged by their other halves. I conclude that's the thing about a wedding – it supercharges all those warm, fuzzy feelings about love and brooding.

A box-fresh baby present is just the emotional MDMA icing on top.

Saturday, 29th September (10:05pm)

William's been an amazing show pony for the last six hours of the wedding. He's yawned, cried a little, stared a lot, slept, sat (well, sure, leaned) awake doing absolutely nothing, and shat himself many, many times. All to the delight of cooing wedding guests. Alice and I have been taking it in turns to look after him (while the other runs off to dance as much as they can, reliving bygone baby-free days), but we're now officially exhausted. Broken. It's hard work looking after a 3-week-old baby at a wedding.

All I can think of are ducks. We, Alice and I, are ducks. On the surface of it all, we seem to be gliding effortlessly through the wedding day. Carefree, projecting a *baby, what baby? It's so easy!* façade. In reality, we're non-stop paddling the fuck out of the water in a frenzied, inconspicuous effort to simply stay afloat. Which is why as I drove us all back to the hotel, Alice and I both weakened to silence and William finally enjoying the meltdown he utterly deserved after today's performance – when the car broke down I wasn't in the least bit surprised. There was always going to be the price to pay for the perfect day.

Karma. And here it is.

I think one of the fuel injection cylinders has blown. We've gone from 60mph to 6mph in the blink of an eye. We're only one mile away from the hotel. I resolve the dilemma in my mind: there's no way I'm having Alice and William sit in a lay-by when we're this close. William continues to cry. I block it out and concentrate. We decide to chance the final mile at 6mph. Alice is using her arm to gesture any late-night cars behind us to overtake (not tricky, given our speed), and I drive with the hazard lights on. After what seems like a very long mile, we roll into the hotel car park. We exchange a look, Alice and I, as William continues to express losing his shit and smile at each other.

'Well done, my love.'

A quick kiss. I feel accomplished. Relieved. Still exhausted.

Alice takes William off for a comfort breastfeed and then bed, while I unpack the endless baby-related kit that now comes everywhere with us. Then, as it's a nice night, I lean against the wheel arch of the car for a bit, on hold to our breakdown insurer, and take in the night sky. I should be furious right now. Enraged. Angry at life. But I'm not. That would've been the old me, pre-William. Instead, I'm simply happy and relieved my little family are safe and sound. That's all that matters now.

How life has changed.

FLASHBACK: THE ROAD TO BECOMING A GP

I didn't wake up one day and decide to become a GP. Far from it. In fact, I thought it all sounded incredibly boring when the idea was raised early in my medical training. All too touchy-feely. Not to mention a notion utterly incongruent with my mum's assessment of me when I announced my intention to become a doctor – *'But, Max, you don't like people!'*

Thanks, Mum.

Instead, as a doctor, I wanted to seek out the drama. The Action. The Blood. To me, general practice offered none of that. In any case, I began training. First, I went to medical school for six years. Then after I graduated from there, I trained as a junior doctor for what they call two Foundation Years (*FY1* and *FY2*) in a number of hospitals. I did these before deciding what speciality I wanted to train in. Essentially, those two years are about learning how to be a doctor *on the job*. And not kill anyone by accident. After all, I was fresh out of medical school – and although yes, technically a qualified medical doctor – as inexperienced (and terrified) as you could get. But critically, it was in those two years where, as I moved around the different medical and surgical specialities every four months, the seeds of becoming a GP started to be unconsciously sown. Extracting the sense that general practice might actually be the unlikely match for me after all.

What follows aren't necessary those seed-sowing moments (that's all rather boring to hear about). Instead, I wanted to share some of the moments when I learned about myself as a person – and a doctor – during my early life as a GP. What accompanies these are some of the unexpected reminders for life that were accidentally acquired along the way. I use the word 'reminder' deliberately. After all, these aren't earth-shattering realisations, it's what we all know. It's just that sometimes we need just that – a little reminder.

Reminder 1: Nothing's ever (usually) as bad as you think

Status: Day before my first day as a junior doctor

I stare at the shirt. Completely creased. My third ironing attempt. How have I made it *worse*? I'm fucked, truly totally and utterly fucked. I'm going to kill scores of people tomorrow, I'm sure of it. I'll be the headline of every *Daily Mail* newspaper for weeks to come.

Doctor too incompetent to even iron shirt – after three attempts – kills masses.

Reminder 2: When you start at the bottom, think positive – the only way is up

Status: FY1 in General Surgery

I'm sure it's shit I smell. Sitting in one of the surgical outpatient waiting areas, I stand by with eight other box-fresh junior doctors waiting for our boss – one of the surgical consultants – to arrive. I scan the area, backwards and forwards, the only thing to keep me busy in the deafening silence. It's so loud. Palpable. I hate it. I decide it's too hard to tell. Either one of my peers has just shat themselves in terror, or it's because we're in the colorectal (*bottom and bowels*) surgical department. My plans to narrow down and sniff out which junior doctor's the culprit with a causal walkabout are pushed aside. In strides, Mr Thornton-Cox, who at a height just shy of official pygmy status looks like he's going to be a real piece of work.

'Just remember, shit rolls downhill.'

That's it. That's the opening line from my first-ever boss as a qualified doctor. If he's the top of the hill, it's not going to take long to reach me then. Let the nightmare begin.

Reminder 3: Self-belief is key, so stick to your guns

Status: FY1 in General Surgery

Tiff the ward nurse looks at me, incredulous: *'You said she was dead?'* I place my clipboard gently down on the nurses' station and work out how the hell to get out of this one. Stick to my guns. There's a rational approach.

'She is,' I state with no confidence whatsoever.

I loathe these weekend on-call shifts – running around hospital surgical wards for twelve hours straight, just you and a skeletal crew of other doctors, mopping up all the unresolved shit from the working week before. In this case, the unresolved shit is that I thought Mrs Higgins *was* dead. I'd been in to certify her death only an hour ago, having performed a full check to confirm death: her pupils fixed and dilated, no carotid pulse, no heart sounds, and no respiratory effort for three minutes (plus, a bunch of other stuff, like checking they're not just asleep because yes, that has happened). It was also an expected death with her clinical condition sadly deteriorating over the last forty-eight hours.

My stomach churns. I'd already called and informed her family. The nurse continues to stand there, nose deliberately pointed down, eyebrows raised – her sign language for *you fucking moron*, I expect. Despite being so exhausted, I realise I haven't even questioned why Tiff here thinks Mrs Higgins *isn't* dead.

'The bed sheet is moving.'

I just stand there, really hoping there's some other piece of evidence she's about to give me – like she rang her bedside call bell and asked for a cup of tea. Nope. Just the bed sheet moving. I look over to the bay where Mrs Higgins is apparently not dead. Being 10:30pm, it's pretty quiet on the ward. I say pretty quiet because I can hear *something*. A gentle *whirr*. And I think it's coming from Mrs Higgins' now curtained bay. Slowly, I walk over, feeling like I'm in some budget horror film, and stick my head into the bay. I make the *whirr* stop. I then come back and inform Tiff that while Mrs Higgins remains dead, the oscillating fan at her bedside is still very much alive.

Reminder 4: Respect your place in the pecking order

Status: FY1 in Intensive Care Medicine

Now working on the Intensive Care Unit (ICU). As a doctor. This is ridiculous for many reasons. Mainly since, as an FY1, it means I'm some proper intensive care doctor's secretary, following them around taking notes and watching them be absolute rock stars of the medical world for the next four months. I say this because intensive care doctors look after the most critically ill and complex patients in the hospital. This means they not only have an intimidating amount of medical knowledge and skill, but they can do it all under pressure. And look bloody cool doing it. Like I said, rock stars. Me, I can't even spell half the procedures they do.

Reminder 5: When life gets scary, dig out your big boy/ girl pants, and get them on!

Status: FY1 in Care of the Elderly Medicine

Death's having a field day. Three patients dead in the last twenty-four hours on the Care of the Elderly ward I'm working on. Maybe a rebrand to *God's Waiting Room* is needed? The day's barely crawled to 08:05am but already, I've had to delay the start of my ward round (my senior doctor will be with me by 10am, I'm told), and am now trying to contact the relatives of Mr Joseph, the latest patient to permanently check out.

I learn from his clinical notes that the on-call overnight medical team were called to his resuscitation attempt at 07:39am, only twenty-one minutes before I stepped onto the ward. Cardiac arrest the final, fatal ruling. It was felt it would be better for one of Mr Joseph's regular doctors to inform the family. *How kind of them to think of me.* As the phone continues to ring, I perch on the nurses' station desk, gazing at our ward entrance doors, my brain still warming up. I'm not particularly looking at anything, my mind too distracted by the monotony of the dial tone and wondering if anyone else will die before lunchtime. My gaze of the clear-glass ward door windows disrupts. There's a mass of movement – enough movement, and enough mass, in fact to snap me fully and immediately out of my telephonic trance. I refocus on the door. *Shit.* Ten clearly distraught individuals are now banging on the ward doors.

Not taking my eyes off them, I place the phone receiver down, knowing full well that Mr Joseph's relatives aren't picking up the phone – because they're too busy banging on the buzzer-controlled doors in front of me. That extra Weetabix would've been welcome in hindsight. The senior nurse, Shelia, tells me not to open the door as the relatives don't know Mr Joseph's dead yet. Skirting over the fact they look like they've a pretty good idea, I explain that it's just a bit awkward if we don't. As I open the ward doors, I get a taste of what being on the streets of the Pamplona Bull Run feels like. All ten stampede past me into Mr Joseph's bay, where cries of despair, devastation, and realisation now echo.

As much as I'd love to ignore a day like today, preferring perhaps to be climbing back under the covers of this morning's warm duvet, I guess it's time to be an actual doctor. Something I'm slowly realising doesn't always involve medicine. Instead, it involves communicating. I stand at the curtained opening of his bay, more than a little terrified. *'I'm so sorry for your loss'* leaves my mouth, turning ten heads towards me. One head turns more than most. Like an olive branch being held out, this particular head tells me what I really needed to know, that he's Mr Joseph's brother, Samuel – and importantly, his next of kin.

Despite vocal protests from the other relatives, all understandably wanting information, Samuel agrees to step outside so I can first explain to him what happened. I sit him down, get him a cup of tea. I explain. Re-explain. Twice. I check he understands (he does). I then let him first go back in alone and explain to the rest of the family. I might be still very new to this job but even I know that it's not my role to explain things to ten relatives, nor is it the best way to get information across. I leave them to grieve, asking Shelia and the other nurses to give them some space, and we get on with the other jobs on the ward.

An hour later, as they all start to leave, Samuel comes up to me and does something I wasn't expecting: he thanks me. I shake his hand and wish him well. Then, I just sit and stare. Stare at my hands more than anything else. Silly, when I think about it now but I really do remember a feeling of exhilaration at the time. Overcome by a sense of purpose. It might not even be 10:30am yet, but already I've had a day to remember.

Reminder 6: Sometimes people will try and ride you

Status: FY2 in A&E Medicine

I wish this Terry would shut up. Nobody, absolutely nobody, wants to hear him. Not the A&E department staff, not the other patients, and definitely not me despite him being *my* patient. After a month working in A&E, I get how chaotic it looks from the outside – staff running around, people shouting, endless machines alarming, windowless artificial strip lighting disorientating you from night and day, and of course, a stack of sick people without the space to put them all somewhere. And that's about right. But I'm not running, I'm sitting. Sitting at the nurses' station, working very hard to ignore the fact that Terry, the vocal shit in Bay 12, is my next patient to see.

The fact that it's 2am on a Saturday means I'm a long way off finishing the shift. And that, sadly, means I can't put Terry off any longer. I draw back the Bay 12 curtain. Terry paces the bay, repeatedly banging his right ear.

'There's a fucking spider in my ear!'

I nod, thinking how that'd probably upset me as well. After taking a few more clinical details – all very sketchy, I might add – I reassure Spider-Man that I'm confident we'll be able to remove it. Only a fraction after I've left his bay, Terry begins his next chorus of *'Do it quick! It's burrowing into my fucking skull!'* to fill the now-quieting A&E department. Grabbing a pair of long crocodile forceps from one of the equipment trolleys, I wonder whether to make him wait even longer as punishment for this, his terrible cheerleading attempt at encouragement. The collection of nurses hovering at their station, all glaring, all sporting crossed arms as if in collaborative unison, answers that question.

Back in the bay, Terry's truly lost his shit. He's not listening to anything I'm saying now, so I shout back at him to sit down and I'll do it. Childlike behaviour requires a parental approach, it seems. With Terry now sitting on the trolley bed, I pull back his right ear and with the spotlight behind me, peer into his grubby pierced ear. I pause my breathing and stare a little harder.

You bugger, Terry.

Unless spiders have evolved to look like rocks of cocaine wrapped in clingfilm, I'd say Terry's pulling a fast one. As I continue to try and grip the drugs clearly stashed in this moron's ear, I ask if he'd got a look at what kind of spider it was – some clearly being much, much more dangerous than others, I add. Terry's quiet.

Of course, you fucking are.

With the cocaine clamped, I withdraw it slowly, careful not to rip the clingfilm, and giving Terry's ear canal one hell of a Saturday night. Now I'm impressed as even for a little fella, the next bit happened pretty quick. When I pull out the rock of cocaine, Terry springs to life, pinches it off the end of my wax-covered forceps, and sprints out of the department. As I write up Terry's clinical notes, I can't help but wonder if, when A&E departments were first designed, the creators realised this is what would fill it: the Terrys of this world.

Well, have a good night, Terry. I'm sure you will.

Reminder 7: Never leave home without a sense of humour

Status: FY2 in A&E Medicine

Just had to insert a urinary catheter into a 78-year-old woman with suspected chest sepsis – a severe, life-threatening infection that's spread from her chest into her bloodstream – in our resuscitation bay. This, by the way, is the part of the A&E department, where the critically ill patients go to be stabilised. A death avoidance area, if you like. Now there are some things in medicine that no amount of training ever prepares you for. I've just learned a new one: it's that when you're passing a thin rubber tube into an elderly lady's urethra (that's the pipe millimetres north of her vagina), you *do not* expect to hear the giggly words, *'I haven't had a man down there for ages!'* I just couldn't bring myself to reply. Partly because I was holding my breath. Partly because I was about to make a wholly inappropriate joke about *charging by the hour* – and my consultant was standing right behind me. Still, that wartime spirit, you've just got to love it.

Reminder 8: Teamwork, banter and sugar, the recipe for success against *any* odds

Status: FY2 in General Medicine

There can be something quite exciting and dramatic about weekend on-call ward-cover shifts like this one. I'm sitting on a box of nondescript files in a cramped, tiny office on the Acute Medical ward. It's pouring down with rain and a grey gloom dances into the shadows of wards and corridors. A perfect Saturday to charge around the hospital.

Our hospital. *Our* patients. *Our* responsibility.

In the office are two teams. The nightshift team, who look somewhere between dead and asleep, and the more fresh-faced, chatty team of dayshift doctors, including myself. Our job this weekend is pretty simple: keep as many of the patients alive as possible until Monday morning. Then it becomes somebody else's problem. And the key to this – and some might argue *all* – success? A fry-up, Haribo sweets, banter, and unlimited caffeine.

As the night team begin their handover, I look down at my three sheets of blank A4 paper, numbers one to thirty listed down the side. My pen hovers, ready to take down patient details, jobs, and priorities. It doesn't take long to fill. It never does:

- Five arterial blood gases
- Seven furosemide medication reviews, once blood tests are back
- Ten drug charts to rewrite
- Four specialist teams to contact at other bigger hospitals

- One family meeting at 2pm with angry relatives (always interesting)
- Two palliative care discussions with relatives of patients who are nearing the end of life
- Eleven blood tests to perform (and then check the results)
- Three acutely unwell patients to review (that the night team didn't get a chance to)
- Two urinary catheter changes for patients with large prostates (nurses can't do these)
- And the five more newly deteriorating patients to review that have just come through on the pager system as we wrote down all of these other jobs
- Plus, all the other jobs generated throughout the day
- Last, but not least, the cardiac arrest call that's just gone out over the pager system in the opposite bay.

(Meeting promptly over.)

*

Those two Foundation Years left a lot for me to digest and think about because once they were over, I had to decide which speciality to now train in. By the end of them, I had my answer: I wanted a career as a GP. It was the result of a collection of individual gut feelings. Feelings that must, with hindsight, have been bloody strong given that I hadn't set foot inside a GP surgery as a doctor for those first two Foundation Years.

So on I marched. I completed a further three years of Specialty Training (ST1, ST2, and ST3) in General Practice. Here, I rotated through different GP-related specialities every six months for the first two years (ST1 and ST2). In the third year of the Specialty Training (ST3), I worked solely in a general practice surgery (you may meet these trainee GPs, called GP Registrars, at your own GP surgery). That year was to consolidate my skills and to make sure I could actually do the job of a GP when push came to shove. Again, over those three years, I had some incredible moments. Moments that brought with them even more new reminders about life, and how I wanted to live it.

*

Reminder 9: Fake it before you make it

Status: ST1 in Paediatrics

As the obstetric consultant approaches the knife-to-skin stage of Mrs Blenheim's Caesarean section (C-section), she'd be forgiven. Forgiven if she looks around the busy theatre room – seeking comfort in the skilled professionals around her – to land on me, the on-call paediatric doctor standing next to the neonatal resuscitaire. For most C-sections in our hospital, a paediatric doctor is always present to receive the newborn at this, a sort of chest-high small table with a heating light over it, as well as equipment like oxygen masks (very tiny ones, obviously) and suction tubes. As it happens, she does catch my eye. I give a reassuring smile, inside paradoxically terrified.

Everyone else in this room knows I'm just a GP trainee on my paediatric rotation, waiting to receive this baby, box-fresh from Mrs Blenheim. What they (and definitely Mrs Blenheim) probably don't realise is that it's my first one on my own. As I check the equipment for the hundredth time, all to the sound of Mrs Blenheim's abdomen being pulled open, I can't help but think how I'll never open packaged mozzarella balls in the same way again. I wait for the scream. Instead, they hold up a blue, wet, floppy object. I stare, unblinking, at this scene at odds with the Lion King's iconic Simba presentation.

No scream.

My heart rate doubles. The theatre team bring him over to me.

No scream.

Scream, please.

No scream.

Please.

Nothing.

The first step in this boy's newborn life support is to stimulate him to breathe by rubbing him with warm towels. I still can't get over how the first step is a rub-down. Also, I don't think I've blinked yet. I definitely haven't exhaled. The light he's under is harsh, artificial, generic. Nothing like him. I toss another amniotic fluid-drenched towel on the theatre floor, replacing it with a clean one to dry him more.

Fucking breathe.

Please. Please, God.

I glance at the red timer in front of him: thirty seconds has passed. I assess his limb tone, breathing, heart rate. All absent. This isn't happening. I know I've got support from the theatre team but what I really need is for this newborn baby's dad not to be watching me. If his son is about to die, I don't want him to see him like this. Without even a gasp yet, it feels like time itself has stopped, here in a theatre desperate to be filled with the sound of a crying newborn. To fullfil the narrative we all want right now.

I position his head neutrally and apply five inflation breaths via a tiny mask. A tsunami of relief floods me. He breaths. I continue to stimulate. To reassess. And then reassess again. My eyes don't leave him. He keeps breathing. He cries.

What a cry!

His heart beats. Mine restarts. He goes from blue to pinkish-blue to pink. He keeps breathing, he keeps crying. *I want to cry.* I keep my shit together long enough to swaddle him in clean blankets before handing him over to the midwives to pass to Dad, and then Mum. Some bizarre relay event. While Mrs Blenheim's abdomen is being put back together, she, along with her husband – now parents of a newborn baby boy – thank me. I smile, informing them that Max is a very strong name. And that's it, I leave – my baby drying duties complete for today.

Reminder 10: Do everything you can to protect love

Status: ST2 in A&E Medicine (*again*)

I wish I could take them home, they just don't make them like this anymore. Mr and Mrs Hobag are eighty and eighty-two years old respectively. They now find themselves lying on two hospital beds in our A&E department at 1am on a Thursday. Both were found at home on the floor – Mr Hobag on the landing, Mrs Hobag on the bathroom floor. It's seems wrong to allocate myself as the A&E doctor to only one of them, so I take on both. I feel like a police detective. Mr Hobag reports *he* definitely fell first. It was *his* entire fault that Mrs Hobag then fell as she was coming to rescue *him* in the dark, having heard a thud.

I nod. Like a detective's nod, giving nothing away. I leave Mr Hobag in Bay 3 and wander across the A&E shop floor to Mrs Hobag in Bay 10 to get her version of events. Naturally, Mrs Hobag reports *she* definitely fell first. It was *her* entire fault that Mr Hobag then fell as he was coming to rescue *her* in the dark, having heard a thud. Both ask how the other is. Incessantly. Married for sixty-one years, never a day apart. Respectful. Kind. Loving. Which is why it feels wrong that Mrs Hobag is wedged between some twat who's drunk too much in Bay 9 and a snowflake-generation moron who's just scratched their arm yet screaming out for morphine in Bay 11. This isn't on. Annoyingly (but predictably), all the other bays in the department are full. I stand there, two sets of notes in my hands, two different stories, but in the words of Bob Marley, *one love.* That's when I realise what needs to happen. Popping back into Mr Hobag's bay, I stamp off his trolley brake and push him to the side of his bay. I leave before he can ask me again how Mrs Hobag is and jog over to Bay 10. Where I kidnap Mrs Hobag.

The department's nurse in charge, Sal, asks me what I'm up to as I casually wheel Mrs Hobag around to Bay 3.

'Restructuring.'

Two minutes later, I'm standing at the entrance of Bay 3, admiring my handiwork. On the right-hand side of the bay is Mr Hobag and on the left-hand side is Mrs Hobag, holding hands in the middle. Not only do I now have to walk less between my patients but they can now ask each other how they are to their hearts' content. This leaves me to get on and see if we can't patch them both up, and get them home in time for breakfast. Together.

As Bob would've probably wanted.

Reminder 11: Be the clarity in the confusion

Status: ST2 in Care of the Elderly Medicine

Breaking bad news is never fun. Yet by now, I know I can do it pretty well, strangely relishing the responsibility to do it right. Maybe it's the risk that it can so easily be done wrong that's the draw, or perhaps it's an arrogance in me that I think I can do it better than others. Hopefully the former.

Sitting down in a poky side room off the main ward, I'm opposite three brothers, the last remaining family of my patient, Mr Smith. I'm about to explain that we, the medical team, feel it's time to withdraw active treatment; that it's time to let him die peacefully. But of course, I can't just come out and say this, there's a process. When I did it for the first time, breaking bad news as a doctor, it was conscious, deliberate, scary. Today, it's different. I'm confident in my ability to do it. I think patients and relatives are, at the very least, owed this when they receive the news that time has run out.

Already I've taken the first step and got them into the right setting – a quiet room, undistracted from the chaos outside. Now the next step is for me to learn what they understand about their brother's condition. OK, they know he's unwell. Ah, but they think he's responding to the antibiotics. *He's not.* I offer up an invitation for me to give them more information. A weird step I used to think, but I learned now that some families just don't want to know anything about what's happening to their loved ones. Sometimes it's all too much. Others want to know everything and then, of course, there's everyone in-between. So, for that reason, I invite – rather than just give – more information.

The brothers sit opposite me, their faces a cacophony of emotions. They nod in invitational agreement, now leaning towards me, awaiting the news. I give the warning shot, *'I'm afraid it's not good news about your brother . . .'* I pause. They don't blink once. I then go on to explain that his infection has gotten worse, that he's required additional escalating medical interventions overnight, and that it's felt he won't survive the day. I pause. Silence is one of the hardest environments to exist in sometimes. As humans, we're desperate to fill it. But silence is important. It's needed. To be embraced.

Heads drop. Tears flow. Shoulders are comforted with loving brotherly hands. When the time's right, we discuss more about his condition, the discussions had with the Intensive Care team (and why he isn't suitable for that level of care), and I explain what'll happen next. Every family takes this news differently. Some are completely silent for what feels like hours, others thank you, some hate you, some blame you. Mr Smith's brothers are unanimously accepting, thanking me for explaining it all. We go over it again and agree the next steps one more time. We'll keep Mr Smith comfortable, pain-free, anxiety-free, and I'll inform the hospital palliative care team. They can be by their brother's bedside for as long as they need, visiting hours not applying at this stage. No more blood tests, scans, blood pressure or temperature checks. It's all about comfort now.

Before I take them to their brother's bedside, I warn he'll look frail and may not even be responding at this stage. Importantly, though, he'll still be able to hear them. This final bit of information is so, so important. I'll never forget when I was told this as my grandad was dying. It still brings me huge comfort knowing this. Finally, I take them to their brother's bedside so that they can spend those precious final hours together. As a family.

Reminder 12: Develop a thick skin for when life gets bumpy

Status: ST2 in Care of the Elderly Medicine

I wish Mr Smith's brother would put the fire extinguisher down. Turns out the middle brother, Simon, has decided I murdered his brother yesterday. He's bumped into me, by chance, on the ward as he came to collect his brother's belongings. Lucky me! I glance at the other patients sitting up in their hospital beds (well, the ones who can), jaws slack, bearing witness to this stand-off taking place by the nurses' station. I try to give them a reassuring nod but expect they'll be sleeping with one eye open tonight.

After a minute of shouting at me and me saying very little – static, standing there, hands raised in a sort of suggestive *'calm down'* posture (which he didn't agree with) – Simon slams the fire extinguisher down, calls me a *'fucking murderer'* one more time, and storms off the ward. Grace, our ward's student physiotherapist, by this point is having a comprehensive meltdown, screaming for the police to be called. The more experienced head of Charlie, our amazing ward sister, casually asks me, while still typing on the computer, if I want a cup of tea – or hospital security called. It's an either-or question. I decline both, preferring instead to begin a hearts and minds campaign with my patients by doing a walkabout to see if everyone's OK – and to let them know I don't murder patients.

People grieve in all kinds of ways. For Simon, he bumped into me. It was a freak event while on an emotional rollercoaster those last twenty-four hours. And while what he said was wrong, I don't bear a grudge. He's deep in grief – and that does funny things to people.

Reminder 13: Admire others who do what you can't

Status: ST2 in Psychiatry

Now more than ever, I admire psychiatrists. I've just finished a clinic for patients with complex personality disorders and feel like I've been emotionally dragged over hot coals, naked, backwards, before being stabbed in both eyes with shards of glass. And I'm the bloody doctor! I can only imagine how these patients feel. The complex emotions, demands, challenges, and struggles they face must feel utterly overwhelming and confusing. Incomprehensible, in fact. That these are also often physically intangible conditions, wrongly stigmatised, and not easily treated, makes it even worse. And when you step back to see that as the bigger picture, it's not hard to admire those who try to help them, day in, day out. And sympathise with those affected. Directly. And indirectly.

As I leave the clinic, a pang of self-annoyance strikes me. I realise I'd never be able to do their job. I'm just not strong enough.

Reminder 14: It's OK to be cruel to be kind

Status: ST3 in General Practice and Out of Hours Care

It's a fucking cold. All of them, yes, have fucking colds. I close my eyes, phone receiver still pressed to my left ear, forehead now resting on the edge of the same painfully generic office desk I've had to see twice a month throughout my final year of specialist GP training. I inhale deeply. Angrily. This phone call with Mrs Stockley has already run its course. It feels like I'm trying to break up with her and she doesn't want to hear what I'm saying.

I exhale. Nobody wants to be forcibly blunt but it's going that way if she doesn't see the light soon. It's also 11pm on a Thursday night, so naturally, I'd rather be anywhere but here. To add insult to injury, this total non-drama is unfolding in a decaying industrial estate, in the middle of bloody nowhere, where the Out of Hours (OOH) medical care triage centre happens to be based. Every time I get the bus and walk to it, I wonder if tonight's the night I'm getting robbed, beaten unconscious, and tossed into a dumpster. Anyway, that's a whole other issue. Back to the service . . .

Basically, between 6pm and 8am, if a person needs medical advice and they're not already in an A&E department, they can call NHS 111. That's where they're triaged by a trained call handler, who may then end up putting them through to me in an industrial estate. Unless I'm in a dumpster that night.

Grey's Anatomy, eat your heart out.

Mrs Stockley asks for antibiotics for the third time. Once again, I recap to her, working hard not to sound as annoyed as I absolutely am, that if her *entire* family have runny noses, are sneezing, and generally feeling a bit shit (admittedly my description, not hers), it's most likely a simple upper respiratory tract infection, i.e. a cold – just as I've been telling you for the last twenty minutes. Even my reassurances that yes, I do indeed expect they'll all survive the night before being seen by their regular GP tomorrow for a face-to-face review falls on deaf ears.

The fourth request for antibiotics from Mrs Stockley crackles down the receiver into my exhausted ear. Enough now, the velvet gloves come off. The iron fists beneath them are ready. I explain to Mrs Stockley that my final decision is that she and her family will not be receiving a bumper pack of antibiotics from me to help them get over their colds. That she should in fact be thanking me for helping her to reduce her family's collective risk of becoming resistant to some very helpful broad-spectrum antibiotics. Antibiotics that, were they actually to become very ill in the future – and *actually* need them to stay alive and not die of sepsis and multiple organ failure – will be incredibly helpful. Not to mention supporting the control of overall rates of global antibiotic resistance, and therefore stopping *other* people dying of sepsis and multiple organ failure. And for all those reasons, Mrs Stockley and her family need to yes, keep a lookout for red-flag signs and symptoms of more serious illnesses but ultimately suck it up, buy some paracetamol, and drink hot honey and lemon like the rest of the sodding universe!

I probably softened the *actual* vernacular used but that's the crystallised message she needs to read between the lines. And with that call successfully ended, I pick up the next one. Again, starting the process of explaining why meeting patient expectation does not, can not, should not, and will not always be the status quo. After this, I think I'll need to step outside for some air. Staying away from unlit spaces and dumpsters, of course.

Reminder 15: The pain always fades (usually)

Status: Training complete

Thank fuck for that.

*

After those three years of Speciality Training, that was it. I qualified as a GP. An 11-year journey, all to get to the start line of my career. Yet in this alone, I'd already seen so much. Love. Hate. Joy. Sadness. Tragedy. Surprise. Fear. Naivety. Frustration. Desperation. Acceptance. Confusion. Anger. Bargaining. Nostalgia. Craving. Awe. Warmth. Coldness. I felt I'd already begun to learn a surprising truth about life as a GP – that the hardest part is often everything in-between the medicine. It's those raw, unforgiving emotions. It's learning how to navigate the medicine alongside them, fighting against the constant potential derailment of one another. In all the cases above, unbeknownst to me, I was learning the trade of being a GP – even though for many of the training years, I was in a hospital setting. Communication being as important as clinical knowledge.

Worthy bedfellows.

From that very first day I stepped onto the surgical ward, a box-fresh junior doctor, I began to see that. Sometimes it's obvious, other times less so. But the more I saw of it, the more I began to understand. Appreciate. Connect with it. I'm certainly not a clever doctor, far from it. For six painful years I struggled endlessly through medical school. Now I also realised that what I can do well (at least I hope so) is read people's emotions. I also think I can often do this before others might – and respond to them in a way that connects me to them. Perhaps this is the emotional intelligence inherent in me (making up for my lack of common sense, so Alice tells me). That's not to say I make any better or worse clinical decisions than my colleagues. More that perhaps the way in which I do it – and the way I engage with them – *that's* what makes me different. My unique selling point (USP), I guess, if I were a brand.

And you know, maybe it's all this that makes my patients – unbelievable as it may sound for a paunchy little man who swears too much – like me as their doctor. Great for me! Because becoming a GP *is* the dream job I didn't know I wanted. In the beginning, I thought being a GP was for the doctors who couldn't really hack the perceptibly tougher career choice as a hospital doctor. Yet I learned by the end of my training that tough medicine *is* in general practice – and the doctors that do it are fucking tough to match. I'm only three years down that road at this point, but I suspect it's a road well worth travelling for the rest of my career.

OCTOBER 2018

Monday, 1st October

There's no getting around it, some patients you instantly like. Namely because they smile at you as they enter and so you know they're (probably) not about to try to take you over a barrel. Other times, it's just a vibe. When Hattie and long-term partner Tom entered thirty seconds ago, I got the vibe. As an aside, this initial reading of a patient is part of the job that I love the most. It means I get to try to engage in some sort of emotional intelligence covert warfare and figure out how I can *tick* to their *tock*, something I've enjoyed trying to improve over the last three years. Partly, because I love the immediacy and intimacy of the face-to-face contact as a GP – and partly for the race that follows to read them and the situation quickly. Anyway, I digress . . . Back to Hattie and Tom. They're about my age and I decide have the same style – confirmed by how they're just edging themselves out of fashionable clothes and into more sensible, comfortable ones. They're also clearly very much in love. What's not to like about that? You can feel them bounce off each other, like a non-verbal game of love ping-pong, as Hattie describes her symptoms.

Tom nods in earnest support with every word leaving her mouth. She's felt bloated and had a crampy pain in her abdomen for the last nine weeks. There's nothing clinically sinister in her history, like weight loss, night sweats, or a change in appetite. Sensibly, she's chalked it all down to her irritable bowel syndrome (IBS). A condition that can, yes, easily give all those symptoms. With the history done, I guide her over to my examination couch and expose her abdomen. I pause for a second, taking in what I'm seeing, before continuing with the examination. Hattie stares down her chest to me feeling her abdomen, neck craning. Tom, arms folded, looks on, unaware that I'm about to totally shake up their world.

'All done.' I smile.

I let them sit there for a minute as I type a note on the examination, a gift of sorts, before my world-shaking begins.

'I don't think this is IBS, Hattie . . .'

They hold hands that little bit tighter. Look to each other, before coming back to me, sharing a collaborative, nervous, blank look. Wow. They even blink in unison. Seems a good time to shake.

'Any chance you could be pregnant?'

Silence.

They look to each other again. There it is – that's what I'm looking for, that nervous smile. It breaks out across them both. Always a relief. Because although it's not always the case, it's nice when you know the thought of a pregnancy is a positive one. The nervous smiling continues as they play dumb, shrugging their shoulders in a *we're not sure* – but definite – *that would be AMAZING* kind of way. One urine pregnancy test later, Hattie and Tom's lives have changed: Hattie *is* pregnant. They're both thrilled. Turns out Hattie had *overlooked* the fact she hadn't had a period for two months. I roll my eyes jokingly. As I refer them to the local antenatal services, and give them endless links to the NHS pregnancy webpages, they tell me how they decided to come off contraception a few months ago – but were just taking a *laissez-faire* approach in trying for a baby. I point to her stomach and smile: *'Seems a successful approach for you two.'*

As they leave, I let the door creak shut under the weight of the safety bracket and smile to myself, knowing full well there's no way Hattie ever thought that was IBS. It brings back memories of when Alice and I first found out about William. Goosebumps prickle my neck.

What an adventure they've got in store.

Tuesday, 2nd October

Hew's finally died. About time too. RIP, Hewlett 'Hew' Packard B5L25A – a loyal servant.

Friday, 5th October

I want to call him an arrogant prick but I know deep down, this would be unprofessional (not to mention a bad way to end the week) so instead, I clear my throat one more time and again repeat, *'Sorry,'* (I wasn't at all, but I'm British and we're always sorry) *'I didn't catch that. What was your name again, please?'* Again, the neurology registrar on the other end of the phone line not only choses to ignore the question but somehow seems offended. *'My name?'* I want to calmly tell him – *yes, of course your bloody name. Like how normal humans introduce themselves to each other.* How this guy has made such an innocuous question sound like I've just politely asked to tickle his balls, I'll never know. I move the phone receiver away from my mouth and exhale. If there's anything that's going to well and truly irk me, removing a person permanently from my Christmas card list, it's bad manners. All I want is some advice on adjusting a complex patient's epilepsy medication. Important since they're having more frequent seizures.

'I'm the neuro reg.' His full, unedited answer to my seemingly overly challenging question. *God.* I stop short of asking if he was bullied at school with a name like that. I see the clock, and realise the time. Afternoon clinic kicks off in five minutes and I still want to call Alice to see what she and William have been up to today. I exhale once more.

Be Zen, Max, be Zen.

Fine. Biting my lip and moving on from the *name game*, I get the advice I need and promptly hang up, making sure I'm extremely clear on who – and where – I'm calling from. Then, while on the phone to Alice, hearing how William has been having some good naps, long feeds, and big shits (the only activity list of any 4-week-old, it seems), I write an email to the local neurology department consultants. As I click send, I smile and cackle inwardly at my pot stirring. The email enthusiastically highlights the need for some further communication training for one of their trainee registrars – only known as *the neuro reg.* These neurologists may be super-duper bright and amazing at what they do, but manners cost nothing. No matter who you are.

Sunday, 7th October

Despite knowing full well the futility of the exercise, his ears and eyes barely unpacked from nine months in the womb, I can't help but play a re-run of the famous, the glorious, *Jonny*

Wilkinson 2003 Rugby World Cup Final-winning Drop-goal for William on YouTube.

Alice is having a much-earned nap – the only reason I can get away with this without being called a tit.

Tuesday, 9th October

No words in the English language can capture what I'm seeing. My jaw hangs slack, a little more than probably professionally acceptable, as my eyes absorb the flat of 70-year-olds Mr and Mrs Leigh. At first pass I count sixteen dreamcatchers hanging from the ceiling. I stop counting the dreamcatchers for now as my eyes consume the framed photographs on the wall: Barack and Michelle Obama (at his inauguration), seven Alsatians (all individually framed), Cilla Black, and my favourite, Will Smith as The Fresh Prince of Bel-Air. Mind-blown. I'm speechless, lost in the wonder of their world. I'm not even sure the fact I can't remember why I'm here even matters now. And sorry, Benny, but after only four months since I met you, the Leighs haven't just bumped you off my top spot of all-time favourite patients – you've been spear-tackled and dumped unceremoniously on your head. And by the way, I'm pretty sure these two will have an answer to your *meaning-of-life dilemma*, judging by their living room.

I put my medical bag down and sit on their sofa – next to about fifteen boxes of singing garden gnomes (batteries thankfully not included). I get out a printed (from my new unnamed printer after Hew's passing) summary of Mrs Leigh's medical notes, trying to bury my excitement at this wonderland and suppress all the many, many questions

I have and be more *GP-like.* I'm here for her first diabetic review (most long-term health conditions have some kind of annual check-up scheduled by the GP). She's received this recent diagnosis of type 2 diabetes mellitus, picked up on a set of annual blood tests by the district nurses.

Mr and Mrs Leigh sit in front of me, taking in the information about what diabetes is, how it can occur, what the treatment will entail, and what an annual review – like the one today – involves.

'Do you like Home and Away, *Max?'*

I'm already on first-name terms. Bloody love that. There's something about these two that really makes me want them to like me. Slightly blindsided by the question, I explain, while trying to professionally complete her diabetes checks, that while I don't get a lot of time to watch it (given the fact I'm no longer fifteen years old, have a job, and moved out of the 1990s), I'm sure it's still great. Fighting the urge, I stop short of telling them I'm *sure* I could probably still sing its theme tune.

God, I want to impress them.

Mrs Leigh asks if her diabetes might be causing her vaginal thrush. I'm kneeling in front of her, having just been checking the sensation in her feet.

Shit, I think I prefer the Home and Away *question.*

Facing me, dressed only in her Dennis the Menace sleeping T-shirt (a few sizes too small and critically, short), her knees flap gently from side to side now. Bile meets my throat. I bet they wish they had their batteries in, because if the 15 or so garden gnomes *could* turn around right now, I expect they would.

I stand up, positioning myself clear of a vaginal line of sight, and explain it probably could, yes. Luckily for her (definitely for me), we can treat that presumptively. That is, there's no need for me to take a lower vaginal swab today. Mind you, I'm not surprised she might have it. It's not uncommon for elderly women like Mrs Leigh (and Elsie from last month) to suffer vaginal-related problems.

Mr Leigh reappears as I pack up my bag, the diabetes review testing now complete. He has a photo for me of their wedding day from fifty years ago. I'm really touched, if not slightly confused as to why he has this handy for such an occasion. I listen with a warm sense of happiness for them as they speak about it with such reminiscent love. A wave of pessimism sweeps over me – *shit, am I being groomed?* It'll be sweets in the bedroom next. I bat it away (putting it down to lunchtime hunger) and accept the photograph graciously, not quite sure what else to do. I wonder what Alice will say? Maybe not one for the family photo wall. Still, a caring gesture nonetheless. And with that, I say goodbye, leaving the Leighs' wonderland. I really do hope to come back soon, this being one of the most fascinating home visits. EVER. One thing's for sure, these two need their own television show – I even know a theme tune for it . . .

Wednesday, 10th October

Wow! The last four months really have flown by. It seems my annual performance appraisal at the surgery is already here. I rub my eyes with forgotten alcohol rub-covered hands and wince wearily with infantile groan. It's the end of a long day, William's not sleeping well at the moment (by default, meaning Alice and I aren't), and it all means I'm dog-tired. And it's naturally spilled over into work. The result? I snapped at patients all day long. And reception staff (which went down as badly as expected, judging by the overzealous eye-rolls I received). And Alice on the phone earlier when she told me I wasn't listening to her properly (I'm not sure I was, to be fair).

I open my stinging eyes again, partly in self-punishment, partly to read the email one more time. Serious-looking New Times Roman in bold tells me I'm requested to meet with two of the senior clinical partners (including the dementor) and the practice manager, Jasper, on Tuesday, 23rd October at 2pm. I stand up. These things are usually fine, yet that still doesn't stop them being a ball-ache to go through. I stretch. I switch off the desktop screen and slope off to the bus stop, ready for home – albeit via the florist – to buy some apologising flowers and spare myself a LIB (Lecture In Bed) later from Alice.

Thursday, 11th October

I nearly swapped to Velcro shoes last week, the thought of laces being too demanding. That's the level of tiredness I'm at since William was born, a mere five weeks ago. So how the hell Gale and her husband Tony had the energy, or even the carnal inclination, to have sex three weeks after giving birth to their daughter, Felicity, I've no idea.

I'm working hard to unscrew my face, the saving grace being that Gale's busy tending to Felicity, and Tony's out feeding the meter for the car since I'm again running late (a Mrs Tally phone call special, of course. The carers are still shit, of course). I nod and smile, still digesting the details. I mean, there's not only the logistics of finding the time to do it, but what about permitting some recovery from the naturally occurring structural changes that would have gone on down there following her vaginal delivery of a 9lb Felicity?

As I scan Gale's medical notes, I can't help but think that Tony really needed to give her some breathing space to let things return to normal. Gale looks a little sheepish and as she changes Felicity's nappy, filling my consultation room with the sweet aroma of baby shit, now a *home from home* smell. She asks if she needs the morning-after pill. She's fully breastfeeding. Good news for her. I explain that won't be necessary as she won't be ovulating yet. Fully breastfeeding very much protects from this. Gale's looking over her shoulder now, one hand on Felicity laying partly changed on the examination couch, and gives me a look of unrestrained relief. She tells me it was only the once.

'A special occasion?'

I can't help myself.

'Nothing like that!' She laughs.

Turns out, they just wanted to give it a try. I hope it was worth it. To be fair, as they leave, Tony rushing down the hallway to meet them, I can't help but think how I'd much rather have the extra five minutes of sleep – or longer, of course – depending on Tony's performance status.

Friday, 12th October

'Are you an English doctor?'

That's Mr Jones's opening enquiry to our phone consultation. Clearly a member of the English Defence League.

I explain that I'm one member of an international team of healthcare professionals working across the NHS for people like him and that my nationality is irrelevant.

'You sound Australian.'

For. Fuck's. Sake.

Saturday, 13th October

'Doreen, can you drop this off to Mr Grafton at number 11 for me, love?'

I'm speechless. Speechless because I'm currently sitting in the front passenger seat of 72-year-old Mrs Gray's car, holding her neck perfectly still. Specifically, I'm sitting in-between Mrs Gray, who's sitting in the driver's seat – airbag now deflated – and Doreen, her neighbour, who's standing outside my open front passenger door – holding two blankets and a cup of tea. Three minutes ago, I was in the pub across the road having a pint with Alice, William, and the friends we're visiting in the Cotswolds. That was before we heard the *crunch*.

Turns out the *crunch* was Mrs Gray driving her car right into the rear of a parked van at well over 30mph (judging by the fact that her front car bonnet has now halved in size).

'Do you remember what happened, Mrs Gray?'

She ignores my question. Instead she shouts *'Yes please, love'* to another nameless neighbour gathered outside the car, who's offering to take her food shopping in from the back seat before it defrosts.

I mean, come on, love, priorities!

I'm ready to give up and go back to the pub. A viable option had Mrs Gray's driver's side of the car not been wedged tight up against an old stone wall. Besides, having made the decision to place my hands on her neck (due to the risk of a serious neck injury being high at such an impact – and considering the age of the patient), I'm basically stuck here until the ambulance comes to take over and get her out safely.

More neighbours appear. *More* blankets offered. Something tells me this is the most action a Saturday night has seen in this tiny village for quite some time. I take another punt at getting some history from Mrs Gray. That is, since the neighbours are either posting her letters, taking in her shopping, or grabbing more blankets, it seems she finally does have time for me – the Good Samaritan off-duty GP (*I mean, what was I thinking?*). Turns out she suspects that she fainted momentarily after getting some chest pain. I ask if she's on any medicines.

'Only paracetamol.'

I don't believe her for a second, so ask if she's got her paper prescription slip in her handbag (for some reason, a lot of elderly people still do this routinely). She does. I get a neighbour to get it out (remember, my hands are still on her neck for the foreseeable future). Right, so she's not only on paracetamol medication for pain, but on one for thinning her blood, two for controlling her blood pressure, one for lowering her cholesterol, and another for controlling her irregular heart rhythm. Bit more than *just* paracetamol, I'd say.

Ten minutes later, after a quick speakerphone (*hands on neck, remember?*) conversation with the ambulance service – and several more blanket contributions from the entire village, all now standing outside – there's an air ambulance helicopter hovering over us. Today was meant to be a relaxing countryside walk and a quiet pub lunch. Not a TV episode of *999: What's Your Emergency?* In the end, it took several hours of the combined efforts and expertise of the air ambulance crew and the fire brigade to safely cut Mrs Gray out of her car and transport her to hospital. But that wasn't the only thing that was impressive: equally impressive was the way in which this small rural village rallied together. There was a sense of community. They all knew each other, they all wanted to help one of their own. I've never seen anything like it, not where I live anyway. And I have to say, it left me quite envious.

Monday, 15th October

The weekend's drama is barely over and already, I'm working hard not to cry. I've just asked Adam to come in and see me. I meet him at my consulting-room door and he smiles politely, asking *me* how I am. He doesn't need to be doing any of that, it certainly doesn't matter how I feel. Now sitting opposite me, he wears the face of a man who is using all his will not to burst into tears. For his sake, I need him to. That way, we can properly talk.

I smile benevolently.

'How are you?'

I doubt I can even scratch the surface of how he must be feeling. Katie, his wife of only eleven months, has an aggressive form of cancer that will likely kill her before their second wedding anniversary. Those three words are all that were needed. I can feel the lump in my throat and glaze on my eyes as I watch Adam drop his head, disinheriting the masquerading smile, and begin to sob uncontrollably. He looks up at me, a face that holds despair, desperation, and disbelief in equal measures. I put my hand on his.

Despite best efforts, I cry too. The first time in front of a patient. With a patient. Unashamedly. It was always going to happen at some point. It just so happens that it took three years since qualifying as a GP to find the case that really exposed my own emotional vulnerability. I think of Alice. I met Katie before I called Adam in to discuss what the specialists had said about her cancer (*advanced, invasive, incurable*). Her main concern was not what would happen to her but for Adam and how he was going to cope. To have their dreams of a big family, exciting adventures together, and a long life full of love ripped away is both cruel and dangerous.

Adam and I sit in silence, wrestling only with the vocal methodical ticking of the wall clock. He looks up, tells me he's sorry. I tell him not to be an idiot. We both smile in mutual support. With the emotional charge of the first fifteen minutes fractionally easing, we talk through the practicalities of the next few months, namely getting time away from work, managing medical appointments, and what their immediate plans are. Adam relaxes some more, which is to be expected. We often find discussing these more tangible aspects of any traumatic situation easier – there's something to grab hold of, to handle. Emotions, on the other hand, can be colourless, odourless, intangible. They want to arrange a trip together to a few places they always talked about visiting. With life's revised timeline, that's all been brought forward. Every time Adam talks about Katie, he smiles to hide the part of him that's clearly cracking. It's not heartbreaking, it's devastating.

As the conversation comes to a natural close, and the fatigue of the consultation strikes us both, I finish by giving Adam some information about support groups. He thanks me, both of us knowing full well it's a token gesture for something unfixable. A child's plaster for a fatal arterial wound. I shake his hand and we hug.

Katie's outside the door. As Adam leaves, she steps towards him, seeing the tear stains on his face. They embrace. I close the door and give them their privacy. Five minutes later, I'm still sitting at my desk, staring at the empty clinical entry on the screen, the impersonal, dispassionate black vertical text bar flashing impatiently. Waiting. Waiting for words to be typed from it. To summarise what just happened. I find none to do it justice. Something with that much emotion deserves more. More than to be reported with cold, functional medical language. So instead, I just continue to stare. Drained.

Tuesday, 16th October

It's 3:18am the next day. That drained feeling still hasn't gone. Sleep hasn't found me either. Leaning against the door-frame to our bedroom, I just watch. Watch as Alice and William sleep, accompanied only by their beautifully personalised noises, movements, exhalations. A tactically silent nocturnal exhalation of my own escapes.

I take a sip of one of Alice's leftover pregnancy-friendly chamomile herbal tea. My taste buds remind me why I don't normally drink it. I haven't been able to shake the meeting with Katie and Adam. People come to see me *for help* and

I do my best to provide that. But when I see so many people, day in, day out, I now realise how blinding it can all become. With that much density, I forget that patients also teach me. *Help me.* It's moments like I had with Katie and Adam that remind me of this. Bringing a sharpened focus into my own life. And its priorities.

I look back through the darkness to Alice and William. Mere silhouettes. I honestly don't think I could go on living now without those two. My whole world, fast asleep, just five feet away from me. Safe. Happy. Loved. Unharmed. Not everyone has this. Life, no fairy tale for all. The penny drops, soundless. That's what's keeping me awake – bearing witness to the fragile, vulnerable, and cruel position that life can choose to unexpectedly put people in. Cancer. Trauma. Accident. Death. It scared me. It scared me because there's no reason why what's happening so tragically to Katie and Adam couldn't happen to my own family. A selfish thought, I know.

I go to put the kettle back on. I expect I'll spend the rest of the night now trying to figure out how not to let it consume me.

Friday, 19th October

I delete the word *shit.* Both of them. And replace *demand* with *strongly encourage.* I then re-read the letter. Yep, firm but fair. The Consultant Orthopaedic Surgeon should appreciate it. Actually, they won't. But that's not the point. The point is my patient, Stanley, a retired 69-year-old carpenter, has had his total-knee replacement cancelled four times now. Being a gentleman, Stanley is polite and reflective each time. *Fuck that.* I'll be his fist banging on the orthopaedic department door in that case. Because while he so politely waits, he wears the other knee down in anthropometric compensation. He increases his risk of functionally declining as he moves less and less. He loses his confidence. He loses his independence. All these increase his chances of an early death. A *polite*, early death.

No, Stanley.

I fire off the email with an angry but satisfying bang of the mouse. Now complete, I walk off down to Jasper to let him know another complaint might be coming the surgery's way.

Tuesday, 23rd October

Is this happening?

I'm sitting opposite the dementor and Dr Phil, two of the senior GP partners, and Jasper, the practice manager. I nod slowly as, after fifteen minutes of positive praise for my work at the surgery, they gently pull the pin on my appraisal hand grenade: they tell me there are concerns that I may not be very much of a team player. Talk about blindsided. I didn't see this coming. My immediate visceral reaction is one of shock. I want to get up and leave. Run away from this criticism. Something I've struggled to take even from a young age. Then I realise that running may be rash – not to mention odd. Instead, I choose to sit in silence, trying to ignore the inner reactive monkey in my brain (we all have one) that encourages such rash decision making.

I remain seated. Speechless. I try to slow my breathing. Slow my now-racing heart. The dementor fills the void, expanding on their concern. They explain that perhaps I don't use the resources I have access to, namely the senior GP partners, who can lend their years of clinical experience to optimise some of my patient management plans. That is, had I just chosen to discuss them (especially for the more complex cases). I nod slowly. Deflated. Bruised by the verbal blows.

'Right.'

Dr Phil puts on his boxing gloves and takes aim at my head, continuing to explain how there are concerns this lack of team engagement and discussion has led to some more unilateral, less orthodox management plans. I nod again, asking if they had any examples, to help me better understand. They have none. Jasper winds up his arm for a verbal uppercut.

'It is rather a general observation,' he explains.

Closing the notepad in front of me, I don't even bother nodding to this nebulous comment. I'm either about to be fired, in which case I won't need a note to remember that, or I do still have a job but am so apparently flawed as a GP that I won't have time to write all the problems down. Shock makes way for brief defiance. And it's hard not to show this. I work hard for my patients and I always, always do what's best for them. I never take shortcuts and I always pick up the slack when I see others dragging their clinical heels for patients.

The defiance, as it turns out, is fleeting. Hurt replaces it, pride now scrap metal. Part of me actually wants to cry, pathetic as it sounds. I've always taken pride in myself as a team player – following and leading – and this has never, ever been a criticism of me. In fact, historically, I'm praised for it. Which means I'm so overwhelmingly confused by what they've just told me. I take a breath. I think of Alice and William. After a minute or two of zoning out from their comments, clarity. Clarity emerges, replacing the melting pot of more negative emotions. This job isn't just about me, it's about them too. It's about being supportive to my family.

Personally, and financially, I need this job. *We need this job.* Which is why, after taking a further moment to collect myself, I inform them that I'll wholeheartedly take on board everything they've said – as well as any advice or guidance to support self-improvement. They all thank me for doing this and with that, I leave. Being British, I of course thank them for the criticism as well.

Returning to my room, I check the clock: my first patient is in five minutes. I pray it's a simple blood pressure check, I'm not in the headspace to do much else right now. I need to call Alice. I want to hear her voice, for her to tell me that of course I'm a team player. That I haven't misinterpreted who I am for so long. Silly as it sounds, I feel weak. Exposed. No wind in my sails at all. But I can't call her. After a quick pat-down of my trousers, I realise I've left my bloody phone somewhere. I opt for Plan B and instead just lie on the examination couch for five solitary minutes, wondering what the hell I'm going to do about all this.

Wednesday, 24th October

Dead calm. Still no wind in these sails today. Turning yesterday over and over in my head. I did find my phone though – left it by the confidential waste bin.

Friday, 26th October

I approach the same GP surgery – distinctive in its new-build appearance – bright blue NHS sign worn above the entrance.

I enter the same large brown front door. Walk up the same flight of stairs. Unlock the same consultation room. Turn on the same computer, and forget to water the same chronically dehydrated pot plant. Yet it *all* feels different now. I'm conscious. Conscious of how I speak to the other doctors. Conscious of how I interact with the reception staff. Conscious of not being perceived a team player.

Conscious of fucking everything now.

Despite my clinic already starting, I don't call the first patient – I don't want to. Less than forty-eight hours after my performance appraisal meeting, crushingly low self-confidence and self-doubt still dance loudly in my head, jazz hands held nice and high. Which is why all I want to do right now is go home and do something that won't wreck my confidence any further.

Like breathe.

I can still do that, can't I?

Sunday, 28th October

Apparently, I need to stop being a total drama queen about my appraisal.

'Thanks for that, my love.'

One of the reasons why I love Alice so much: she knows how to get to me. With momentum on her side, she goes on to tell me that of course I'm a team player – and that they (the senior GPs) just want to make me as good as I can be.

It was *constructive criticism.*

I nod, outstretched from the sofa with a pillow over my face, as she tells me this. Then, pushing all the right buttons, she explains that it's really (she stressed this part) not attractive to see me give up so easily – and to pull my bloody finger out and do something about that, please.

Buttons not just pressed, buttons smashed.

She knows that behind a somewhat overconfident, borderline arrogant affront is someone who crumbles when criticised. She makes me see sense when I can't. And she's right: I need to dust myself off and get on with the job, trying to address their concerns. I look to William: he offers no such words of wisdom. Instead, he just fingers a little patch of his own vomit on the carpet.

Charming.

Monday, 29th October

I agree it looks manky. Daniel's right big toenail is thickened, yellow, and certainly fungal-like. I explain that we'll need to get a cutting of it first to confirm the diagnosis before considering any stronger tablet-based antifungal treatments. He can do this at home himself. Despite all our training with sharp objects, it's felt that GPs aren't qualified to take a nail clipping. For the time being, he can continue with the nail lacquer to try to minimise its spread.

'At least it's not sandals weather,' I tell him as he puts his sock back on and I type his notes up. The room fills with the polite laughter of relative strangers and I look over to his 6-year-old son he's brought with him for a smile too. No such luck. He's been very good though – sat there, reading his book quietly in the corner, not making so much as a peep the whole consultation. Be nice if William turns out like that.

'Is it alright if my wife, Natalia, drops the cutting off tomorrow for me?'

The room temperature plummets. My neck prickles. Natalia isn't a common name for these parts of the country. I only know one. With Daniel busy sorting out his laces, I discretely check the linked family names listed under his address.

It *is* her. And that means I'm sitting opposite the man who abuses her, beats her up, demeans her. I keep typing, forcefully digesting the fact I want to wrap the keyboard around his head, before responding with a *'Sure, not a problem.'*

Their son, whose name I remember now – Ethan – glances up from his book. Is he quiet because he's afraid, I wonder. He's wearing a T-shirt. I look to his arms for bruising. None. Hardly a full assessment but given the context, it's better than nothing. I do some clinical fishing and ask if he and his wife had a nice weekend. He's casual and nondescript in his answer. The thing about being a doctor is you can't pick and choose who you treat. You should also, in theory, treat everyone the same, no matter how vile, abusive or despicable you might find them. And yes, as much as it feels wrong in every possible sense, that means treating him the same way I'd want my own family treated. Internally, however, I can only dream of how the *C*, *U*, *N*, and *T* keys would fly off the keyboard as it makes contact with his temple.

I get up, shake Daniel's hand, double high five Ethan, and tell them I'll look forward to catching up soon. Then I sit down, and fire off another email to social services, telling them to hurry up and speak to Natalia.

Tuesday, 30th October

It's Alice and my wedding anniversary today, the first one with William in tow. And by tow, I actually mean the dead weight around any ideas I had of romance and seduction. Instead, we're sitting in formula milk-stained pyjamas, physically and emotionally exhausted, at 7:20pm watching BBC's *The One Show*. The romantic dinner downgraded to pizza delivery and Häagen-Dazs.

We talked about anniversary sex but both agreed we'd prefer to have the extra sleep.

Wednesday, 31st October

The last patient of the day leaves just before 5:40pm as day makes way for evening skies. Mr King shakes my hand, thanking me for his Viagra. I tell him to have fun. As I sit down, watching my desktop power down with all the absent pace expected of an NHS computer, I feel a sense of calm. You see, I've had time now to think more about my performance appraisal, a full eight days ago. The dementor, Dr Phil and Jasper *were* right. And my reaction more than just a little silly.

It was wrong. *I* was wrong. I think I do need to be more open-minded to opinion and advice from my colleagues – I had become too sure of myself as a GP. So, with the benefit of hindsight, I'm actually thankful for their words. Hard as they were for me to take initially. After all, what's wrong with trying – wanting – to be a better doctor? That's a goal that should never stop. And this, I realise, means not only being privately self-critical of your own ability but having the balls to stand up and take criticism publicly (and allowing yourself time to process it before reacting in a way that may be regrettable) – something I've fundamentally always run away from.

William, you've made me grow up, haven't you?

NOVEMBER 2018

Thursday, 1st November

I'm not sure I can medicalise foreplay. Lea looks at me, presenting a face that packages all the awkwardness of a parent trying to discuss sex with their child for the first time – who aren't getting the Rabbit hole analogy. Her problem is pretty simple: Greg, her new boyfriend, has a huge cock. And it hurts during sex. She's also five foot nothing, which probably doesn't help this engineering predicament. So much a problem in fact that it's already putting a strain on their fledgling six-month relationship.

I nod in detached sympathy, thinking this is a problem I've definitely never had. Lea sits opposite me alone today, Greg, I imagine unable to get his beast through the front door of the surgery (one of the door hinges is jammed at the moment). I can't think of anything immediate to say.

I'm so sorry, how awful. Poor you, poor Greg.

All seem a little off-key. Is this even a health issue? I sigh inwardly as I know it probably is, especially if I've resolved to taking a total health approach for my patients. Still with no words to offer, I opt for a sympathetic GP head tilt to buy me some added time. Not enough, it seems. Instead I inaugurate the world's most spectacularly slowmulti-stage car crash.

'Well, how do you get, er, warmed up?'

My indirect, utterly coded question for what's your foreplay skills like? We both shift in our chairs. Well, this quickly got awkward. Lea looks up to my pinboard behind me for inspiration. Sadly, I doubt the HIV: GET YOUR FREE CHECK TODAY poster will fuel it. Expectantly, she finds none, her mouth opening but with nothing to exit. It's at this point that I gently lay down the spade for digging my hole and replace it with a JCB digger: *'Do you play, er together, before the, er, penetration?'* The moment the words leave my mouth, I want them back. Forever.

She looks at me, mortified that the word – penetration – was just uttered in reference to her. How is this ten-minute appointment still not over yet? Sweat clusters along my neck. If only the professional boundary could be dropped for a mere split second, I could say it like it is – but as it turns out, that's impossible. She's yet to answer my *play together* question, though I now realise I don't even want the answer. This consultation is stalling. I wish Greg was here. At least there'd be another talking point as he sits, legs four feet apart. Maybe he knows Kev, my Basic Life Support (BLS) instructor, who ingratiated himself on the surgery last June?

I regain control, and switch off the JCB's engine, explaining to Lea in the most professional, asexual, and detached way possible that I'd recommend three things: *'The first is to spend more time being intimate in other ways like . . .'* (*the JCB powers up*) – I retract, realising this isn't quite the right forum to be offering specific sex tips – instead saying, *'in ways comfortable to both you and Greg.'* The second is to try some vaginal lubricants to help reduce friction. We both break eye contact at this point. The third – and probably most critical – is to go and have a good old-fashioned alcohol-fuelled disinhibited chat about all this with a close mate. Basically, they'll give the unedited version of the advice I'm trying to professionally give – shouted up from the depths of the large hole I've dug. Remarkably, Lea leaves, happy with this trio of advice.

Who would've thought I'd have discovered the inner sex therapist in me – on a Thursday mid-afternoon of all days?

Friday, 2nd November

William's getting his first set of vaccinations today. Poor bugger. Still, great for me, as it means only a half-day at work. A fair compromise. After all, Alice and I have done everything for him in his first eight weeks of life. In return? He wakes us up every three hours crying and demanding food, has put our social life in a shallow grave – and our sex life in an even deeper one. So, he can take a few needle scratches to win me half a day off work.

Just as I'm about to shut down the computer and meet my family team at *his* GP surgery (since he can't be registered at his dad's surgery – slight, but very obvious conflict of interest there – and also why GPs, including myself, must be registered at another surgery from the one they work at) nearer to home, an email *ping* fills my room. With an unfamiliar sense of digital diligence, I decide to check it. Well, I never! A reply from Stanley's orthopaedic team about his cancelled total-knee replacement operation. They've apologised for his cancellation, chalking it down to a bed capacity problem (which isn't Stanley's problem), and they've rebooked him for the operation in two weeks.

I'm filled with volitional obligation and call Stanley to give him the good news. The orthopaedic team are clearly feeling sheepish since they've beaten me to the punch and already called him. I tell Stanley it's because they're feeling *fucking guilty.* Like me, Stanley loves a swear word and we both laugh, victorious. He thanks me for writing an angry letter but I explain there's no need, it was a pleasure.

Sometimes I feel I can't do enough for patients, my hands tied by either NHS system barriers, my own work capacity, or referral waiting times (or all three) – frustrations I've grown to accept. So today, this news is fantastic: I've managed to slip the knots, so to speak, for at least one patient. And with the call ended, a smile on my face, I finally close down the computer and off I go to watch William get the smile wiped off his.

Sunday, 4th November

Pushing a sleeping William around in the pram while Alice takes a well-earned nap at home is surprisingly rewarding. With the hum of the city in the throes of a sunny but cold weekend around me, I negotiate the uneven pavement in an attempt to keep William asleep – a little fella who was, unsurprisingly, fairly indignant after his set of vaccinations on Friday (he rewarded us with a couple of pretty rough nights).

This walk also has an alternative agenda: I need to think. You see, last month's performance appraisal (*sorry to harp on about it*) threw up more than just a little self-analysis and reflection. It seemed to open the floodgates, leaving me with a Noah's Ark of thoughts. I felt so strangely positive and rewarded by the process of (finally) reconciling the constructive criticism from the appraisal, pushing me towards becoming a better GP, that I started to look at the single most important aspect of my life: Alice and William. *My family.* I started to ask the same sorts of questions: *How can I make it – life – better for us?* From what felt like nowhere, a single thought enters my mind – moving out of the city and heading for the countryside. This hasn't been a concrete idea in my head until now. And it's one that feels like a new pair of shoes – uncomfortable and unfamiliar at first but, once broken in a little, surprisingly quite snug.

But I love this city. In fact, it's all I've ever known, born and raised by my wonderful family. The same goes for Alice. We are, we joke, utter city rats, urbanised to the bone. So, *where* did those thoughts of leaving behind everything we know suddenly appear from? Could it just be a knee-jerk reaction – something Alice would tell me I'm famed for – to a few rougher months than usual at work? Or perhaps the seeds of departure have been there longer than I thought? *Push* and *pull* factors insidiously working in collaboration over the last six months. Fate making itself heard.

I smile as I pass another relieved dad pushing his equally comatose child around the park. I breathe. I deliberate. The pull factors feel very obvious when I think about it – in the countryside we'd . . . I pause, I need to write these down. I detour William and I off the path to a nearby bench and get out a scrap of paper . . .

Pull Factors

1. We could afford a bigger family home
2. Space. Lots and lots of green space for William to play and explore
3. Cheaper cost of living

4. More golf courses (note: don't tell Alice this one)
5. Slower pace of life and time to enjoy the simple things
6. Cheaper nursery
7. Finally, finally, have the chance to get a pet dog (can imagine William being dragged along by a fox-red Labrador)
8. New professional challenges – the countryside would offer lots of different hurdles from isolation of patients to access to services (think of Mrs Gray and her car crash last month!)
9. Being part of a smaller but well-connected community (we don't have that here . . .).

I pause for a second, surprised at how many reasons have just poured out of me. Stored up, now unpackaged into my stream of consciousness. I begin to think of the factors that are pushing me away from the city and towards a more rural life . . .

1. Not spending thousands of pounds on a new house in the city for a few measly extra square metres of space
2. The pressure bubble that city life can create sometimes (something only realised with trips out of the city, like our mini babymoon to the Lake District last July)
3. Growing work pressures from being a city GP and the imbalance it has on family life and stress levels (not sure how different it would be in the countryside, to be fair)
4. Increased awareness of crime where we live. Sense of security lessening.

All food for thought. Stuffing the paper in my jean pocket, I get up and cruise the pram around another corner, back on the path towards home. Just as I do, a whimper stirs from beneath the dark red of the pram hood.

'I know you're there, pal.'

The little boy who's changed how I see it all.

Tuesday, 6th November

Flying start to the week – I finally killed off the second pot plant Alice bought me.

William, you're definitely fucked.

Maybe I'll say it died of shock after last night's Guy Fawkes fireworks. That sounds better than chronic dehydration.

Wednesday, 7th November

Elizabeth wears a confidence beyond her thirteen years. With her father, Andrew, next to her, she sits opposite me, hands neatly and deliberately resting on both knees. Poised. She looks relaxed with it too. I study the surrounding picture – crease-free matching clothing, hair neatly tied back, and iPhone placed perpendicular to the edge of my desk. Maybe it's a generational thing but when I was thirteen, I looked like an extra from *Oliver Twist* despite parental best efforts.

I kick off proceedings with the open question of *'How can I help you today?'* It's the default opener of any customer-facing job, mine included. A good one too since as a GP, I very rarely know what the problem is going to be when someone sits down in front of me (also, part of the thrill of the job). Besides, I want to give Elizabeth an open playing field to tell me what she wants. She's had tummy ache for the last few weeks. I nod in a manner which encourages her to continue, yet as the minutes tick by and I wade deeper through her clinical issue, I realise I'm finding very little. In fact, I find nothing.

I recap with her, a GP's tool that says either I'm confused, unsure or zoned out for a second. The problem has been ongoing for a few months, worse after eating quickly, and then gets better. It's the same at the weekends as it is on weekdays (important since if it's just occurring during school time, it can suggest anxiety or being stress-related – or the provision of very shit school meals). My clinical fishing yields no bites, so I decide to branch out and ask what she does outside school.

Gymnastics. A ton of it. Six times a week. Elizabeth does the thing with the ribbons particularly well, apparently. I've no idea what that is, but tell her I do. Andrew lends me a subtle nod of encouragement as if playing a non-verbal game of clinical hotter or colder. Interestingly, we're five minutes into the consultation and I've only just properly digested his body language. It says *I'm dying to tell you what I'm worried about – but don't want to betray my daughter*. His eyes will me on. The clinical history largely wrapped up, I check her observations and casually suggest we check her weight as part of the assessment. Important, I add, because with all that gymnastic exercise, we want to ensure she doesn't lose too much weight and risk impairing her performance through excessive fatigue or increased illness and injury susceptibility. She doesn't want to measure her weight. *Bingo*. Andrew adds how they no longer have weighing scales at home – they can upset her.

'What do you see when you look in the mirror?' Bearing in mind this 13-year-old girl has a perfectly healthy body shape and eyeballing her, a healthy weight, the answer is a massive red flag: *'That I'm fat.'* The contributing factors to that answer are, likely, endless. Social media, advertising, magazines, celebrities, school peer pressure, and sadly, even the sport she loves, to name but a few. I'm not going to reverse her perception right now. Andrew glances at me with a mix of heartbreak and relief: Elizabeth's finally shown her cards. At this age, the way in which we interact now isn't all that different from skating on thin ice – too much pressure and it's game over. Elizabeth presents herself as a person who wants control, despite her young age. This includes control over body image.

It will seem really unsatisfactory for Andrew (and understandably so) but I wrap things up with no real intervention. I need Elizabeth to trust me a little, this being only our first meeting. I'll get her back in to see me soon and continue to explore this more (including offering to speak to her alone without her parents since she may have things to share that she's unable to do in front of them – for many reasons). For now, though, this hasn't to my mind taken a landslide into disordered eating. This is a young girl who feels the same pressures as many young people do about their body image. At a time too when they're undergoing all the confusing physical and emotional changes that encapsulate puberty. She is at risk, yes, but part of a GP's job is to differentiate between a natural emotion or perception and a disordered one.

Today, Elizabeth doesn't need to be medicalised, she needs to know she can trust me first. As I close the consultation,

I can't help but wonder if my seniors at work would consider this an irrational, unorthodox, and unilateral decision.

Perhaps.

Thursday, 8th November

If I could make any wish, I'd wish people to have the foresight to tighten the lid of their urine sample pots before giving them to me. I stand here, mesmerised as three strategically placed blue NHS-issue paper towels excitedly absorb a stranger's urine from the deep grooves of my keyboard. After a long day, I dig deep for a silver lining, glancing around the room for inspiration.

Found it. My box of stool sample pots.

At least it wasn't one of those.

Sunday, 11th November

Woke to find our car's been keyed again, no doubt by some of the local fuckwit delinquents. I'll need to keep an eye out. Then again, realistically, what am I going to do? Beat them up? Unlikely. I can barely touch my toes, let alone swing a punch. It could be some of my patients for all I know. How ironic would that be. Still, it's something else to firmly add to the push factors to leave for the countryside. We, my family – no family, in fact – should ever have to feel unsafe outside their own front door.

Alice and I spend the rest of the day (like many of the days since I raised the idea of leaving the city to her earlier this month) pulling apart and putting back together the arguments for and against whether we should stay in the city – or go for it, and have a rural adventure. We are, unsurprisingly, still undecided (slightly paralysed by the mammoth weight that comes with such a decision). Instead, we decide to put on the fabulous classic song by The Clash – 'Should I Stay or Should I Go' and have a dance around the kitchen.

William loves it.

Tuesday, 13th November

People can place some unexpected things on my consultation table. A dead mouse wrapped in supermarket-strength clingfilm is, however, a novelty – and a first. Mrs Chambers explodes into tears. It's only 09:10am and there's a lot of clinic left to survive so I decide to pace myself here and let her cry it out. I check my to-do list as she sobs into the table, head next to her dead mouse.

As the crying subsides, I feel out the answer to my first question: is this a pet or a pest? Mrs Chambers looks at me like I've just asked her if she needs bereavement counselling.

'A pest!'

Of course.

She shakes her head in disbelief at this question. With only a few remaining sobs escaping as she regains her composure, it seems the right time to tell her to remove the dead mouse from my table.

'Now, please,' I add with a smile.

She does as she's told, albeit looking slightly put out by the request. As a fascinated spectator, I'm speechless how anyone can think that to bring in a dead mouse to their GP is in any way normal. The best part is as she puts the clingfilmed mouse back in her bag, she pulls out her bottle of water and takes a sip.

Hygiene not a priority then.

Corpse now in its shallow grave of Mrs Chamber's handbag, I sit and listen as she laments how her private rental flat has mice everywhere and she's had to write to her local council (twice) since her landlord won't do anything about it. This is definitely one of those consultations that I don't type up as I listen – mainly as absolutely nothing of medical pertinence has even begun to materialise. So far all I've learned is that Mrs Chambers has no concept of boundaries or hygiene. That's not a diagnosis, that's just people.

I settle into my chair, one eye on the clock, monitoring how long I need to grind this out for. Finally, the patient agenda materialises.

'I need you to write to the council.'

Before explaining my answer is to be an unwavering *'No, thank you, Mrs Chambers,'* I let her explain why she *needs* me to do this. It seems she's under the impression that GPs have some sort of magical power given to them on qualification that means I'll be able to whip her local council, private landlord, and pest control services into frenzied and immediate action. Not my first *you need to write me a letter* rodeo, I nod in understanding of her predicament, before confirming that I won't be doing that.

Why? Easy. Because it's not my bloody job.

Jaw hanging, Mrs Chambers looks at me as I deliver this news with an albeit more sensitive choice of vocabulary.

'No?'

I nod slowly.

'No.'

She has the all-too-common misinformed preconception that if you've got a problem (with absolutely anything), if you see your GP, they'll fix it. I'm a doctor and what Mrs Chambers is actually saying is that she wants to use me as leverage.

I'm not a bloody bank!

She starts to sob into the table again. Tacitly, I groan. Not wanting to be a total dick (yet wanting to stick to my guns here), I redirect her to some local support agencies including the Citizens Advice Bureau. Of course, I end the consultation with the most obvious suggestion of all – *'Mrs Chambers, just move out!'*

Wednesday, 14th November

Teri is fifty-four years old, and my favourite alcoholic. Now that's mainly because despite the setbacks, she never gives up the fight. Quitting alcohol is far from easy for those in the grip of addiction. To understand the battle is near impossible as an outsider. I've supported her journey to abstinence over the last couple of years. Every time our paths cross, the story runs a similar course: it starts strong. Inevitably though it's then derailed by some negative life event or trauma. Sometimes it doesn't matter how many Alcoholics Anonymous (or similar) meetings, therapy sessions, medications, or GP appointments a person has, if their resolve to abstain gets dented for even a second, that can be enough to open the door to a drink.

I'm sitting scrolling through all the consultations I've had with Teri, phone receiver clasped to my ear, waiting for her to answer my call. It's the third time I've called today since she missed our face-to-face appointment earlier. My moral compass is clearly strong today as I'm beyond exhausted after a long night with William (*who seems to have lost his off-switch*) and should really be going home now my clinic is over. Long finished, in fact. It's nearly 7pm, but I want to make sure she's alright. Besides, I also know I'll have a bit of a laugh with her, both being on similar wavelengths when it comes to humour.

I flick to my personal email account while I wait. Yet more spam emails from this Prince in Africa telling me he needs to share his financial windfall with me – and URGENTLY, for tax reasons – just needing my bank details for the transfer. What websites have I stumbled on to get this shit?

''ello, Doctor!'

My thought process stops abruptly. There she is – and somewhere very noisy by the sounds of it. Guilt percolates down the phone line as I ask where exactly she is. She hesitates a fraction too long. Now, in the ideal world, following our last meeting ten days ago, Teri should be seven days into a reducing regimen of alcohol consumption (I've lost count how many times we have done this). In the real world, she's definitely in the pub.

'I'm on the non-alcoholic beer, I promise.'

Her words slur. I explain that we both know that the kind of pubs she visits don't know what non-alcoholic beer is.

'It's my birthday!' she protests.

Again, I explain to Teri that, as her GP, I've got all her personal details and so unless she's morphed into the Queen, with two sodding birthdays, her celebrations are four months overdue.

'I'll start next week, I promise. Gotta run, thanks, Max!'

And with that, the phone line goes dead. Another battle lost. A war still to win.

Have one for me, Teri. On your new *birthday.*

Thursday, 15th November

Just bumped into Dr Phil. He asked if I was alright after my appraisal last month. I feel like he was genuine with his concern. This means I probably looked at the time of the appraisal like they'd gone full-on *Deliverance* on me, taking my pride, dignity, and self-belief. As I've said before, a massive overreaction on my part. And although I'm not quite sure where my head's at with work at the moment, I give him a nod.

'Never better, boss.'

He sets my mind once again turning over the key question about leaving.

Is there enough here in the city to stay for, or too much out there in the countryside to ignore?

I click the call bell for my next patient. Whatever it is, one thing's for sure, 5-year-old Jessie with ear pain is unlikely to have the answer.

Friday, 16th November

'Are you on Twitter? I'll follow you.'

Who asks their doctor that? I mean, really, come on.

Monday, 19th November

It's a *Daily Mail* headline in the making. I glance away from my computer screen back towards Mr Wells, waiting expectantly to hear when his ENT (Ear, Nose and Throat) consultant outpatient appointment will be. I inhale. Look back to the screen. Back to Mr Wells. Exhale.

'You're not going to like this, I'm afraid.'

He sits back, coat crumpling against the back of the chair. Now, I think he volunteers in the local Oxfam? In fact, I'm sure I've bought some of William's books off him there. Still, maybe a chat for another day, given the bombshell I'm about to drop.

'Well,' I pause, not really wanting to continue, *'the next available routine appointment is on 24th May . . . in 2019.'*

I'm so embarrassed for the NHS right now. Mr Wells doesn't move an inch. He just blinks for second and then looks down, frowning, his brain processing the timeline. I feel like telling him optimistically that a cancellation might come up before his current appointment – some six months away – may be pouring buckets of refined salt into his fresh gaping wounds even more. Knowing what comes next, I get comfy in my chair – a chair, by the way, I'm beginning to realise isn't comfy at all. I make a mental note to ask our practice manager, Jasper, if he'll buy me one of those big leather high-backed *power* chairs.

Ah yes, here it comes: The Rant.

Off Mr Wells goes. Usually, as is the case today, it starts with total denial that this timeline can even be possible. Disbelieving laughter peppers his statement. Then the anger rises. First, he blames the Government. Then the NHS. Before more conveniently (I'm in front of him, after all) blaming me. A mention about how he pays his taxes is tossed in (it usually is). I nod in agreement to nudge the process along. Next, comes the bargaining. Always a non-starter, but I listen anyway. I explain that no, even if I were to write an *extra-*, *extra-special* letter about how his chronic recurrent ear infections need to be seen sooner, it will not speed up the process. Then comes the sulk. Often, much like today, followed by the guilt approach. How their life will be *on pause* while they wait for their appointment. When I was perhaps a little greener behind the ears in my first year as a qualified GP, I'd buckle at this and make promises I couldn't keep. Nowadays, a smidge more seasoned with two more years' experience, I know bending to this isn't an option: my hands are as tied, as are theirs. Finally, zipping up his coat and shouldering his bag, Mr Wells gives me a nod and a *'Well, it'll have to do'* – the acceptance stage. I smile and wave him off.

Sometimes the hardest thing as a GP is not to buckle. It's ingrained in you to want to help, to do everything you can for a patient, but the reality is you have to moderate that, be rational, realistic, and manage expectation – hard as those conversations can be. As I type up his notes, it strikes me the process I went through with Mr Wells mirrors the five theoretical stages outlined in the Kübler-Ross Grief Cycle: Denial-Anger-Bargaining-Depression-Acceptance. My head throbs. This lesson about accepting what is and isn't in my control has taken time to learn. Even so, it still doesn't make absorbing a patient's disappointment and frustrations at the system – a system I don't control – any less exhausting. You feel like you're not doing a good enough job. Basically, it's like someone telling you they're disappointed in you and we all know that can cut the deepest.

My next patient is running late so I take a minute to continue my search for car-scratch removal products.

Tuesday, 20th November

Had an email back from Jasper, the practice manager. Apparently, he won't be buying me a big leather high-backed *power* chair for my consultation room – because I'm not Lord Alan Sugar from *The Apprentice.* They *will* find me a cushion though.

Victory!

Thursday, 22nd November

Tricky. I scroll through Patsy's notes. It's fair to say I've been out of the loop with her for a while now. In fact, it was over four months ago when I last saw her. I digest the recollection.

Yes, the home visit when I discovered intertrigo lurking within her abdominal skin folds.

How she's escaped me for so long, I've no idea – she was fantastic! I make a note to go and see her soon for a catch-up and a dose of her unbelievably sunny disposition. I scroll further through the last four months of documented consultations and phone calls made by other GPs to Patsy or the community services I referred her to. This happens sometimes in general practice. You have a frantic period of involvement with a patient and then just like that, they drop off your radar. When this happens, it can be for lots of different reasons. You go on holiday, they go into hospital. Yet sometimes the truth is that it's just because it can get really hard to keep an eye on all the plates you've got spinning in the air at one time. I, along with every other GP, simply have too many patients to properly maintain a fully engaged role in their lives on a weekly basis.

Dialling the community occupational therapy (OT) lead, I can only wonder what this is about. Five minutes into the call with Ben, the OT lead, I feel like I'm in some warped version of the TV show, *The Crystal Maze.* Our puzzle: how to weigh a patient unable to get out of bed and the ambulance crew unable to get her through the front door (due to her width) on some zoo animal scales (*I'm not kidding*). The OT team cannot install her wall-mounted hoist until this is all done. She's likely very close to the maximum weight limit. That translates to: *She might rip the ceiling down if our estimated weight is too inaccurate.*

Again, not something they teach you in medical school.

I think of all those cool TV shows where the fire services cut holes in the front of houses and crane people out. I agree with Ben when he drily tells me that he doubts the council would thank us for that.

How can this happen? I wonder. *A person has eaten themselves into a homemade prison.*

With Ben still on the line, I go back through Patsy's clinical notes to see if there are any other weights for her that would be acceptable. Nope, as was the case in July, the last recorded weight was two years ago when she was in hospital. So, I tell Ben I've no idea. We may even need to get the ambulance and fire services to come and work it out for us, like an emergency services multi-disciplinary team meeting. How I even organise something like that is beyond me. Especially at 4:50pm, a good three hours since my last coffee. So, I tell Ben I'll have to get back to him on this one.

I shake my head at the frustration of this naturally defaulting to being an issue for the GP to figure out. Out of ideas for now, I decide that maybe I'll write to *The Crystal Maze* team for some advice.

Friday, 23rd November

The plot thickens in the surgery. One of the partners has reportedly gone off with long-term stress (the unofficial, rumour mill version). On the back of this, there's to be a compulsory *must attend* GP meeting next month to discuss the current working climate in the surgery. It'll either be some very polite British disagreements, or a few GPs will throw the gloves off and go toe-to-toe.

Right now, given my ongoing discussions with Alice about city life and work, I can't help but wonder what side of this I'm going to fall on.

Saturday, 24th November

I was enjoying this weekend. Until tonight, when I was told off by Alice. We took William to his second wedding. I was in charge of him (Alice's first mistake) and so decided to carry him around in the harness so he could sleep against my chest. It happened to be a stand-up buffet cart rather than a sit-down meal. And oh, my God, they had the most amazing beef brisket in wraps with horseradish that I just couldn't get enough of! Bit messy to eat though. So much so that it appears I may not quite have got all the food in my mouth. As Alice extricated a sleeping William from the carry harness to get into the car, he had half the buffet stuck to him.

My joke about early weaning at eleven weeks old went unwelcomed. I'll get a further LIB (Lecture in Bed) later, no doubt – Alice's standard operating procedure when I don't show remorse.

Tuesday, 27 November

'That is a terrible present to yourself' is what I want to say to Rachel. She stands, leaning against my consultation wall in floods of tears. Nobody's ever cried into my wall before. It's usually the desk, the perceptibly more comfortable option. I sit there in silence, exhausted (*again, I know*) and Rachel's the last patient I'll be seeing as the duty doctor today. She hits pause on her sobs for a moment, turning to me, telling me she'll really do it – she'll really kill herself this Saturday – the first of December – *her birthday*.

Gently, I get out of my chair and perch against the consultation table, hands loosely wrapped around the lip of it. I ask why. She feels awful. That's why. She hates her life. Her boyfriend has not only just dumped her but revealed that he cheated on her repeatedly. She hates her job in the supermarket and is on a professional conduct warning for persistent lateness. She hates where she lives as the neighbours are noisy. I say nothing, letting her get it all out, uninterrupted.

I peer briefly at the summary information from her clinical notes. I've seen Rachel a few times on and off over the past two years. She suffers severe depression and is under the community mental health team. She's undergone talking therapies of various types and cycled through most of the common antidepressant medications before arriving at some more exotic antipsychotic medications via her psychiatrist.

I also know she's taken a deliberate overdose of paracetamol and codeine twice before and cut her arms and inner thighs with an opened safety pin, requiring stiches in the local A&E department.

Basically, she's not fucking around. She means it. She is very unwell.

I hand her some NHS-issue tissues – a bit like rubbing glass on your face. She takes them and dries her eyes. I sit down, hoping she'll take the hint and join me. She does. Finally, nearly ten minutes into the consultation, we sit opposite each other, neither crying. Progress. I can feel my phone vibrate in my pocket: it'll be Alice wondering if I've finished yet. I let it vibrate to voicemail. After all, it doesn't take a medical degree to know it's not the time to show Rachel what a nice life I have with a happy wife (now that I've been forgiven after the weekend) and baby waiting for me at home. She sniffs again before quietly saying, *'I'll do it, you know.'* I tell her I know she will, I believe her.

The brutal, unvarnished truth is that if a person wants to end their life – short of being sectioned under the Mental Health Act (where they're detained against their will for assessment and/or treatment) where they're under 24-hour watch (which can, even then, fail) – you cannot stop them. All you can do is help them as best you can – with the time and resources available – to improve their mental health. Rachel's triggers today don't require a detective: her life isn't what she wants it to be. And with her boyfriend now out of the picture (despite sounding like a useless twat), she's feeling unloved. Shit for anyone, but a dangerous thing for someone suffering depression. I know she has family though. She has a sister and a dad (who raised her as a single parent) that she adores. She's also recently become a new auntie. I talk to her about them and her new niece. She breaks into this beautiful smile. Then she starts to cry, telling me it's all too hard.

I can't possibly understand what she's going through so I don't bullshit her by pretending I do. Instead, I tell her that *'it sounds shit'* – and I'm sorry she's going through it. The truth. And then I just do what I can – ask her if she'd let me get her some help. Naturally, she tells me nobody can help her. I ignore that. She's in a dark place right now and no matter how bright I try to shine light on her, she'll turn away in favour of darkness. I tell her to sit here with me while I call the on-call emergency mental health team. Reluctantly, she agrees. I give her some water in a dusty plastic cup and my last bar of chocolate (meant to be my reward for finishing these typically awful duty doctor shifts but she's won the Toughest Day award for today).

After fifteen minutes of waiting, I get through to the team. They know Rachel well and agree she needs urgent review and support. They'll see her in person within the next forty-eight hours and will also call her tonight. *As long as it's before her birthday*, I stress. And with that, I go through the same well-trodden steps I always do when someone comes to me in mental health crisis. I tell them there's always hope, however small. I tell them not to give up. I make them put the Samaritans and the local 24-hour mental health helpline numbers into their mobile phones. And I book them in for a phone call with me when I'm next in. And then they go.

And I just hope to see them again. Instead of their coroner's report.

Thursday, 29th November

Well, I never. Turns out Patsy's social worker had quite the epiphany when she visited her this morning. Called for an ambulance straight away and sent her to hospital on the basis that *she was too fat to live like this.* I'm not sure that's a valid clinical reason for an ambulance crew to be called out. Anyway, it's done now and she's in hospital.

The incredible thing isn't necessarily the social worker's reaction but that the ambulance crew actually got her out! I wonder if next time I visit there will be a Patsy-sized hole cut in the wall. Perhaps it'll be filled in with fresh bricks and mortar, forever an embodiment of a less-glamorous version of *The Great Escape.* And I suppose, now in hospital, at least the OT team will get that up-to-date weight they need for her hoist to be fitted.

I delete the task – *The Weighty Conundrum of Patsy* – from my jobs list.

Friday, 30th November

Currently on the phone with Mrs Tally, hearing how her carers are not only *still* just as shit as ever, but also now breaching her human rights as a tax payer. None of which makes sense.

Perhaps I should break the news that she's a month too late if this is meant to be my Halloween phone call.

DECEMBER 2018

Monday, 3rd December

The best twenty quid I've ever spent on Amazon. On the changing mat, as I work to make his feet clean from the shit he's managed to stamp in, William stares, transfixed, like some infant stoner, at the projected blue, red, and green sea creatures floating around on the ceiling. The fact that it's 04:27am – or that the whale projections are the same size as the seahorses – is academic.

After feeling the grind of my GP clinics lately, I've decided to take a week off work, joining Alice on her maternity leave. That means tonight, despite the time, there's no dawning realisation of a next day's clinic to run – exhausted, irritable, and angry (well, more angry than usual). Instead, it means in a few hours' time there'll be a longer-than-usual Breakfast Club with Alice and William. This, our morning ritual of tea, cereal, and breastfeeding in bed, all to the sound of BBC Radio 2's Chris Evans.

As I strap William's explosive arse back in his nappy, he looks at me. Patiently. Words can't describe the feelings that thunder out of my heart at the sight of my boy, crystallised by the calm dead of the night. I often wonder what he's thinking. I glance at my watch: it's late. Or early, depending on your perspective. Still, as William seems up for it, we decide to disrupt the calm and have a little (very) early morning boys' club meeting. I quietly play his favourite song, The Beatles' 'Twist and Shout'. He goes crazy for it, clasping his hands together in front of him with joy and the best full-facial toothless smile money can buy. Sadly, it's all too much for him. A little *shart* punctuates the air.

Never mind, pal, we've got nothing but time this week.

Wednesday, 5th December

Alice just stares at me, bemused and incredulous. To be fair, I knew it was the wrong thing to say. I work to back-pedal but she knows I was being serious – she knows me too well. She's also set out using her skill as a human black-box recorder (handy for her, never for me), and recounts verbatim what I said: *'You said that you want us to go to the neighbours around the corner for a drink – but take William's baby monitor with us – so he can continue to sleep at home? Alone. At thirteen weeks old.'* When she says it like that, it doesn't sound the most sensible idea. I let the grey peak of my very old but very sentimental baseball cap obscure my eyes as I'm stared down by my wife.

Judge. Jury. Executioner.

I wonder if this is what my patients feel like when I hear *them* say something stupid? I hold back on the urge to make a joke about wanting to build community bonds. Perhaps build early independence in our son? No? Too soon, I resolve. Instead, once again, I deploy good old-fashioned GP tactics and stand here, nod earnestly, drinking in the silence. Alice softens (*she always does, thank* God), calls me a fucking idiot (*I love her so much*), and we then take William out for an evening stroll. It's surprising how being a GP can teach far more than just medicine. So many lessons for life. For one, I never knew it would get me out of a bollocking so many times.

Worth all the endless days of training for that alone.

Thursday, 6th December

William bobs around in front of me, a potato overboard from a shipping container. Poor boy, he's a bit dazed and confused right now after we crashed into the swimming class pool ten minutes late. On the upside, this did mean missing the terribly awkward thirty seconds where all the parents join in to sing the welcome song to their babies – *as if they really give a shit; they're just wondering when bathtime got so scaled-up*.

I explain to Hal, our swim instructor, that we're late as traffic was heavy. In truth, it was Alice. She did a proper number on me, and as I wipe the watery congealing snot from William's face, I make a note to take it up with her tonight. I mean, to give me *zero* warning that getting William's thunder thighs into his waterproof swimming shorts (*that are, to all intents and purposes, stripper hot pants – just with colourful fishes on them*), is next to impossible. That's not just cruel on her part, that's premeditated.

As William continues his potato-cum-stripper look, I smile at the other grown-ups, trying to refocus and erase from my mind that I've just had to lubricate my child to get him into swimwear. Even harder to swallow is the guilt that I decided to chance him in a normal, non-seafaring nappy.

God, I hope it doesn't absorb the whole bloody pool.

Twenty minutes later, and with the water level still roughly the same, the lesson's over. I say 'lesson', though I'm not sure what I actually learned for my £12. I'm pretty confident that I could push William around in the bath and splash water in his face for a lesser fee. As we get out, one mum mentions she recognises me. In my foolish head this means I immediately think that I'm being hit on. Given my tight, faded, pink flamingo swim shorts that somehow collect my gut into neat abdominal puff pastry rolls, I realise this is highly unlikely.

'Dr Skittle?'

Rumbled. And me, clearly mistaking that being a GP equals some kind of rock star, return with a *'You got me!'* Complete with cheesy smile.

You, dickhead, Max!

She introduces herself as Mrs Western, who turns out to be a patient at my practice. *Lucky me.* As I wait for Mrs Western to spit out whatever the hell it is that she wants, I juggle William in my arm, who by this time is cold, hungry, and unbeknownst to him, likely needing to be cut out of fishy stripper hot pants. His vocals ramp up. A sign of increasing frustration. We're close to an emotional meltdown, so I ask Mrs Western if she wouldn't mind hurrying this up a little. She wants me to check her son's belly button. He's three months old. Boring, but also tricky. I don't want to be a dick about this and could indeed have a look, but in what capacity? This is a classic GP trap. If I peer at her son's wet, manky navel here, and think something's wrong, what am I going to do about it? Nothing. Why? Because I'm standing poolside in a pair of tight, faded, pink flamingo swim shorts, holding my hot-panted son. The result of such informal consultations, in the worst-case scenario (i.e. I mess up and then Mrs Western takes me to court and says, 'B*ut Dr Skittle said . . .*') is that you don't have a legal leg to stand on. The sad truth of our increasingly litigious society. Which is why all GPs will be paid up to one of the many very good medical legal unions to support them when those unexpected events do occur (*and they do*). It also highlights why GPs have a lower threshold for risk – making a mistake now comes with a much higher risk of legal action. More importantly than all this, however, is that the patient doesn't get a good and thorough consultation.

In the end, I fold and take a peek. It looks fine to me but will, I explained, need a proper review when not soaking wet with heavily chlorinated pool water. And by a fully-clothed clinician. As fate would have it, there's a walk-in clinic tomorrow so I signpost her to that. And with the lesson over, Mrs Western satisfied, William and I slip away to the changing room.

For the fight of our lives.

Sunday, 9th December

What a week off! I feel amazing. It's like someone's reached into my life and fixed the broken spirit level. Equilibrium restored, life and work equal partners once more. Sat on the sofa, panting, I flop two sweaty forearms over my knees. William just stares at me from his play mat, effortlessly permitting a trickle of curdled milk to escape his mouth before squealing at absolutely nothing – he can be very weird at times.

The thirty-second interval alarm sounds and so in quiet protest, collecting up the 12-kilogram kettle bell, I start swinging again. I'm fifteen minutes into the workout led by The Body Coach on YouTube but remain mindful to keep a strong grip – and avoid sending it through the window.

Or flattening William. Alice would be mad at me for either. Talking of windows, that's partly why I'm putting myself through it. This week, away from the chaos of work, has allowed me to reflect on my own life window. It wasn't pre-planned activity either. More an insidious, subconscious process that evolved, gathering pace over the week. I spend so much of my working life peering through patient windows that perhaps I'd neglected my own. Don't get me wrong, I'm not annoyed at myself for not doing it sooner, it's the collateral damage of being a GP in a climate where there's suffocation by demand. Work is noisy, angry, emotional. All too easily, it can drown out your own life's needs. Until that is, you pause, breathe, and take a step back.

That's what this week was for me: a step back. An opportunity to reframe, refocus, and refresh. And that's what I've done. I pushed work right to the back of the priority list, caught up with my family, drank beer with my friends, even took Alice on a date, leaving William with a babysitter for the first time. Terrifying for us. And him.

Basically, I *lived.* We *lived.*

I did all those home improvements I'd been putting off. William's nursery shelves are now put up (*successfully, after a couple of attempts*), the garden paving stones have been power-washed, the external windows all cleaned. Once more I let the kettle bell crash into the cushion on the floor – there, as Alice would positively castrate me if I marked our wooden floor – and flop onto the sofa. This is the other revelation this week. I need to look after my own health – physical, mental, and social. That's why I'm breathing out of my arse right now, and will do so every week from now on. Because, just like with many sedentary desk jobs, as a GP I need to fight the urge to sit slumped over a desk all day, snacking on shit processed food, before finally going home and collapsing on the sofa. None of this is helpful to my health.

To anyone's health.

William just lies there, curdled milk cementing itself on his chin. I wonder what he makes of this life so far. Is he bored? Does he want new parents? What does he *really* think when he shits himself? All questions I'll ask when he's older. We have friends over later for dinner, so it's time to have a shower and scrub up.

Everything I've just said has been about washing away the dominance of work. Alice and I haven't even talked about our *to move or not to move?* saga (yet to be resolved). And this week, it's worked. The proof in the pudding will be to see if I can carry this new, healthier, more balanced perspective into the months and years ahead.

For now, let's just keep our fingers crossed for next week.

Monday, 10th December

First job now I'm back at work is to call Rachel. Turns out she did survive her birthday and while not quite skipping carefree down the Yellow Brick Road, she's feeling a little better than two weeks ago, and awaiting further input from the mental health team.

For now, I can't really ask for much more than that.

Tuesday, 11th December

I should just keep my door shut. I hear the screaming. I hear the commotion. I hear the thud. It would be the sensible thing to do. Yet, I know as the duty doctor for today, whatever chaos is materialising outside in reception, it's about to be unceremoniously (and unapologetically) dumped in my lap. I decide to confront the storm and open the door. Sarah and Dan, two of my salaried GP pals, are holding up some skinny fella in his early twenties, legs dangling under him like party popper strings in gale force nine winds. Their eyes lock on me.

'You're duty today, aren't you, Max?'

I nod. Noting their subtlest of smiles.

Cocks.

I make a mental note to book Mrs Tally in for phone calls with them.

For the foreseeable future.

Together, we drag all nine stone of our limp stranger to my room and he collapses on the examination couch. I stand and stare at him, deeply unimpressed. He's hyperventilating, writhing around, retching, all while grabbing his chest, screaming something about his heart being about to explode. I've never seen a heart explode, and doubt today's the day either.

As Sarah and Dan leave my room, Sally from reception rushes in with the oxygen cylinder and emergency box of medications. I can see the look of morbid fascination and excitement etched over her face as she no doubt wonders if she's about to witness her first death.

'His name's Ryan,' she tells me with breathy excitement, having sprinted up the stairs, handing me a printed summary of his clinical notes. I glance over them as Ryan continues to play out his death in front of me. I ask him to put

all his focus into his breathing – three seconds in through his nose, followed by three seconds out through the mouth. He ignores me, and continues to scream that he's about to die. He's not. I know that. I tell him that he's having a panic attack and unless he's really unlucky, has some rare heart condition, or snorted a bucket of cocaine, his heart isn't going to stop. Or explode.

God knows why he's having the panic attack. I expect we'll find out once he calms down – or dies of a rare heart condition. I toy with the idea of doing some basic clinical observations on him – heart rate, oxygen saturations, respiratory rate, and blood pressure – but decide against it, realising it'll be pointless. For one, he clearly has a blood pressure good enough to send plenty of blood to his brain and muscles to be carrying out all this screaming and fuss. That's a blood pressure good enough for me. Plus, his heart and breathing rates will be through the roof while he's in this state. I don't need machines to tell me that. I do, however, order him to lie down some more, my only really concern that he's going to hyperventilate, blow off a large amount of carbon dioxide in his exhaled breath, subsequently faint, before finally rolling off my examination couch and breaking his neck.

That would be an ambitious one to explain away to the General Medical Council.

Against my better judgement, I give him some supplemental oxygen via a face mask – partly just to muffle the bloody screams. Harder to achieve. Then, like most panic attacks, I just watch. This is peppered with encouraging the breathing exercises and generally trying not to get too impatient (*a bad trait of mine, Alice informs me*). Fifteen minutes go by and

Ryan's still a complete mess. Quite impressive really, since he must be exhausted. I decide to wait some more. A full thirty minutes on and he's still no different. I check the duty doctor list: seven patients now waiting to be seen. And I'm stuck with him. Time to pharmacologically speed up this recovery.

I give him 10 milligrams (mg) of diazepam. Fifteen minutes later, Ryan is way more Zen (diazepam does that to people). Now that he's not banging on about his heart exploding, I get a bit more information. It turns out he broke up with his girlfriend of three weeks (*I mean, really*) and it sent him into a spiral this afternoon when she changed her Facebook status to *single.* He's now just sobbing, which isn't a medical emergency, and so I move him into another empty consultation room for some quiet reflective time. That means I can get on with seeing the growing queue of other emergency patients, occasionally popping in to see how his heartbreak is doing. Every time I do, he's a little better.

Poor bugger.

Now fully calm, I offer him some general advice about how while being dumped is shit – and we've all been there – he'll bounce back, I'm sure.

As long as his heart holds out.

Thursday, 13th December

The salaried GPs WhatsApp group is on fire this afternoon with excitable conspiracy theories. We've all received an email from Jasper, the practice manager, confirming next Monday afternoon there will be a two-hour mandatory meeting to discuss, amongst other items on the agenda, *employee morale.*

Juicy.

Friday, 14th December

End of the week. Now, Western superstition would have us believe that Friday the 13th is the unlucky day. I wonder if in fact it's Friday, 14th. Mrs York uncrumples her sheet of paper, no doubt listing her various ailments. As I sit here in the consultation room, this petite and unassuming 61-year-old former librarian draws a slow deliberate breath in (I'm holding mine) and glances at her sheet, smoothing out the paper's wrinkles as she does so.

Totally fucking unnerving. She's either going to pull out an axe from her recyclable hessian supermarket Bag for Life, or do what I think she's about to. Her eyes meet mine. I exhale in preordained acceptance. Then it comes: *The Patient Blitz.* She rushes me with six different problems, barely pausing for breath between each one: her diabetes medications are upsetting her stomach, she's had six weeks of constant headaches and absolutely nothing makes them better, her left ankle hurts (but only in the morning before 11am and before *Loose Women*), she thinks she might be losing her memory, she's had a rash on her groin for the last two years that she wants me to check, and finally, the *pièce de résistance* and final nail in any GP's coffin – she's got *all over body pain.*

I want to get up and go hide in the staff toilet. Instead I smile. Because it's my job. You see, the issue with the patient blitz is that it can be utterly impossible to see any one individual patient concern or condition with any perspective. When you rationalise it, that's basically one hundred seconds per issue in a ten-minute (six hundred-second) consultation. And half of that's taken up by how fucking annoyed you are at yet another patient *saving up* all their ailments for one appointment – because they think it helps the NHS. I'll say this one more time.

IT. DOES. NOT.

Luckily, through tragic experience, I've developed an emergency strategy for just an event such as this. I take out a piece of paper, divide it into six, tell Mrs York that I've listened and hear her concerns but I'm now asking the questions and I *only* want short, succinct, and closed answers. No waffle. If she doesn't do this, she'll need to keep hold of that list for another time because I won't be able to deal with them all today.

She sits back, surprised by the counterpunch, and nods. And with that, we smash through all her issues in fifteen minutes, leaving just the clinical notes to write up on the computer for later on. A decent result. Sometimes the reality is that the bedside manner needs to be sacrificed if you're ever going to get the bloody job done.

Sunday, 16th December

This weekend I took William to a Christmas-special baby sensory class today.

Another MDMA (ecstasy) session for babies, basically.

Monday, 17th December

Well, there's certainly no fucking Christmas spirit in this room! It's the big staff meeting we've all been waiting for. We're an hour and twenty minutes in. So far, we've had lots of *I feel that . . .* monologues coupled with fantastically awkward silences. What I'd give for a phone consultation with Mrs Tally right now – happy to listen to every one of her individual (and many) concerns about the quality of her carers. Yet, I decide to pitch in to the meeting myself, mainly because I figure if I do one solid *I feel that* . . . monologue, I'll have done my bit. Then I can sit back and watch the other car-crash conversations.

The overall outcome of the meeting is that the younger salaried GPs (myself, included) feel they aren't supported enough by the senior GPs. The dementor takes a few swipes of flesh from the more fragile GPs, telling them that they're not going to go around hugging them and saying how wonderful they are all the time. Eyes water, tears even flow.

Oh, my God, this is gold.

I sit back in my chair (positioned in the corner for optimal panoramic view) and take it all in. Everyone in the room shares the same look like a uniform.

Unhappy. Stressed. Despondent.

I think of Alice and William. Any of that uniform worn by me immediately escapes into the ether. Of course I would never say this to my colleagues but for me, none of this matters. Not *really* anyway. I think some more about this as Dr Phil asks how the senior GPs can make things better. Sarah and Dan suggest Employee of the Month, Best Diagnosis of the Month, and team socials. I look out the window and sigh.

Is this what it's come to? We've become American.

As the meeting limps through its final few minutes, like a one-night stand awkwardly looking for their other sock, my thoughts turn once again to the future.

To my family.

God, now I sound as wet as the bloody Americans.

Tuesday, 18th December

How anyone can get into trouble for offering a child a sticker for being brave was, before today, beyond me. As I'm learning now, it's when you offer the *wrong type* of stickers. My ears ache as Mrs Holiday (her misleading jovial namesake) lectures me on how I should be offering *all* children *all* types of stickers – and not gender stereotype.

Wow! Punchy.

I hold back from pointing out that her son, Freddie, clearly loves the Batman sticker he's picked, as does her daughter, Sophie, her Princess Elsa sticker. However, I'd rather avoid a complaint. So, I concede the oversight. Apologise. And offer her children another sticker each, laying them *all* out in front of them. Freddie now leaves with a Batman sticker and a Supercar sticker. Sophie now has *two* Princess Elsa stickers. Love it.

Wednesday, 19th December

I couldn't have ironed a shirt that well if I had all day. Let alone, square a tie off that neatly and pair it perfectly with a buttoned-up blazer. Also, I don't think I can stand up that straight. As I hover in Mr Cheema's living room, I'm acutely aware that my shirt's creased, definitely not tucked in at the back, and my trousers (yet again) are covered in William's regurgitated milk from this morning's feeding frenzy. I also find myself straining to stand up straighter, aware of my comparably inadequate posture.

Mr Cheema's incredible: he walks over and shakes my hand, eyes evidently still full of twinkle. He invites me to sit, and I do so in silence, a little stunned by the amount of life in this man. At one hundred years – *'and two weeks'* (he adds, exuberantly) – he looks forty years his junior. I wasn't expecting to find the answer to eternal youth on today's home visit.

'What's your secret?' I have to ask as we sit here, imagining all the changes that he's lived through in this world.

'Being kind and happy,' he says without hesitation, not a beat missed.

A little disappointed at the intangibility of his answer, I probe for anything else more tangible – like cheese. Or holidays to Bali. Sadly, he says that's it. I make a mental note to remember this. Aware that this afternoon's clinic is only half an hour away, I get down to business. Now clinically speaking, there's not much wrong with Mr Cheema. To be honest, at his age, I've also no interest in poking around to find something to sour his remaining years. This visit is rather a general check-up as we haven't seen him for a while. Remarkably, he still lives alone with only one weekly carer doing some odd jobs for him. I take in how immaculate his compact first-floor flat is, while the blood pressure machine tells me that he still has the blood pressure of a 21-year-old Olympic-level gymnast. Yet, as with all of us, if you scratch deep enough, you'll always find something. I can feel the quiet of his life, strange as that sounds. The flat a cacophony of newspapers, books, and crosswords.

'Do you see many people?'

Mr Cheema's veneer didn't take much scratching. It turns out he is in fact incredibly lonely, and has been for years. He sees hardly anyone at all, with no family nearby (all largely dead, including his wife some twenty years ago), and a community that he doesn't really recognise or understand anymore. This upsets me for two reasons: first, this man clearly has so much to give. Second, we've become the kind of non-communicable society that's perpetuated and fostered loneliness despite being on top of each other in bricks and mortar. It's something I'm seeing more and more in the patients I meet. Yet Mr Cheema's clearly still up for life – I love that about him. We can all take a leaf out of this centenarian (and two weeks) book.

He agrees for me to get in touch with the local Age Concern organisation and some of the other local services that plan social activities like tea and cake mornings (though I do promise him that they do other things a little more exciting too). Before leaving, I ask him to show me the secret to ironing his shirt so well. Thankfully, his advice here is a little more tangible than *being kind and happy to your shirt.*

Thursday, 20th December

'I need the cock.'

More than a little puzzled, I hesitate in my reply.

'The cock?' She shoots me a confused look. *'Yes, the cock.'*

I'm not sure what services our surgery's new website is showcasing but I'm pretty sure this isn't on the list. Knowing I'll probably come to regret the question, I turn my chair around to face Anastasia and while truly fighting the childish smile that wants to explode from me, ask if she can explain a little more.

'To stop baby.'

Bloody hell, now I'm really confused.

Tilting my head to one side, I say *'to STOP baby?'* like some confused parrot. The cogs of my brain, grown rusty as the day's stretched on, grind away. Hang on . . . The COC! The **C**ombined **O**ral **C**ontraceptive (COC) pill. Relief now floods me as I realise any breaking bad news strategies (*you can't have cock, sorry.*) will not be required. A few minutes later, Anastasia leaves with her COC prescription, ready then to protect her against, well, you know what.

Friday, 21st December

Last day of work before the Christmas holidays. I can't believe how fast the last six months have flown by. Today it's all going smoothly with the usual pre-Christmas rush for repeat prescriptions and antibiotic pleas to cure people of their clearly viral colds before the holiday madness kicks off. I've noticed too that since the meeting last week, it's like working in *High School Musical* – everyone super peppy and upbeat. All the GP partners (even the dementor) are being supportive and friendly (though I've yet to witness any hugging), and the vibe amongst the younger salaried GPs is that things are going better, that the meeting has genuinely caused a positive shift in team morale. It really is great news – we even have two social events in the diary now.

Discreetly, though, I explain to our newly appointed social secretary that one per year will be sufficient. The cherry on top of all this good news is that I've had a pretty good pre-Christmas present haul from my patients: three boxes of Celebrations, one Ferrero Rocher box (from my only posh patient), two bottles of wine, a bottle of Prosecco (sorry, *two* posh patients), and even a toy for William. This means that you can't help but be caught up in all the positive festive spirit, and I start to think maybe working life at this surgery, in this city, isn't so bad after all. I shove another Celebrations in my mouth before calling in my final patient of the day. No wait – of the year.

Like I said, that went quick.

Sunday, 23rd December

Today is Alice's birthday. We celebrated it by being sleep-deprived, covered in William's regurgitated milk, vomit and paste-like shit throughout various stages of the day – before then tidying it up, along with all the paraphernalia that comes with having a baby and somehow spreads of its own accord into every bloody room in the house. We then continued the day of celebrations by inhaling a frozen pizza (*each*), some Ferrero Rocher (as it's a special occasion), and necking a bottle of Prosecco together (*thanks, Mr and Mrs Pecksworth*), before collapsing into bed.

Alice thankfully had the energy to unwrap my birthday present to her – a necklace with a *W* inscribed on it. We did conclude, however, that despite our best intentions, our collective marital energy levels for birthday sex tonight did *not* meet a sustainable threshold and so went to bed at 9:08pm.

Rock'n'roll! Mr Toska would've been proud.

Tuesday, 25th December

The first Christmas with my little family. It's everything I could have wished for – and more.

Monday, 31st December (11:50pm)

Sitting on the floor by the fireplace at my in-laws, Alice fully outstretched on the sofa, and William obligingly fast asleep, I take another sip of whisky. I know I've said it before – and I know it's probably getting really boring by now – but looking at Alice and picturing William upstairs really does make my heart burst.

I smile in the room. A smile for no one else to see but Alice. She knows what it means: it's a smile that summarises our 2018. So much happened. And while yes, work provided questionable turbulence and disquiet, the arrival of William eclipses it all with casual ease, providing what was a life-changing moment. In the blink of an eye, I went from son and husband to son, husband, *and* father. I top up my glass with a few more fingers of whisky.

No matter how much people tell you having a child changes your life, nothing prepares you. The centre point of life, of priorities, of purpose, of sheer being, just gets smashed with such unimaginable force that it's sent careering to this new location you never knew existed. If I was being honest with myself (and I know Alice and my parents would probably agree), my centre point for years, if not decades, had been my career. It was what defined me. I leaned on it. Relied on it. Hid behind it, even. And in fractions of a second, as William was born, it moved. To family. Perhaps where it should always have been. My new obsession. My new drive. My new reason. Emotions that both overpower and incapacitate.

You're telling me there's a job that could match that? No, I think back to life before William. While I can visualise it (conceivably a fraction hazier as the warmth of the whisky envelops me), I realise I'm finding it harder to *feel* what it was like. As if it was perhaps someone else's life and not my own. Hard to explain, even without the whisky.

The clock ticks ever closer: 11:59pm. Alice and I stand, holding hands, ready to welcome in 2019. We've agreed that we both only have one New Year's Resolution, one that's from the heart. A gift from me to Alice, and Alice to me: we're both going to learn how to do that fucking annoying flossing dance right!

Midnight arrives. 2019 arrives. A kiss. A YouTube video on flossing.

Goodnight, 2018.

JANUARY 2019

Tuesday, 1st January

You might expect life-changing decisions to come in some profound and technicolor way fit for Hollywood. This one didn't. This one had a slow build-up over months of conversations between Alice and I. During walks in the park, while collectively bending over William's changing mat, wiping shit off his flailing feet, while brushing our teeth before bed. You name the situation, and we were probably taking about it.

The scrap of paper which I wrote that list of *push* and *pull* factors for moving to the countryside back in early November last year, is now unbelievably well thumbed. And it's led to now. To New Year's Day, 2019. Where, somewhat unceremoniously, our final decision was made. In bed. With a cup of tea. Fighting last night's New Year's Eve hangover. And with a repeat of *Countryfile* on the TV. Given we're on our seventh season of watching its re-runs, the signs were clearly there all along. We just didn't see it. Or perhaps chose to ignore it. So yes, we're going to do it. *This is the year.* This is the year that Alice, William, and I will be moving out of the city and heading off to have ourselves a countryside adventure.

I take another sip of tea. Here we go then . . .

Wednesday, 2nd January

First day back at work after nearly two weeks off. As expected, it's a total, unrelenting, never-ending, stick-needles-in-my-eyes, fucking nightmare. Every single patient turning up has successfully managed to shatter into a thousand pieces, thanks to the perfect storm of too much booze and sugar, too much time with their family, and too much time sitting on their arses. Not to be a hypocrite, I do count myself in this demographic. Still, it's an exciting day with Alice and I reaffirming our decision this morning over another cup of tea. We are really doing it. Neither of us bottling it (just yet). Pursuing a new life beyond *this city*. Beyond *this surgery*. Both total unknowns. A new adventure.

Friday, 4th January

End of the week and already the first complaint of the year. I've outdone myself, it being at least two weeks earlier than the year before. Mr Taylor was expecting a phone consultation with me about some ongoing knee pains. He has this knee pain (as I've explained many, many times) because he weighs 127kg, refuses to change his diet or engage in anything resembling physical activity, and so is slowly crushing his knee joints.

I called him three times. Twice more, I might add, than I'd usually try any patient. I put it down to the fact it was immediately post-lunch, and I must have been feeling energised and good-natured. Each time I called, it went to voicemail. Mr Taylor's complaint was that I didn't let the phone ring long enough. When I finally got through to the grumpy bugger, I asked him to explain to me how he'd like me to let it ring for longer – given that it's set to go to voicemail after five rings.

Own goal, Mr Taylor!

Sunday, 6th January

Quite the sight to see shit come out of the *top* of William's vest. A parenting first, in fact. Alice and I left him in the baby bouncer – basically, a plastic *ring of neglect* for those hands-free parenting moments – for perhaps ten minutes too long while we had breakfast in bed. All the bouncing around must have given him the equivalent of *runner's trots* (think Paula Radcliffe's toileting incident during the 2004 Athens Summer Olympics Marathon). Still, at least he had a massive smile on his face as he thrashed up and down in the bouncer, really mulching that shit into his expensive John Lewis dinosaurs vest that his grandparents treated him to.

Seven wet wipes and one new outfit later, William's box-fresh once again. I give it an hour.

Tuesday, 8th January

'Can you masturbate?'

My question hangs awkwardly in the room like an unsanctioned fart. George studies the ground with all the intensity of a 100m sprinter waiting to explode from the starting block.

'I think so.'

Poor bloke, that's not even an answer. Without pause, I drag him over the burning coals a little more.

'You think so?'

I wait, ever so slightly impatiently. It's a pretty binary question – either you can or you can't. He nods. I nod back, trying to offer a look of male solidarity, but stop short at congratulating him on his ability to have a wank. George, who at forty-one years old is finding this line of questioning all a little bit uncomfortable, finally looks up and meets my gaze. I smile, then hit him with another dick question.

'Ever wake up in the morning with an erection?'

Seems George has got through the 100m qualifiers and is now in the final, returning back to his intense ground stare.

'I don't really pay attention to that sort of thing.'

That, my friend, is rubbish. All men who wake up with an erection in the morning bloody well know about it. It's like a morning salute, for Christ's sake! Plus, you can't pee without significant angulation challenges. I press him more to think harder (no pun intended). Finally, he nods again. I nod again. *God, this is painful.* I sit back and show him an anatomical image of a penis from Google images (found using *very* carefully selected search words), and explain how an erection works. I start by going through the plumbing of his erection. Blood flows into his penis, engorges it, and this engorgement then traps blood in his penis temporarily. The fact I'm using the pronoun, *his,* seems to make him wince every time.

I chuckle a little inside. With that explained, I move on to the psychosexual perspective. I tell him how he needs to be either physically (i.e. being touched), or psychologically stimulated (i.e. visually aroused) to trigger his aforementioned plumbing mechanism. He nods again, body language signalling just how much he hates this consultation.

George has come to me with a common problem: he's got himself a new girlfriend after some time out of the game and on their first sexual encounter, he failed to launch. Since then, he's convinced himself that he's got erectile dysfunction and, as he told me on arrival, *his penis is broken.*

With the clinical history taking and GCSE science lesson complete, I sit back and tell him what I think. The first thing to explain to George is that he can't technically *break* his penis – it hasn't got any bones in it (though I warn him, if it got bent really badly, it's possible to burst the blood vessels within). The second thing I explain is that because he can get an erection while masturbating – and wakes up with them – it tells me that his plumbing, that blood supply, is working just fine. He nods, looking away in utter inescapable humiliation at the topic as we talk about his cock some more.

Finally, we get to the most important point: he's clearly got a mental *cock-block*, essentially out-psyching himself. I pause, swinging my chair around to meet him squarely, feeling the switch from GP to counsellor mode as I do. I tell George that he needs to go into his next sexual encounter confident that everything will work. After all, *'I know it works.'* Again, I watch him die a little more as he digests that his GP is telling him he knows his penis is certified *operational for sex*. Still, to give him that little bit of extra added confidence, I prescribe a single Viagra tablet. Not because he needs it, but because it'll act as a comfort blanket for the first time, easing the psychological pressure he's subconsciously placed on himself. Once he's relaxed, and assuming there's a next time, it'll be business as usual. As he leaves, I can't help but make him wince one final time, telling him to have a good time.

God, this job is fun sometimes!

Thursday, 10th January

Took the day off work today and spent it with Alice and William. Apart from starting to form a timeline and plan for our move, we took our son to another one of those sensory classes – you know, just to keep the process of totally blowing his mind ticking over each week. The theme today was the planets. It was run by the most fantastic New Age hippie I've ever seen, accompanied by a helper who was clearly detoxing from something very hard – I made sure William was on the other side of the classroom to him. Anyway, it was all going well until the adults were asked to name some of the planets. Alice unimpressed by my level of maturity.

Of course, I'm going to shout out *Uranus!*

Friday, 11th January

It's never a promising start when the parents of an 8-week-old baby walk into my room accompanied by a Mother and Baby Unit keyworker. As they trudge in, any hope of an effortless, light final consultation of the Friday afternoon clinic exits unceremoniously. This, I've learned from unpleasant clinical experience, is a consult to take slow, with all the potential to descend into a *he said, she said* affair.

They don't disappoint. It turns out Tiffany is in the local mother and baby unit with her daughter, Maria, working her way through a twelve-week residential stay and assessment after some early concerns about her parenting (very sadly, she already has two other children in foster care). Maria's dad and ex-partner to Tiffany, Travis, currently carrying that well-known *I wanna fuck you up* standing posture, was visiting the unit today. I take him in. Not being a fan of the *I wanna fuck you up* in my consultations, I get up, place a chair next to him, and get him to sit.

Good boy, stay!

Tension hangs in the air, punctuated only by Maria's gentle cries. I turn to Gale, their keyworker, and ask her to explain what's happened. Turns out one of the Mother and Baby Unit staff saw Travis being overly aggressive in his handling of her while she was distressed and crying. I think of William; I look to Travis. He looks vacant now, seemingly totally unaware of what's being said or why it might have been a bad thing. He looks like he couldn't care less, in fact.

So far, I've sat here nodding, listening, nodding some more, all while occasionally looking to the parents to gauge their reactions to what's being said. It's these kinds of cases that are pretty black and white in terms of what needs to be done. This isn't about *what* the parents tell me, it's not even *who* tells me what. And that's because when there's a *single version* of this story that says this innocent little girl *may* have been subject to abuse, then they need to be immediately referred for a full and specialist paediatric assessment in the local hospital. How this makes anyone feel is, quite frankly, irrelevant: it's about the child that can't speak for themselves. And so, with that, I get up, perform a cursory examination of little Maria and explain to her parents that all three of them will be going to see the paediatric team.

Right now.

Tiffany nods in uncertain agreement, while Travis assumes his *I wanna fuck you up* posture. I look at him. But it's too late, it doesn't matter. I stand as he offers some unveiled threats about not going before succumbing to the fact that his wishes count for nothing. And, after one call to the paediatric team, off they go under the watch of keyworker, Gale. Now, despite being a bit of a scaredy-cat outside the workplace, I've never been scared in work (yet) during times like this. For one, I'm surrounded by a great team at the surgery, and two, I've got an alarm on my computer, that at the click of a button, goes to all the rooms if I needed instant assistance, and three, I did Karate for 4 months when I was 9 years old. Well, the first two are helpful.

My room now empty, I sit and lean back, letting the back of the chair take my increasing, post-Christmas weight. Drained, I want to go home now.

Friday, 11th January (6:55pm)

A few hours later, I'm home and listening to William's uncontrolled, excited, gurgling shrieks of joy that seem to pour over me like warm water. Cleansing me of any hardships from the day. His face lights up again as I spin him in the air, faster and faster to the sound of The Beatles' 'Here Comes the Sun' blasting out of the living-room speakers. Alice watches from the sofa, shaking her head in overt disapproval, yet secretly loving seeing her two boys at play.

Bliss.

Monday, 14th January

Ah, Monday, you've delivered once more! The dreamcatchers, Barack and Michelle Obama, the Alsatians (all seven of them), Will Smith . . . Once again, I drink in Mr and Mrs Leigh's living room and remind myself why this is still the best home visit location. Ever.

Mrs Leigh sits in her favourite armchair, still dressed in her entirely inappropriate Dennis the Menace nightdress, fanning her knees back and forth. A wave of nausea. I move from my crouching position – an aborted attempt to be engaging as she sits – and return to a safer eyeline. I'm here to discuss Mrs Leigh's recent blood sugar result that Irena, the practice nurse, had taken last week. It seems her control of her type 2 diabetes mellitus is sliding a little. We need to try to right this wrong before it lands her in trouble with future secondary complications. Important since early control for long-term complication avoidance in diabetes is essential.

'But I don't eat no sugar, Max!' she shouts at me, enthusiastically letting flecks of partially congealed spit spray in my general direction. As an aside, I haven't said it's OK to call me by my first name but since they're such total heroes, daring to have a photo of the Obamas next to seven randomly framed Alsatians, well, they can call me whatever the bloody hell they like.

I nod.

'I believe you.' (I'm not sure I do.)

Mr Leigh steps up and shoves a packet of something in front of my nose. Having heard him only just flush the toilet next door, I pull back from the finger now under my nose.

'See, SUGAR-FREE!' he shouts as well.

Why is everyone shouting?

I sit back next to the fifteen singing garden gnomes that Mr and Mrs Leigh seem to have still failed to shift and examine the packet with less faecal finger distraction.

Dextrose tablets. Otherwise known as the total antithesis of sugar-free since they're essentially a packet of individually wrapped highly concentrated sugar sweets to *boost* sugar levels. So the mystery of why Mrs Leigh's diabetic control is going so totally haywire is short-lived and now easily explained: she's munching on little parcels of pure sugar three times a day.

Waggling the Dextrose tablets in front of her, I explain where she's been going ever-so slightly (massively) wrong.

'Noooo! You're lying!'

I look at her, shaking my head in disbelief (and oddly joy at such engagement from two living legends), *'Why on earth would I lie about this?'*

Five minutes later, Mrs Leigh finally digests what I've been telling her and subsequently begins to blame her husband for buying the wrong thing. A situation that reflects many marriage situations here, I expect. They begin to row in front of me. I sit there, this parallel universe – me and fifteen singing garden gnomes – sixteen of us now awkward third wheels bearing witness to a marital spat. Our surroundings – dreamcatchers, Barack and Michelle Obama, Alsatians, and Will bloody Smith!

I could sit here for hours.

Tuesday, 15th January

Found myself doing a little *property porn* on an estate-agent website this lunchtime. Leaning into my iPhone screen at the houses, I'm totally blown away. I had absolutely no idea just how much more house you can get for your money when you buy outside a city.

I mean, it's insane! Seriously.

I WhatsApp Alice a few houses and spin around in my chair, thinking of the possibilities. A paddock for a horse? A home gym to finally get some of my fitness properly back? A double garage for my soon-to-be midlife-crisis soft-top sports car? *Countryfile*, you've a lot to answer for. It's then that I let my foot slap on the floor, arresting my chair spin, and sigh at my momentary realisation. There's quite the unenviable process between this point and sitting in my midlife-crisis car in my countryside garage. For starters, I'll need to formally hand in my resignation to the surgery (like you would for any job), breaking the news that I'll be leaving the team. This, I expect, will come as a bit of a shock. And I hate break-ups. Then there's all the other equally mammoth tasks that follow. We'll need to sell our flat. We'll need to find somewhere initially to rent in the countryside (we've decided on where we're going now, but as this is *The Secret Doctor,* this bit's a secret as well, I'm afraid!) while we then look for the right house to buy. I'll have to sign up to a local locum GP agency (a 'locum' in this case being a GP who temporarily works at a GP surgery which needs cover for one of their employed GPs, who may be off sick or on maternity leave, for example). Plus, a locum agency means that I can work in a variety of GP surgeries around the area we want to live in for a few months before deciding (based on my experience), which one I might like to work in full-time – if, of course, there's a vacancy.

Oh, yes, so this is probably a good point to highlight that this is why when you go to your GP surgery, you might sometimes see a GP you've never met before – and then never see again – they may well be a locum just working there for the day or week.

I exhale, thinking how all of this is more than enough to keep me busy over the next few months. The size of the task is a lot to take on board and leaves me feeling more than a little overwhelmed.

Alice replies to my message, breaking my train of thought. Worry makes way for excitement once again.

Thanks, my love. Perfect timing.

Wednesday, 16th January

Pronouns. That's the only thought running through my head as I welcome 25-year-old Jessie into my room. *Don't fuck this up, Max* circles my brain, this being classic foot-in-mouth territory for me. Inviting her to sit, she looks at me with a conscious smile and explains that she's here for her Decapeptyl injection, extracting it from her handbag.

'Not a problem,' I say, clawing at my memory to remember what the drug does. Finally it comes to me – it blocks testosterone production and is used in prostate cancer – and gender reassignment. For Jessie, it's the latter and she's the first patient I've met in a long time who's undergoing transition, now fully identifying as female – pronouns (personal and possessive) included – something I'm doing my best not to fuck up on. She's under the local gender identity clinic and the hormone treatment they've prescribed (but I, as her GP, have to give) is to help her further develop female characteristics while suppressing her male characteristics. In time, if she chooses, definitive surgery awaits her.

I look at her as she rubs her right hand up and down the tattooed sleeve of her left arm. She's been on quite the journey I expect to this point and I'd bet my mortgage that it's not been easy. I straighten up and with an rally of added pep in my step, go about the injection, asking her how it's all going as I do. Her shoulders relax. She relaxes. *I* relax. Any preconceived, expected awkwardness evaporates from the room. As it should. Jessie tells me it's been really tough but she's so excited to be on the path to what's meant to be. The needle clatters into the sharps bin. I smile. And tell her I'm always here to help. Or even just listen. She thanks me, and as if the injection has given her more energy and zest, leaves the room with added *pep* in her step – no doubt happy in the knowledge that she's one injection closer, one clinic appointment nearer to achieving her goal. That's one battle. No doubt there'll be a few more down her road.

Good luck, Jessie.

Friday, 18th January

He's really not getting our surgery's consultation booking system. I stand, phone receiver anchored between my ear and neck. To be honest, given that when I last saw Mr O'Keefe he was a heart attack waiting to happen, I'm surprised he's still with us. I draw breath and try again, *'What do you mean, this isn't a convenient time?'* Angry words rush out the receiver, abusing my ear.

What a dick!

As he draws breath for his next round of moaning, I take my opportunity to launch a counterassault. I explain that *he* booked this bloody (I didn't say bloody, obviously) appointment time and no, another time will not be convenient for me – because as I'm sure he can appreciate (though I'm not sure he does), I do have other patients to see apart from just him.

He hangs up. Just for fun, I call him back to say we got disconnected, knowing full well he's deliberately hung up on me. To my disappointment (but not surprise), Mr O'Keefe doesn't answer. Instead, probably clutching his chest right about now.

Monday, 21st January

Not right. That's the only way I can describe Nick. Thirteen years old, super active, rugby mad – playing and training most days – and yet sitting here in front of me with his mum, looking *Just. Not. Right.* The first thing is he looks scrawny. The sort of scrawny that says his body is not only *not* building itself but doing the opposite: *consuming itself, a scaffolding of bone left behind.*

'What position do you play?'

Interesting. For an open-side flanker, he's not built as he should be for the position so either he plays for a team of malnourished midgets, or something really isn't right. He feels tired all the time, sleeps when he can. Thirteen-year-old boys who play rugby every day don't laze around lethargic, like some 40-year-old trucker nursing a pot belly, twenty-a-day cigarette habit, and recurrent gout.

I sit there, tapping my pen on the table, directing it at him every time I fire a question. *Nothing. Nothing makes sense. He just feels tired. Not right. That's it.* I find myself staring at the computer, turning to Nick, opening my mouth to speak, but then returning to the computer screen – seemingly nothing to say. Totally perplexed, I click and scroll his past medical history again. *Nothing.* His mother sits there politely anxious at my apparent lack of insight into what on earth's happening to her darling boy. I straighten up, take a deep breath in, and go over it again, this time going through every single physiological system I can – his neurological, respiratory, cardiological, gastrointestinal, urologi . . .

Stop, stop!

'I guess I'm peeing more than usual.'

I feel myself getting warmer, if of course this was a game of *Hot or Cold.* I ask if he's more thirsty than usual: he is. The heat's everywhere now, thanks to this urological lifeline in the questioning. I jump out of my chair, fetching Nick a urine bottle, and send him off to shake out a few drops for me. A few minutes later, he's back. As I sit opposite, mum and son quietly waiting, I sink the urinalysis testing stick into his sample. This is basically a thin test strip that when dipped in urine can show if there's a presence of infection, blood, protein – or sugar.

The sugar reading lights up: a big wailing diabetes siren.

I smile. Reassure. Explain I need one more test. And so, after showing Nick the small needle-like machine I have called a capillary blood glucose monitor, take a small drop of blood from his finger. He doesn't wince. *Good lad!* The blood sugar result reads HIGH, basically the monitor has reached its maximum level at which it can read sugar, and this young man has type 1 diabetes mellitus until proven otherwise. I nod again – to myself really – and put the machine down.

Mum and Nick look at me, perplexed. I slide my chair from around the table, eliminating any barrier between us, then explain I strongly suspect Nick has type 1 diabetes mellitus. This is the type of diabetes that means his body isn't making the hormone insulin, which gets sugar out of our blood and into our cells. Because he doesn't have this, his blood fills up with sugar. That's why he's tired, why he's scrawny, why the sugar's reading HIGH on the blood test, and why it's cascading out into his urine (blood filters through his kidneys). I pause. They looked shocked. I can read Nick's thoughts as he sits there, head down, tracing his finger around his school's RFC (Rugby Football Club) logo.

'Right now, you will need to go to hospital. I'll arrange for you to be met by the paediatric team, who will assess and treat you. We need to get your blood sugars down quickly.'

They nod, still in shock. I reassure Nick he'll feel much, much better once they've done this. I ask if he knows who Henry Slade is. He does, of course he does.

'He played rugby for England in the Six Nations – and hopefully, in this year's World Cup. He has type 1 diabetes.'

He smiles a little more and nods, knowing what I'm trying to say. As they leave for the hospital, I pick up the phone to the paediatric team to let them know they've got a hospital admission on the way.

Wednesday, 23rd January

'And when Matthew says . . .'

I zone out, picturing a white sandy beach and cold beer. An emptied mug clatters to the table, sending me crashing back into the surgery meeting room, surrounded by all my team. I'm not in Antigua on holiday, I'm on another training afternoon. The current topic's manual handling.

Yes, the one we all hate.

Sliding up my chair, my eyes track to our over-enthusiastic health and safety instructor, Matthew. He stands in front of me, knees bending and rising, bending and rising, all while referring to himself in the third person. Sure, he's no Kev from Basic Life Support training but still, who the fuck refers to themselves *in the third person*? It's just something I can't get on board with. In any context. He stops bending and rising to continue his sermon. Pointing to each and every one of us, getting louder, more visceral, more passionate, he tells us that we all (he stresses *all*) have it within us to engage in safe and effective manual handling.

I might be the wrong side of thirty but I'm pretty sure I've managed to survive this long picking things up just fine.

Oh, for God's sake, no. NO!

I vocalise a sigh in angry protest. Yes, he actually wants us to put this into practice. Right now. This is worse than the usual break-out group work these sessions force us to do. I rise, wearing my best resting bitch face and along with the rest of the team, practise bending my knees.

Well, look, Matty, it's a miracle, these knees of mine . . . Look how they bend, just like the joint's supposed to.

'*As Matthew says . . .*' I shut my eyes in the hope it'll close my ears as well. It doesn't. With nothing for it, I exhale slowly and try to take myself back to the beach. Yet sadly, after all that interruption, the beer's gone warm and the tide's out.

Thanks a lot, Matty.

Friday, 25th January

We've been sitting opposite each other for a few minutes now, Mrs Petrova talking away in a language no way compatible with my GCSE French – the only foreign language skill I possess. I smile and nod, happily telling her that I don't understand her at all. She smiles, nods back. She keeps talking. She hands me what I think is a discharge letter from a hospital in Bulgaria. I take it with all the enthusiasm of somebody expecting to see it's written in English.

Of course it isn't.

My phone speaker we're both encircling continues to tell us that we're on hold for the translator service and they will connect us as soon as a Bulgarian translator becomes available. I see any aspirations of finishing this afternoon's clinic on time and getting home for William's bath (my favourite time of *every* day now) ebbing away with every dull, draining ring emitting from the receiver. I smile, raise my eyebrows, and shrug. Let's be honest, there's not much else to do at this point.

Mrs Petrova laughs. Maybe shrugging shoulders in Bulgaria is some kind of amusing gesture. I could explain to her that in the UK, it just means *I have no bloody idea.* And guess what? I really *do* have no idea what you want, Mrs Petrova. Yet fate intervenes. A ray of hope amongst the darkness. Mrs Petrova unveils four beaten-up medication boxes, tapping on them. As I examine them, it's clear they're empty. I look back at her Bulgarian discharge letter from a Bulgarian hospital, incomprehensible Bulgarian words stamping their linguistic authority on each line, and though I've still no clue what it says, I can read (and therefore put into Google search) the trade names of the drugs she's been sent home with. I nod positively, thoughtfully, all of a sudden beginning to feel like some shit budget medical version of Sherlock Holmes.

Empty drug boxes. Patient tapping on empty drug boxes. Discharge letter dated one month ago.

I smile and speak in pigeon English: *'Empty? Need more?'*

She nods frantically. Jackpot, now we're getting somewhere! I spin around to my computer screen and start re-prescribing these medications, checking that it makes clinical sense and I'm not issuing some fantastically dangerous drugs by mistake (it's happened before, trust me). Yes, they're all cardiovascular drugs to help control blood pressure, lower cholesterol, minimise blood-clotting risk, and maintain good heart function. Maybe she had a heart attack a month ago in Bulgaria? Then again, maybe I'm totally getting this wrong. Meanwhile, the translator service continues to ring: no answer, nobody wanting to help poor Mrs Petrova get her voice across – or me home to William's bathtime.

We can't sit here forever but I can't just give her the drugs without being sure or it's another *Daily Mail* headline waiting to happen: *GP Prescribes Drugs on a Hunch.* I pull out my iPhone, quickly swiping away the box on its home screen telling me William's godfather has sent me an image – no doubt of another highly offensive joke. From there, the next ten minutes are a technological and linguistical marriage of perfection – celebratory even. Using Google Translate, we find out my guess (well, partly educated) was right: she did have a heart attack.

In the end, Mrs Petrova gets her medications, we book her to come back and see me again with her English-speaking relative, and I refer her to the local cardiology department for some cardiac rehabilitation (**Bulgarian translator required** written in bold and underlined. I even manage to get home in time to see William exiting the bath in floods of giggles.

Thanks to Google, everyone's a winner today. Onto the weekend.

Saturday, 26th January

En route to hospital in the car. Alice and I say nothing. I stare ahead. She extends a hand back towards William, stroking his head. William has a high fever and a rash that doesn't seem to be blanching when we press on it.

All of these signs are bad. Like, possible meningitis, bad.

I change gear, wait impatiently at the lights. I shout at the other drivers, carefree. My heart's stabbed with every distressing cry he lets out from his car seat behind me.

My poor boy!

I clench my jaw to quash a lip wobble.

Don't cry. Don't flap. Just drive.

I feel helpless.

Thursday, 31st January

Five long days later, William rolls around on his play mat, butt-naked, having the time of his life.

His play mat. *His* toys. *His* environment. *His* home. Safe and sound.

Alice and I sit on the sofa, physically exhausted, mentally drained. To look at him, you'd be none the wiser. Look closer though and you'll see both of his hands peppered with tiny puncture marks where the cannulas (a small tube through which medicine and fluid can be given directly into the patient's vein) were positioned – and repositioned every time William managed to pull them out.

The little shit!

Although unlikely, the paediatric doctors said there'd been a small chance that he could have meningitis. And so, William had antibiotics this week. He was so, so good. Smiling at the hospital staff, only occasionally looking to Alice and me, as if to check he was doing OK, being brave enough.

Of course he was.

If previously we had the naivety to think for a second that having one parent working in healthcare would help us get through our own child's illness, well, fuck me, we were very wrong. All common sense, rationality, and perspective are ripped out from under you like a cheap rug. When your child's sick, the world around you closes in. It may sound dramatic but that's how it felt. And in the end, thankfully, the amazing paediatric team felt it unlikely that William had meningitis, and after being fever-free for forty-eight hours, the antibiotics were stopped and the cannulas removed.

We're lucky parents. It was probably a virus masquerading as a meningitis rash. Parents who've suffered true loss (through the ~10% of meningitis cases that are fatal, or from other diseases) well, that's a pain unimaginable. William stares at his stuffed dinosaur for a minute before shoving it straight in his mouth. And then, as if reading our minds, sensing the exhausted relief, he turns and looks straight *into* Alice and me. He smiles. That big, gummy, innocent smile that fills us with nothing but love. And in the next *tick* of time, he shows us why that love is exhausting: he shits right across his play mat, even reaching our expensive rug.

We don't mind. Not really. Not today, anyway.

I get up to find the wet wipes.

FEBRUARY 2019

Friday, 1st February

The first day started – and ended – with rectal examinations on patients. Something I'm certain can never bode well for the month ahead.

My poor finger!

Saturday, 2nd February

Funny how the excitement of planning a move to the countryside still trumps the boring practicalities involved. So far I've spent most of this weekend speaking to estate agents, both here in the city (to sell our flat) and in the countryside (to rent a little cottage), locum GP agencies (so I have a way to pay the bills when we move), and drafting a letter of resignation (the least fun . . .). All a little overwhelming. So, it seems a fitting time to play very loudly through the living-room speakers Queen's classic song, 'Under Pressure'. I grab William off the floor and spin him around as I start to sing along. His face lights up.

Monday, 4th February

After a busy weekend, this is a less-than-welcome heart-sink. That's the only way to describe present company. We've a long history, Mrs Grantham and I – a battle of wills, played out over countless phone calls and clinic consultations. You see, after sixty-four years of life, she's given up on herself. *On life.* She sits apathetically across from me. On her lap rests her medications, clinical letters, newspapers, and, from the looks of it, a recent food shop. All meeting one another, undifferentiated and chaotic in her solitary shopping bag.

'I thought it should go to someone who deserved it.'

I want to get up, frogmarch her to the mirror and get her to look herself in the eye when she comes out with this shit.

'What do you mean, deserves it?' I reply, incredulous at her apparent martyrdom. I lean in towards her, an unmasked look of exasperation etched on my face, and invite her to explain herself more fully. Mrs Grantham feels she is a lost cause. That she can no longer be helped. That because her type 2 diabetes mellitus is all her own doing, she didn't want to take up her slot in the diabetic nurse specialist clinic that I arranged for her: she wanted it to go to someone more worthy, so she didn't go.

God, cry me a river!

Like some angry parrot, I sit back and repeat what Mrs Grantham's just said to me. She looks to her bag for answers, shuffling a bit of inconsequential paper deeper into the bag as if to make it safe from my anger.

'I only came in to apologise to you in person for the inconvenience I've caused.'

I raise my hands in mock pontification, telling her she's mad (in the nicest possible sense). Also, I know I can get away with that since we've danced this dance before. She knows I want to help, that I mean well. And I also know she's not had it easy. In the last three years she's lost her husband abruptly to a heart attack, then her dog died (her only remaining companion), and now she's having financial problems and unable to move away from her neighbours who, by all intents and purposes, sound like the type of anti-social pricks nobody wants to live near. And she has no real friends, the ones she did have long since driven away, weary of the morose cloak now permanently worn.

I let out a sigh, tell her I want to check her blood pressure, and scroll through her notes as we both sit in frustrated silence. I nod at the screen, knowing I go through this same reminder process every time I see her – the reminder that Mrs Grantham's had every possible intervention we can offer. Community mental health teams, befriending services, Age Concern input, district nurses' support, specialist nurses' appointments (that she apparently won't attend), and a very aggressive GP taking any and all approaches to try to light, well, anything resembling a fire, underneath her. It seems everything is damp, nothing will take the flame to ignite any light in her life.

Total inertia.

It's tragic. Life, *her* life, is now one lengthy self-bereavement. She starts to get up once I unwrap the blood pressure cuff (naturally, sky-high despite being on three blood pressure medications). I look on, bemused, '*Where are you going?*' She sits back down, professing she doesn't want to waste any more of my time. At this I roll my eyes, tell her I'm paid to do this, and so she shouldn't feel too bad. I sit back in my chair and look into her chronically sad eyes. It grinds me that I can't make this right, that I can't *fix* her: all doctors want to fix people, after all. As such, it disheartens me not to be able to achieve all I want to do for her. I even feel like I've let her down in some way. Then again, it's not about *me*. Not about what *I* want.

With resigned futility, I ask my final question: '*Can I do anything for you? Absolutely anything at all?*' She shakes her head and explains she thinks it best if she's left to her own devices. The truth is, despite how uncomfortably it sits with me, she's right. I have executed my role as her GP as thoroughly as I can. Right now, I have no more support or therapy to offer her. She has the mental capacity, the ability to choose not to accept help, and the ability to choose to live this way. Some people are just not able to be rescued.

Real life. Not a Hollywood movie.

I nod in agreement at her plan but inform her I'll still be calling every month to see how she is. To see if she's had a change of heart. She thanks me and shuffles out my door. Her parting words sum up her world: '*I just miss Herbert so much.*'

For some, heartbreak has no healing process.

Wednesday, 6th February

I can't help but apologise to Caroline, our local district nurse. And to be honest, sitting in our monthly surgery meeting with her and the other community teams (we have one of these meetings, as well as one for the significant events that I talked about back in July last year), I even find myself a little red-faced on Mrs Tally's *behalf*.

Shit! Maybe I'm getting that syndrome where you fall in love with your captor? What's it called?

The rest of my team look on with a blend of amusement and relief (that it's not they who happen to be the apple of Mrs Tally's eye) as I apologise because she wouldn't see Caroline *inside* her home. Because she was *too busy*. Despite being *housebound.* And therefore *always in.* I smile uncomfortably at Caroline, who judging by the adjectives used to describe her encounters with Mrs Tally – through a letter box – loathed every single moment.

'Try being her GP!' I joke.

No returning smile.

Also, I'm not sure it helped that Mrs Tally told Caroline (through the letter box still) that she'll talk to *me* about *her* first – and then make her decision. Like I'm her accomplice. Her co-conspirator.

Thanks, Mrs Tally.

Stockholm syndrome . . . That's the one.

Thursday, 7th February

We all listen as their unborn baby's heartbeat fills the consultation room. I smile at Jenna and Darren, her husband, standing with his arm warmly draped over her shoulder.

'Perfect,' I report, removing the hand-held Sonicaid (used to listen to the baby's heartbeat) from her heavily pregnant abdomen as she lies on my examination couch. At thirty-four weeks pregnant, they're imminently knocking on the door of parenthood. Seemingly prepared, and yet unbeknownst to them (and all parents-to-be), wildly unprepared for the adventures ahead.

I smile at my growing air of parental experience, William now unbelievably approaching five months of age. I think how, at their stage, Alice and I couldn't even begin to catalogue the spectrum of physical and emotional fireworks about to smash blindingly into them, head-on. Some make you stare in awe. Some just tickle, others make you bleed.

Without really thinking, and against what some might feel is better professional judgement (*snore*), I show them a recent picture on my iPhone of William, smiling in his bouncer, head still mimicking a freshly peeled potato. They peer in and both say how gorgeous he is. I drink in this praise with uncontrolled pride before quickly pocketing my iPhone, aware I've just exercised the nauseating action of a boastful parent – not to mention abandoning any form of professionalism.

As Jenna continues to slowly right herself with help from Darren – her unborn child working hard to truly fuck with her centre of gravity in these final few weeks – I explain that she and baby (*and yes, you too, Darren*) are doing fantastically well. I recap to them both. She's got a good blood pressure. Her urine sample shows no signs of protein (a potential indicator of pre-eclampsia, a serious pregnancy-related condition that occurs in the second half of pregnancy with symptoms including headache, swelling of the face, hands or ankles, and visual problems) or infection. Their baby's heart is beating well within the normal range for its age. And finally, her pregnancy bump is a healthy size (called the symphysis-fundal height, basically a rough indicator of the size of the baby).

They sit, fingers interlocked. Smiling, giddy with excitement. It's a joy to see. For their first pregnancy, everything is going great. Right now, I see no reason for that to change. As I write in Jenna's maternity notes (all pregnant women have paper notes, not digital ones so they can carry them to any hospital if needed in an emergency), I see too that all her pregnancy scans have gone well and there aren't any concerns from her midwives. I joke with Darren about nursery colours, knowing from our previous consultations that he'd been put in charge of this. Given they don't yet know the sex of the baby, he's opted for neutrals: greys and yellows.

'*Nice choice, Dad,*' I nod approvingly.

And with the consultation over, I open the door as wide as I can – joking that Jenna needs all the width she can get to navigate that bump through it – and wish them all the very best. After all, now I shouldn't see them again until after their baby is born. By then I expect two very different people will walk in, forever changed. As I do on most days now, I think of William and wonder what he's up to right now.

Friday, 8th February

Good luck if you're a patient seeing me today! You see, in twenty-four hours, I'll be sitting on a flight to Morocco with Alice and William (now inconveniently teething, so no doubt planning to be a total reprobate). And all this means that today, while my body is definitely sitting in this consultation chair, metronomically swinging side to side as I wait for my next patient to drag what sounds like their Zimmer frame very slowly towards my door, my mind is most certainly already on that plane.

Seatbelt fastened. Checking out the in-flight entertainment guide. Rum and coke on its way to me . . . The first Skittle family holiday abroad!

My trance stops. The metronomic swing disrupted. *The knock.* My Zimmer-framed patient has arrived. I open the door. Back to work, even if it's just for a few more hours. As an aside, holidays as a GP can be a faff in themselves. I don't mean the process, as I expect I book my annual leave much as you probably book yours, requesting it formally via some form of human resources department. The faff comes in the extra work I have to do the week before – essentially needing to do what we call a *handover.* Now, a handover is basically a way to ensure that a patient I've been seeing – and let's say, I think needs to be seen again (or have a result or referral checked) while I'm away – gets followed up by another doctor, who now knows what's going on with them. They get this from me in the handover. This might be a verbal chat about the patient while looking at the notes together, or as there's usually very little time for such robust measures, a quick two-line email asking them to read my notes and to please check up on the patient (*usually with an apology if they're a fucking nightmare*). All this naturally means that my clinical notes written for patients the week before I leave for a holiday are usually some of the most thorough out of the whole year.

Lucky them.

Saturday, 9th February (09:57am)

'Max, don't forget William's black bag.'

Alice's words send a shockwave through me. I'm standing next to our taxi at the airport drop-off point, staring at all the bags I've just decanted.

No black bag. I'm in trouble.

I turn to Alice. *'Slight issue.'* The words that she went on to use aren't ones I typically hear leaving her mouth. And with that now out of her system, she looks at me and bursts into laughter.

'You're such a fucking idiot sometimes. How have you ever made it as a doctor?'

I bow my head in relief that I'm not picking fragments of her wedding ring out of my forehead. I'm a lucky man to have a forgiving wife. William looks up from his pram, blissfully unaware that he's got absolutely no food, nappies, or toys, and that his clothing's limited to the overflow buried in mine and Alice's bag. With time against us, we've no choice but to press on and head into the airport.

I walk on, digesting with amazement that I'm still married.

Saturday, 9th February (11:15am)

Just over an hour later, luck still appears to be in short supply. Alice stares at me, the other side of the metal detector, as she cradles William. A bemused smile evolves onto her face as she watches. *Perhaps sheer delight?* Much to the collective impatience of the airport security team and growing queue of travellers behind me, I try one more time.

Fuck this fucking pram, it's supposed to be easily collapsible! That's why we paid a stupid amount of money for it.

Well, despite my best efforts this supposed fucking collapsible pram will *not* fucking collapse. Wonderful! Now, to my shame, an undercover mother (I say 'undercover' since there's no sign of a child) steps across from the adjacent security line, leans in, and clicks some unbelievably well-hidden (albeit bright red) button on William's pram. I stand here, watching in mixed irritation and relief as the sodding thing instantly collapses into one tiny package.

'Tricky bugger,' I joke to my anonymous helper, expecting parental solidarity. She smiles a smile that translates easily

into *'No, it isn't, you moron.'* Still, finally able to escape my shame and re-join my family, I step through the metal detector. It alarms – of course it does.

'Can you step to the side, Sir?'

For. Fuck's. Sake.

Monday, 11th February

The crusted yellow lesions that have set up their home around his mouth are the giveaway. This little snotbag has impetigo, a common – and relatively harmless – bacterial skin infection in children. It is however, pretty contagious through direct contact. Which is why, as Alice and I watch, when impetigo-boy toddles up to William, now plonked on some giant beanbag of neglect in the holiday crèche, our hearts sink.

Impetigo-boy rubs his hands inquisitively (no doubt having just left his grossly infected mouth) all over William's face. For good measure, just to make sure the sharing of infection is total, William tries to suck on one of impetigo-boy's fingers.

Marvellous!

Wednesday, 13th February

I thought about Mrs Tally today. I have no idea why she entered my mind but she did. Patients often do that at the strangest times – just as I'm falling asleep, emptying the bins, or in this case (disturbingly) while applying sun cream to my shoulders.

Mrs Tally . . . Wow, what a head fuck that is. Maybe there really is no escaping her.

Thursday, 14th February

What a holiday week it's been so far. And tonight, it seems those Piña coladas have really done a number on Alice and me. As we wander past the pool, arm in arm (for staggering support, as much for love), we chat away happily, relaxed, switched off from the grind of life back home. During the holiday, we've talked more about our move to the countryside – now very much in the planning stages, and one which, much to our combined relief and excitement, we both remain very committed to since January's decision.

I think about pushing Alice into the pool but decide she's most definitely earned a reprieve, given how understanding she was that I left the entirety of our son's life essentials in a bag, still sitting comfortably on a chair in our spare room.

In England.

We consider a final G&T on our hotel-room balcony and then we remember: William. Our son.

Shit. Shit.

We unlink arms and Alice checks the time: 11:37pm. William was meant to be collected from the crèche's sleep club (a service I can only assume is purely designed for parents to go and get responsibly drunk) a full thirty-seven minutes ago. We'd forgotten about our son! That has to be a black mark in life's results book. Five minutes later, at exactly 11:42pm, we burst through the crèche doors. Uncontrolled. Laughing. The two remaining teenage nannies spin around. Their facial expressions translate to a judgement of *terrible parents* – but the resort policy must have been to let parents do as they please – as they say nothing but tell us how William has been a pleasure. (They mean he's slept and allowed them to check Instagram.)

I look around.

Shit, no other babies apart from ours. I was hoping our irresponsibility would have had some company. We tiptoe (loudly and clumsily) over to William, who is fast asleep in his cot, one ear of his comfort bunny in the clutch of a tiny hand, the other tattered and soaked next to William's mouth. As per the plan, prior to our late crèche entry, I picked William up. It was a simple one. Since we were *both* drunk, I'd be the one to carry William back to the hotel room – because if one of us did trip and fall with him and it was me, I could use my larger body to break the fall. *Screams responsibility*, we thought.

He stirs briefly as I rest his head against my chest. I peer down at him. With any luck the alcohol on my breath will keep him sedated a little longer if he does dare to stir between here and the hotel room. As I turn to the crèche exit, the weight of my sleeping son on me fills me with a sobering tranquillity. I look to my wife and smile. She's definitely swaying – that, or it's me. We apologise for being late (I explained there'd been another guest who needed medical attention and we were helping. A speck of a white lie, really), and thank the nannies (Alice tells me later I may have called them *nurses* but we can't be sure), and exit.

Yes, drunk. Yes, irresponsible. Yet full of love and happiness.

The three of us wander back to our hotel room for the penultimate sleep of what's been a wonderful inaugural Skittle family holiday abroad.

Valentine's Day sure isn't what it once was.

Friday, 15th February

William remains impetigo-free. A definite medical miracle.

Impetigo-boy had to be quarantined after a quiet word with the crèche manager at the start of the week . . .

Saturday, 16th February

Déjà vu. Once again, I stand facing the security metal detectors, unable to fold this fucking pram!

Monday, 18th February

I think hard to remember whether I'd pissed off the reception team before my holiday last week. I'm sure I didn't. Yet somehow, they've managed to book Mr Bonn in as my first patient back.

Fuck you, Monday!

Reluctantly, I lean in and have a closer look at the grainy image he's presenting me with on his iPhone. All I see is something resembling a brown drawstring bag opening pulled tightly shut.

'It's my anus.'

I nod resignedly. Of course it's his bloody anus, what else would I deserve to look at on my first day back at work?

'Right.'

The only word I can be bothered to muster. Mr Bonn explains he took the picture this morning so that I could see his problem. I stop short of telling him that all I see is a brown drawstring bag opening pulled tightly shut and take his word for it – that it's his *actual* anus. If I was being difficult, I could argue that this could be *anyone's* anus for all

I knew. But today isn't the day. If it was a Friday, maybe. Anal itching, that's Mr Bonn's issue.

God, the Skittle family holiday feels a hazy, distant, long-ago dream right now.

Readjusting in my chair, my buttocks only familiar to a sun lounger or well-plumped bar cushion for the last week, I suggest I have a look at the real thing.

'My anus?'

I sigh. I'd hardly mean *my* anus now, would I? I refrain from letting the words escape. Breathe . . .

'Yes, Mr Bonn. Your anus.'

Short of putting a padlock over his belt buckle, Mr Bonn's reaction tells me that is out of the question. I shift onto my left buttock and lean against the chair's arm, unimpressed and tired, as if my body's finding it hard to hold itself upright.

'I can't properly treat what I can't see. You realise that, right?'

After a further two minutes of debate and discussion on the merits of being able to actually see his anus, it becomes clear that he's not going to budge. His argument is that he thinks it's threadworm (because it's itchier at night), and so he just wants a prescription for mebendazole, the threadworm treatment.

I want to dig into what on earth he thought I was going to be able to see in that *selfie*, but don't have the energy in me. My brain left somewhere in Morocco. With as little frustration showing as I can, I explain he needs to buy that medicine over-the-counter from any pharmacy. It doesn't need a prescription from me. To his surprise, this will be cheaper than the cost of a single prescription. Mr Bonn says he doesn't think he pays for his prescriptions. I'm sure that's bollocks. After a quick review of his notes, I confirm it is indeed bollocks: he's not eligible for a medical prescription cost exemption under any of the ten exemption categories. So I break the news. He doesn't fight me on it. Small mercies.

As he shakes my hand, I tell him to come back if the treatment he buys doesn't work – *'But be prepared to let me see your anus.'* A sentence said out of requirement, not choice. As the door closes shut, I can't help but sink my head into my hands.

Nobody, absolutely nobody, should have to say the word *anus* that many times on their first day back at work.

Wednesday, 20th February

If I hear about performance targets for the surgery one more time, I might explode. Like hand in my notice and storm out in a blaze of vernacular glory, explode. Email reminders. Meeting reminders, such as the one I've just crawled out of, in which I've had any joy of my job methodically beaten out of me with each and every target smashed repeatedly over my skull. Then of course those personal, corridor, *quiet-word* reminders.

My favourite was yesterday in the middle of my clinic. I received an *urgent* instant message from Dr Phil enquiring why I didn't complete a patient's foot check (as part of their annual type 2 diabetes screening) when I'd seen them yesterday. Well, Dr Phil, since the patient had come to see me about the affair their husband was having and how her beloved family unit has been shattered into a million tiny divorce-provoking pieces, it seemed more than a tad insensitive to ask them (as they dry their tears) to quickly pop their shoes and socks off so I can press a 10g monofilament needle onto the soles of their feet.

To. Tick. The. Bloody. Target. Box.

Of course, the rational part of my brain (getting smaller by the day, I'm convinced) recognised this could've been interpreted as overly aggressive, so I opted to completely ignore it – just deleting the message instead. The journey to self-improvement continues. To explain, these targets that incite so much frustration in me are called Quality and Outcomes Frameworks targets (QOF, for short), and are how a GP surgery like mine gets additional money (and, *apparently*, helps the patients). For example, if we've got two hundred patients with a diagnosis of hypertension (high blood pressure), the surgery would get an additional financial payment if we can show that, say, 90 per cent of those patients have a blood pressure controlled to a normal level (under 140/90 mmHg). If the surgery achieves even just 89 per cent, that equals no extra money.

I don't have an issue with the intention. After all, a lower blood pressure will reduce the risk of cardiovascular disease and death. What I do have issue with is that we're not being encouraged to work towards better patient outcomes per se by being *proactive* – for example, getting additional money for every patient who *doesn't* have a diagnosis of high blood pressure (because we've promoted physical activity, low-salt diets, and better stress management). To focus on controlling patients who already have high blood pressure is *reactive* practice to my mind, mopping up the problem when we could have worked harder to stop it in the first place. It's a bit why GPs are increasingly focused on *social prescribing* – a variety of activities organised in the community, from gardening and cookery to befriending, healthy eating advice, and sports – as a means to reverse this approach. But for now, if you ask me, we're positively choking patients with these targets – and in the most obscure, inappropriate, and random of times – crow-barring them into consultations in which they have no place whatsoever.

I became a GP to help people. I didn't become one to practise tick-box money-grabbing medicine.

Thursday, 21st February

Opened my inbox this morning: another email about targets.

And Happy Birthday, to me.

Monday, 25th February

'You can't drive, do your job, be in a bath alone, go swimming alone, or be up a ladder . . .' I pause. *'Or anything remotely similar.'* Peter stares through me. Really not a great Monday for him. I can practically see my words settling in his head.

Kicked-up silt on a seabed.

I sit opposite in the midst of a busy clinic, leaning in, pumping clasped hands open and shut, just waiting for his reaction. *Nothing.* I give him more time. This was always going to be a shock. You can peel the plaster off slowly, or rip it off – I'm a ripper. I cough. This less-than-subtle prompt guides his eyes back to mine.

'Do you understand what I'm telling you?'

He nods. I screw up my face, disbelieving. I know he *hears* me but his body language and lack of conversation tells me he might not *understand* me. Peter's had an episode of losing consciousness while walking to a restaurant last week with his wife. He didn't see it coming (that is, he had no warning, like feeling dizzy or light-headed), he fell forwards (a body tends to fall backwards as a protective mechanism if there's time), he couldn't remember where he was for a few minutes after he woke up (he actually thought he was in the garage where he works as a car mechanic), and felt drained for a full three days afterwards.

If you've just had a simple faint, where your blood pressure drops temporarily and therefore stops getting blood to your brain, you *don't* get those symptoms. As I gently recap these unpalatable facts to Peter, he blinks more and more into the room, coming out of his personal headspace and back with me. I carry on, momentum now gathering with his regained attention. I explain this means we can't exclude other causes for him losing consciousness – and that includes a seizure (a *fit*). I can see Peter's lightbulb moment and, seeing an opportunity to reverse his entire nightmare, he tells me that he *definitely* didn't jerk his arms or legs.

Nice try – I would've done the same.

I explain that unfortunately there are lots of different types of seizures – including types where you *don't* jerk. If he was a balloon, I was the giant needle right then. As a result, I've referred him to the First Fits Clinic at the local hospital to be seen by a neurologist. And until he's seen, I explain, the blanket policy is that he can't do anything which, if he were to lose consciousness, could endanger him or others. Thus, no solo candle-lit soaks in the bath for now.

I lean back, feeling shit, knowing this will be damaging for him. And while it's so tempting to say, *Yeah, this is probably a simple faint, so don't worry about it, mate*, there are red flags (warnings of a more serious condition) in the history I can't justifiably ignore. To make matters worse, I know his work will want to know what's going on – any mention of *fits* or *loss of consciousness* on his sick note a sure-fire way to a fast-tracked P45 (no doubt via some *other* employer reason). The reality is, you can't shake off words like that sometimes, even if the neurologists do give him the all-clear.

I stand, shaking Peter's hand, and explain I've done all I can to minimise this impact for now, using the most generic medical terminology known to humankind on his sick note – '*so they won't ever be able to guess this is about a possible fit under investigation.*' I like Peter and really hope the neurology team finds nothing. If they do, however, I'll be obligated to inform both his employer and the Driver and Vehicle Licensing Agency (DVLA), if he didn't do so. Something I really hope neither he – nor I – ever have to do.

Tuesday, 26th February

I'm sitting here, wondering how to interrupt *Mrs* Wells and tell her she really doesn't need that *prostate* blood test she's demanding.

Ever.

Wednesday, 27th February

It's a misconception that doctors in the UK take the Hippocratic Oath. In fact, we take no oath at all. There's not even a law to say we must help people in medical need outside of work. Nowadays, it's all much more sterile and we simply adhere to an ethical code outlined in the General Medical

Council's *Good Medical Practice* book (as well as another set of guidance for us GPs from the Royal College of General Practitioners). Here, they talk about *obligations* and *professional behaviour* to patients and the wider society. It's an artificial moral compass, if you like. Which is why, when I stood at the top of the train station steps, watching this middle-aged woman swan-dive head-first down a flight of stairs, I knew I couldn't really just politely step over her.

When I finally arrived at her landing spot, she was essentially kissing the concrete of the bottom step. My immediate thought was, *thank God she's made it to there.* To manage this halfway up a flight of steps would've been a logistical ball-ache. She was conscious. *Tick.* The left side of her face was, well, not like the right side of her face anymore – the surrounding concrete now a crimson tide. *Half a mark.* This was tricky for a number of reasons. The first was that she was still pointing *down* the stairs – her head on the bottom step, feet still resting on the sixth. That means she's bloody hard to move. Why? Well, given she's just taken a low-scoring swan-dive off a staircase, the risk of her having a spinal injury has rocketed.

The second is that she's clearly incredibly pissed. The result being that she's very keen to totally ignore every instruction I give her – such as the current *'Please. No. Please. Oi! No! NO! Do Not. Do Not Bloody Move!'* The irony is that although being drunk probably contributed to her fall, it's almost certainly giving her a lot of pain relief right now.

The third is that I'm actually trying to get to a dinner reservation for a rare night out with the boys. And I'm starving.

As I lie in front of her, my body outstretched, grumbling tummy flush (well, not six-pack flush) to the ground, I hold her head in-between my hands. The goal, once I know she has an airway (a *yes*, since she's screaming hysterically), is to keep her cervical spine (her neck, basically) as still as possible while awaiting the local ambulance crew to come and fully immobilise her spine and *only then* move her safely. In doing so we minimise the risk of damage to her spinal cord and so prevent any potential for irreversible paralysis.

It's the same kind of reason why people sometimes get left in cars after a road traffic accident – only being moved once there's a trained team to remove them (unless of course the car is on fire or about to explode). Since my swan-diver isn't on fire – or about to explode, and still breathing, I opt to wait in the position she's in until the ambulance arrives – which, I've been told by the station staff, was en route. Fast.

An hour later, when I finally get to the restaurant, the boys are having their starters cleared away, the bread basket has been pillaged, the first bottle of wine drained. I order a beer and briefly think of my swan-diver being carried off by a very impressive ambulance crew as she lay on a spinal board, head and neck firmly immobilised, taped between two orange blocks, and sporting a fetching blue and white collar. While I get why they're there, I don't personally feel I need a sterile set of guidelines to tell me how to be ethical. I'm happy with my own moral compass just as it is. I look around the table at old friends and smile, *'Sorry I was so late, boys – transport issues.'*

Let the belated birthday catch-up begin.

Thursday, 28th February

Finally found my work contract tonight (*back of the wardrobe. Logical place*). As I take a sip of beer, I scan through and find what I'm looking for – I'll need to give at least six weeks' notice to my employer that I'm leaving the job. I sit on the bed and drum my hands on my thighs, deciding if I'm sick with excitement – or nerves.

I look to Alice for comfort. According to her, it's not nerves but the half-tub of Ben & Jerry's that I've just polished off.

Supportive as ever.

I look to William for backup, but he's just face-planting the carpet.

FLASHBACK: LIFE AS A PRIVATE GP

This was admittedly a short-lived venture. Throughout 2018 I worked on an ad-hoc basis at a private GP clinic. Here, complete strangers can walk in and pay a consultation fee to see me. No clinical notes on record, just what they tell me. Now I could sit here and list the many, many reasons why it didn't work out, but on reflection, it boiled down to one simple fact: *I fucking hated it.* And to be fair, when I look back, this isn't too much of a surprise either. After all, I didn't go through eleven years of training, dreaming of the day when I could generate a patient's invoice in front of their very eyes (as they fish out their platinum credit card), before finally taking payment with the card machine living symbiotically next to my stethoscope. Like toothpaste and orange juice, two objects not belonging together. Not in my life anyway. So, at the end of the year, I quit. And with all that in mind, what follows are some of the more memorable straws that broke *this* camel's private GP career's back.

Enjoy!

*

Monday, 27th August

Thank God I don't have this every ten minutes in my NHS clinics. I hang up the phone and wait for the fourth private client of the morning to come back in so I can take their credit card payment. I read from the tired, unenthused tone of Lisa, my gum-chewing, Instagram-loving, teenage private secretary that she's given up all hope of me ever getting the hang of having to generate an invoice for the client – *and* take a card payment from them – at the end of each consultation.

There's a knock at the door. Back comes Teddy, yet another twenty-something game player needing his sexual health screen after a busy few nights unsheathed. I smile, inviting him to sit.

'Won't be a minute.'

A total lie. I scrabble around the super-flashy Apple Mac in front of me, searching for the digital catalogue of how much each test costs, then turn and smile. I would say things had gotten awkward by now, but Teddy's already busy swiping right on his phone, seeking out another adventure of the flesh. I could take all day and it wouldn't matter to him.

Bingo, found them.

I fill out the invoice with renewed confidence, happy in the fact that I don't have to go to Plan B and make up the costings.

'Right, Teddy, that'll be £127.00,' I announce, handing him a copy of his bill. He doesn't blink. I stare at him. Not one blink. *Really? What the hell's wrong with this guy?* I just billed him over a hundred quid for something that's (fine, with a bit of taxation) essentially free on the NHS. Total madness. With his platinum credit card (the kind of card that's overt code for I make a LOT of money) in my hand, I run it through the portable card reader. Unwelcome bile climbs my throat. I battle it back down. Never, ever in my medical training did I think I'd be using the same type of card reader as my coffee shop.

Teddy takes the card and receipt and thanks me once again. I stare at him, wondering if I should tell him he's totally mad and to go back to the wonderful, if not slightly tired NHS, but I stop myself, realising I'm the one with the massive chip on my shoulder. What a hypocrite. Especially since I take a percentage of everything else he gets billed for after the initial consultation fee. So, having realised the irony and hypocrisy of it all, I let him go without a lecture.

Lisa walks into my room, passing Teddy as she does with a flirty smile (if only she knew what I was testing him for . . .).

'Your next client's here. Please try and remember to charge them.'

I thought she might at least say it with a smile. No such luck.

Tuesday, 28th August (09:15am)

'My wife and I are worried we've got urine infections.'

Henry is thirty-nine years old, well built, sharp suit. He's a business type, clearly switched on. Which is why I'm surprised that the next sentence leaving his lips is said with nothing but unadulterated innocence, *'she suggested we both get a urine test for infection.'* A pause and then, *'Including for chlamydia.'* If Henry had come in with a big red alarm bell over his head, right now it would be ringing like there's no tomorrow. His wife, Yasmin, is at a different private GP clinic nearer her work, having the same tests, he tells me.

Convenient, if not suspicious. By now, clinical experience allows me to keep a straight face, internalising the expression of deep concern that this might not end well for Henry and Yasmin. Both have a three-day history of some burning when passing urine. They've had sex in the last week – with each other – Henry reports. Importantly (for many reasons), Henry denies having any other sexual contact outside of his marriage. He has no concerns that his wife has either. After I've summarised his case, he nods, looking on at me patiently. I look back at Henry, perplexed more than anything else. Nodding, I tell him fine, that's not a problem, we can do all this. I explain the costs of the tests (which would, of course, all be free at his NHS GP, I add), and he agrees to them.

Five minutes later he's back from the bathroom, smelling of some fancy branded handwash left out for him and the other clients. Oh yes, didn't I mention, we don't call them *patients* in the private sector. Wanky, isn't it? You'd get a bar of Poundland soap at my NHS GP surgery. Works just as well. Henry hands me his urine sample, lid on tightly.

Well done.

He pays for the express service – results within three hours. While I sit there generating the invoice and taking his card payment with the machine that sits on my desk like some inanimate object giving two fingers to the NHS (and yes, again, I do realise the hypocrisy of me saying this), I can't help but say a little prayer that these results come back negative.

Tuesday, 28th August (12:45pm)

Fuck!

Tuesday, 28th August (12:47pm)

A little over three hours from our first meeting, Henry's back sitting in front of me. I opted to forgo a lunch break as the bro-code made me want to deal with this one immediately. He looks like a man who knows where this story – *his story* – leads.

'You have chlamydia, Henry.' It's my turn to pause now. *'I need you to be fully open with me. Have you had any type of sexual contact with anyone other than your wife?'* I add in that the importance of this is not just about treating his chlamydia, but assessing his risk for other sexually transmitted infections that he may have caught from someone – including HIV and Hepatitis B and C that we haven't yet tested for. Without moving a muscle, and barely a blink, he answers, *'Absolutely not, I'd never do that.'*

With the false positive rate of this test crushingly low, that leads to only one conclusion: *'I think you need to go home and sit down with your wife in that case, Henry. I'm sorry.'* The words leave me with a heavy heart. I hand him the prescription for antibiotics and advise him to go and have a full sexual health screen at the local NHS sexual health centre (for free). Shaking my hand, I can see he's a melting pot of anger, sadness, confusion, heartbreak, and denial. He doesn't need to say anything. Neither do I. We part ways and I wish the poor bugger good luck.

Wednesday, 17th October

I stare at the instant message sent out to the other private GPs working today. *This must be a joke. Surely. Please.* That, or someone's having a very stupid day at work. *Do we test for carbon monoxide exposure?* The Times New Roman text flashes on my screen. I look away in disbelief and look back again. No, I haven't misread it. No, it wasn't a mirage. A GP working here is really asking this question.

To be clear, carbon monoxide exposure can kill you. That means, you don't trot along to your local private GP for a warm handshake, fancy branded handwash, and a platinum consultation – you take yourself to A&E to make sure you don't die. You see, carbon monoxide is an odourless gas that binds to your red blood cells and that means your oxygen can't bind to it, so you're starved of oxygen and then you can die (if severe enough). Which is why I'm speechless at the organic stupidity of this message. Thankfully, I can see one of the senior GPs writing a message – I expect they'll give them a sensible answer.

Yes, we do. It's listed in the test catalogue on the shared drive.

What. The. Fuck. Seems everybody's having a stupid day today. As my fingers start to tap an instant message back to the group, asking if anybody actually went to medical school here, a reply pops up from another GP, suggesting they send the patient to the local A&E department. A flurry of messages later and they do. I lean back, relieved the desire to make a bit of extra money hasn't just overruled common sense.

Today, at least.

Monday, 22nd October

He's got the shits. But because he's got the shits. he's desperate for an answer more than *'you've got the shits'*. And that's why Mr Kelly is now sitting opposite me, trying admirably to stop the explosion desperate to erupt from his frantically clenched arsehole. He's already seen his NHS GP this morning, who told him he's likely got viral gastroenteritis (*aka, the shits*). When I get more of the history, it turns out he's got the same dignity-stripping symptoms as the other three guys at his office, all whom ate at the same kebab stand last night. So, I'm with the NHS GP here – viral gastroenteritis is the diagnosis.

The problem with this conclusion for Mr Kelly is that it means it's pretty much a waiting game now. There's no real quick-fix to restore gastrointestinal order and decorum, he just needs to ride it out. As I try to explain this, Mr Kelly's demeanour shifts acutely. Tension worn over his face. Knees pressing together. Distracted. Like a man, I fear, who has just shat himself. I choose not to ask: it won't change my decision making and will only air a fact that I expect he'd like to keep between him and his clothing. Instead I smile and lean back a little, relying on the fancy plug-in air freshener behind me to buffer against any olfactory abuse.

Once Mr Kelly's moment seems to have passed, I assume a more vertical position and explain my stance. Since his NHS GP has already sent off a stool sample to test for the presence of any bacterial infections (something that's very kind at such an early stage of a diarrhoeal infection – I would have waited much longer, given the clinical history), I really don't have much else to offer him. Private practice does not equal better practice. Which is why I'm unsurprised at his polite recoil when I deliver my simple advice: stay well hydrated, eat simple dried, plain foods when he feels ready, ensure good hand hygiene (to minimise potential spread), and buy over-the-counter oral rehydration sachets if he feels the need for them. All advice he could have found for free on the NHS website, importantly, while sitting on the toilet for safety.

Finally, I explain – and most critically – he should position himself near a toilet for the foreseeable future. I charge him for the same information he got for free five hours ago. On leaving, he goes to shake my hand. My body language (hands in pockets) tells him that a courteous nod is probably better for today (and less cross-infective). And then, as the door clicks shut cordially (private practice doors seem to shut very quietly), I move to the sink and begin washing my hands. More than once.

Monday, 5th November

I'm tempted to just give him the bloody antibiotics so I can breathe again. The aftershave Mr Hunt bathed in this morning chokes the oxygen from my room. I knew before I met him, on reading his appointment booking note – *I urgently require antibiotics for my cough* – that he had the potential to be one of life's fun sponges. Paired with his inability to judge just how much *too much* aftershave actually was, is his inability to sit with his knees together, and generally it seems, to be a decent human being.

I sit opposite him, stone cold in warmth by this point. Some people you just take an instant dislike to. You can dress them up in icing sugar, stick a cherry on top, but still they're no more palatable. Mr Hunt just started off badly, telling me what to do – *give him antibiotics.* I suggest, with a more than reasonable mix of politeness and authority that we start at the beginning with his symptoms. He scoffs.

Scoffs! Who still does that nowadays? It's like rubbing a cat's fur up the wrong way, you're going to get bitten. Fast forward a few minutes and here we are. Much to his impatience and displeasure, I've now taken a full clinical history, examined him, and recorded his observations. The diagnosis is a viral upper respiratory tract infection. I break the news that he has the common cold. Unfortunately, it turns out he thinks he went to medical school as well. Red-faced, he instructs me to prescribe antibiotics.

Only Alice is allowed to *instruct* me.

I raise my eyebrows, surprised at the audacity. Facing him, I find myself working hard to remain calm and keep that feeling of a kettle below its boiling point under control. Then, out of nowhere, Mr Hunt goes ahead and says something so ridiculous that I laugh out loud: *'I paid for my right to antibiotics!'* The room falls silent, my face fixed in a mock smile, head still shaking in an incredulous and metronomic *no, you silly bugger* manner. Mr Hunt sits, confused by my outburst.

Time to clear the air: *'This is not a demand service. We do not give you what you do not need.'* I let him digest this for a second before continuing, *'So, I suggest you seek a second opinion if you feel my diagnosis does not meet your expectations.'* With that, the consultation ends (on time, conveniently for me). Mr Hunt promptly storms out.

Private practice. NHS practice. It really doesn't matter. I will not be bullied into prescribing unnecessary treatments. Ever. Once again, I forget to charge. Seems I may just not be built to bill people, no matter the reminders from Lisa.

Monday, 12th November

Just completed my eighth sexual health screen of the morning client list. Seems there was a lot of love in the air this weekend. I think back to mine – watching William float around a swimming pool, cleaning the shit from his feet he'd managed to stamp in while lying on the changing mat, and then doing his laundry pile with Alice.

Overall, a slightly different kind of love.

Wednesday, 21st November

Mr Seymour flattens out the medical sign-off form from his jacket pocket. A sinking feeling grabs at me. He's agitated, sweating, and sitting opposite with the kind of wild look in his eye and pressure of speech that says this isn't a simple blood pressure check type of consultation. Stabbing a sweaty finger at the form, he tells me (repeatedly) that he needs this signed today – because he's on a flight tomorrow to join a *save the rainforest*-type charity in South America. And by the way, they won't receive him officially if he doesn't have the forms signed. He's bought his ticket already.

'My GP wouldn't sign it.' His words blow a hole in the bottom of my sinking feeling and suck me straight down. I nod slowly, taking it all in while trying to piece together what exactly it is that I'm getting dragged into here. To make matters that little bit trickier, because this is a private GP clinic – one that Mr Seymour hasn't attended before – I know nothing about him. So, knowing that to dive into a line of questioning of *and why hasn't your NHS GP signed it?* (and therefore, *what on earth makes you think I'm going to?*) may yield a less than favourable response, I go back to basics with a clinical history. It buys me time. I explain that I need to know if he's any current medical conditions or symptoms under investigation. He shakes his head vigorously from side to side. I nod – with much less vigour – not believing that for a second.

'On any regular medicines?'

(A bit sly, really – if he's not got any medical conditions, he shouldn't be on any regular prescribed medicines.)

'Just Olanzapine.'

Ah, an anti-psychotic drug. I hit the bottom of whatever murky waters Mr Seymour's trying to drag me down to.

'So, you're on this medication but don't have a diagnosis?' I ask with more of an Australian-infused inflection at the end, making it sound more like a question than a confirmatory statement (*which it absolutely fucking is*).

'Yes.'

Mr Seymour's my last patient (*sorry, client*) of the day and I'm not sure I've got the willpower to tell him that doesn't make any sense. Another sweaty finger stabs at the medical form that basically says he's alright to get on a plane and run headfirst into the rainforest wearing some organically made T-shirt.

Mr Seymour, I realise, is not a well man. If I were a betting one, I'd say he's got a diagnosis along the lines of bipolar affective disorder and is sitting in front of me in the throes of a manic phase. I also realise that he may well flip his shit when I tell him in about thirty seconds' time that I'm not going to be signing his medical form. Callously, I decide to buy myself some time (once again). I ask Mr Seymour to have a seat outside in the waiting room (I'm sure Lisa can entertain him for five minutes with her sparkling chat while her iPhone leaves her hand momentarily to go on charge) while I gather some more information. He looks troubled by the fact that I haven't put pen to unscrunched paper, though not concerned enough to fight me on it.

As he wanders out of my consulting room, I jump on the phone and dial his NHS GP surgery. The verbal rolling of the eyes I sense from Mr Seymour's regular NHS GP that I'm speaking to tells me all I need to know. Turns out he's completely disengaged with the local mental health service who were supporting his bipolar affective disorder (now confirmed) – and last week had a falling-out with the GP surgery after multiple GPs refused to sign his medical form on the basis of his current mental health. I'll give him credit, it was a savvy move to try to get around this by seeing a private GP. Sadly, he just came to the wrong one.

I rest my head against the desk, ear still to the receiver, realising my predicament. I'm not Mr Seymour's GP. In fact, I'm just his one-off dial-a-doc for cash. And yet the moral compass in me is saying I can't just throw him out without trying to help him at all. Question is how? I run all this by his usual NHS GP still on the phone to me, who is clearly utterly fed-up with the situation. I stop short of telling him that it's still his job to help him – even if he does annoy him – but also stop short of showing any complicity in his pathetic perspective.

A plan is made: his usual GP will contact the community mental health's rapid response team and try to get a review this week. I will *not* sign his form and will therefore not be permitting him to go anywhere leafier than the local park (which may still also need saving, anyway). This also means he's lost a lot of money on a plane ticket that wouldn't have been cheap.

I hang up and feel frustrated though I know the reality is there's really not much else I can do. Well, there's one thing, but it'll likely (once again) not go down well with the management here. Opening my door, I call Mr Seymour back in. He enters. Sits. Looks to me. Looks to the scrunched medical form. Unsigned. Never to be signed. I lean forward and deliver needed, honest blows: *'The good news is that there is no charge for this consultation. The bad news, Mr Seymour, is that I cannot sign your medical form.'* I pause, waiting for the tsunami of anger, frustration, and discontent. He blinks a few times. Frowns. And then just says *'OK.'* I hold my breath. Nothing. He looks at me, downtrodden. Sad. I lean in a little more and, shaking my head, explain that I'm really worried he's not very well – and so is his usual GP. He nods again, resigned and showing no signs of being resolute to fight me on this – I think he probably knows he's not well and this trip to South America was an impulsive escape. One I wonder if he ever really thought would happen.

I feel shit. I watch as he scrunches the form again, shoving it back in his pocket, history from last week once more repeating itself. He tells me he only wanted to help. I believe him. His sadness transfers onto me. I feel it. Now, everything in me wants to say he'll get there one day, but I don't know that and it's not fair to plant false hopes – the view through the window into Mr Seymour's life merely a fleeting snapshot, never to be repeated. So, I swallow the words and just say, *'I know you did.'* I explain that the community mental health team will be in touch this week and urge him to re-engage with them and his usual GP (though I did also suggest he find one at his NHS surgery who he might like a little more/be more compassionate to his needs). Mr Seymour asks if I can be his usual GP. With a shake of my head I let him know sadly that won't be possible. I write him a letter for the airline in the faint hope that he might be able to recoup some of his ticket cost back. He leaves, globally deflated in every sense of the word.

If this was the NHS and he was registered as a patient at my surgery, I could have seen him again tomorrow, made him my patient, and given him the support that he deserves for what can be a challenging condition. But the fact is he's registered at another NHS practice (and you can't be registered at more than one) and they need to take the lead on this. In the private world, in this GP clinic, that just isn't possible. And that, I resent. Deeply.

Wednesday, 12th December

NHS GP, undercover in the private GP sector . . . That's how I feel today. Mainly since I've spent the majority of the morning telling my clients that they don't need all these silly extra tests and that they're better off going to see their NHS GP, who knows them best. Basically, I'm doing the clinic (and, ironically, myself) out of earnings.

The inside man.

Right now, I'm sitting in front of 39-year-old Harriet. She's got a background of anxiety but in the last few weeks has developed new palpitations in her chest. These are naturally worrying her. After taking more of a history, it turns out these coincided with a work promotion. Harriet's now heading up a new sub-team in the recruitment company she works for, and as she's starting earlier and finishing later (trying to impress the bosses), she's nailing the coffee like there's no tomorrow. Apart from that, she's otherwise fit and well, with no family history of early heart disease and not on any medications.

I explain that her palpitations are likely driven by her anxiety and that a medication to help control her heart rate – a beta-blocker drug called propranolol – during heightened times of work anxiety is one way to help with this (if more conservative non-drug measures fail). Now as I say, to really get a handle on it, this needs to be matched with some seriously aggressive reduction in her caffeine intake (she's drinking so much, I'm surprised she's not bouncing off the white-washed clinic walls here) and breathing relaxation exercises during those high-stress work moments.

Harriet looks confused. I know why: she's been told on booking with the private GP surgery that she'll likely need a blood test (to check the function of her thyroid gland), an electrocardiogram (a tracing of her heart's electrical activity), and then a referral to the endocrine (hormone) and cardiology (heart) specialist teams. I shake my head, lean in, tell her all that's excessive, disproportionate, and unnecessary at this stage. She stumbles over her response, unsure what to say.

'I promise you, I want what's best for you – and your bank balance – as all those tests and referrals are going to add up,' I joke.

She looks like she's coming round to my way of thinking so I roll on and explain that if, despite the treatment I'm suggesting, she still gets palpitations, then she can see her NHS GP and get the blood tests, electrocardiogram, and referrals on the NHS. For free. Sure, perhaps a little more slowly though.

She nods more enthusiastically this time. After another five minutes chatting about other non-pharmacological ways to help manage her anxiety and how, much to her surprise, it can manifest as multiple physical symptoms (including palpitations), she leaves with a much lighter bill than she might have had.

I sit back, relaxing into my big padded leather high-backed chair (just like the one Jasper won't get me), look at the shiny art on the wall and tasteful pot plants (fake, so they stay bright green, and require little real effort) – and I thank God that it seems I haven't been bought out by the veneer of private practice. That, in fact, I am a NHS GP, through and through. To the core. Moral compass in good working order.

Which is why it's no surprise that this turned out to be my last-ever private GP shift.

*

For ages, I couldn't put my finger on why life in the private GP sector didn't work for *me.* And no, it wasn't just because some days I might well have been working at a sexual health clinic (despite the stories being great). I mean, some GPs absolutely love the private sector, carving out fantastic and fulfilling careers. For them, it gives them something they seek. For me, however, I realised that it did the opposite: giving me things I didn't want.

After much discussion and dissection with Alice (William, watching on intently, as if a key member of this process), I've rationalised it down to three key conclusions.

Number one: I love the raw nature of public sector medicine

What's not to love about the raw, challenging, and gritty medicine that an NHS GP surgery gives rise to? More than that, I bloody well like the fact my chair has one wheel broken and is unbelievably uncomfortable. That the walls are covered with cheaply printed A4 flyers promoting everything from flu jabs and weight loss to free condoms and mental health park-walking groups. That my room can smell of anything from expensive perfume to a motorway service station urinal on a Saturday night. And of course there is always the latest in a series of increasingly dead pot plants (*sorry, Alice!*) next to my computer which predates the abacus.

Real dead plants, not *fake* dead ones.

It's chaotic. Because life is chaotic. And thus reflects the health landscape that a GP surgery serves. The NHS also battle hardens. Doctors, healthcare assistants, nurses, ambulance crews, all the other many incredible healthcare (clinical and non-clinical) teams and staff that serve it. And it is a *serving*. You don't do it for the glamour, the money, or the working conditions, I can tell you that. I want that battlefield, it makes me good at my job. Sitting comfortably in some oversized sterile room, surrounded by framed paintings of obscure Italian hills at dusk, and a vase of fake sunflowers, all outside a reception with *Mozart Piano Concerto No. 21* gently calming the atmosphere does not reflect real life. It does not reflect the chaos I'm seeking, it sanitises it. A veneer covering the truth. That our health can be ugly sometimes. And sometimes, to do the job right, you need to stare ugly in the face. And smile.

Number two: I'm not a fan of monetised patient expectation

Don't get me wrong, not every person who uses a private GP is like this. But, as my encounter with Mr Hunt highlights, it is out there. And that's just something I can't ever get comfortable with. We can all appreciate that money can act as a distracting magnet when placed next to a person's moral compass. In medicine, all of a sudden, not only is there a moral obligation to act in the best interests of the patient's health (which of course should be the *only* justification ever needed) but there's now a pressure, for want of a better word, *to give them their money's worth.* This has the potential to lead to over-investigation and unconscious bias. The result? The fires of patient health anxieties are stoked. At unnecessary expense.

That's just not how I want to practise my medicine.

Number three: I need to have that continuity of care

As a GP, I have the continuous privilege to look through the window of my patient. Every time I see that person, I take in more information through it, getting to know what makes them tick, what their ideas, worries, beliefs, and expectations are. I get to know their total health inside and out, no stone left unturned. That concept should fundamentally remain at the core of what being a GP is about. Why? Well, because it means that I can see when a change has occurred. I can see when something I've looked at through their window for years is suddenly different. It builds relationships and a trust for which their health (and my job satisfaction) are the beneficiary.

In my experience, the private sector doesn't facilitate this nearly as well. And in some cases, not at all. I can hear your shouts at this passage (assuming someone other than my mum and Alice are reading this) – at the fact that this isn't even possible in your NHS GP surgery nowadays. Never enough appointments. Never the same doctor. I appreciate that. It's not like previous generational relationships with GPs. But personally, when I go into work, I fight to ensure that continuity, best I can. I also believe general practice has the potential to be amazing again in this regard. Yet for now, it's a problem far bigger than me – compounded by the fact that year on year, fewer doctors are choosing to go into full-time employment as a GP. A tragically complex problem that will require a shared, measurable, and realistic plan from NHS leaders and government to fix. Even then, it'll be an uphill battle. One beyond me.

Still, we march on.

I want to remain a public servant – that's ultimately what my time in the private GP sector taught me. I want to be available to *all* of our society, not just the ones who have the financial ability to pay for my time. Yet ironically, I also conclude that I respect, and thank, the private sector for being here. First, because it means those who want it can have it. It's their choice after all, and so why shouldn't they have the option if they have the means? Second, it can deliver timely and convenient care suited to you rather than at 11:23am on a Thursday when you should probably be in work. And third, it helps skim off a little fat from the current burden on NHS GP surgeries, beyond capacity to cope with demand as it is. But still, despite all this, yes, it wasn't for me.

I want grazed knees at the end of my day, not soft, moisturised hands.

The NHS is one of this country's best and most loved institutions. Yes, fine, it's far from perfect, but then again, being British, that suits us down to the ground. To this day, the three core principles of the NHS, developed for its launch in 1948 by then Minister of Health, Aneurin Bevan, are ones that we should remain deeply proud and protective of:

- That it meets the needs of everyone
- That it is free at the point of delivery
- That it is based on clinical need, not ability to pay.

With such real-time seismic changes in our health burden, society, economics, and politics compared to the creation of the NHS in 1948, we can all probably understand why the NHS is struggling to meet these core principles now. The country has changed. Health has changed. The NHS has not. *Not really.* But it is trying – trying to evolve. All while holding on to these three core principles where possible. And personally, I love having the moral and professional obligation to work to these principles. I will work to hold on to them. Which is why being on the coalface of health is where I intend to stay. For the remainder of my career.

MARCH 2019

Monday, 4th March

The marker for today is that I've wanted to sit down on the toilet for just a few minutes of solace since 3pm. It's now 7:15pm.

Tuesday, 5th March

A simple discussion with 7-year-old Ryan and his mum about his sore knee shouldn't be this hard. He jumped off the top bar of the climbing frame at school this morning, as you do when you're seven. No big deal, he'll be fine. But because of the arrival of one solitary bloody wasp camping out in my room, it was just that – hard.

As Ryan's tying up his shoelaces, ready to head back to school, I start explaining to him and his mum the principles of his treatment for a strain to one of his knee ligaments.

'Active rest, icing the knee once a . . .' – *buzz-buzz* – I lurch back as this tiny fucker screams in front of my face before zooming off to head-butt the strip lighting a few more hundred times. Having just pathetically shunted myself back in fear of my 10-millimetre black and yellow invader, as casually as I can, I return my chair to its original position. Ryan's mum looks at me, more than a little surprised. Well, unimpressed. Ryan hasn't even noticed. I smile, aware of the indignity that a wasp's completely emasculating me right now. Clearing my throat to find some deeper, stronger tone, I continue with Ryan's management plan, *'as I was saying*

before I was SO rudely interrupted,' gesturing to the wasp, a joke clearly not well received, judging by the blank faces in front of me, *'active rest, ice, and elevate it in the evenings if it feels swollen, but overall, you . . .'*

I stop talking. Instead, find myself violently ducking down, shaking my head like some wet dog trying to dry itself. The wasp is once again invading my headspace. Any professional credibility I have just left with the squeal I discharge. Working to regain some air of composure (yet knowing it is, in reality, long dead), I watch as the wasp makes its way over to Ryan and his mum. They don't blink. Both demonstrate amazing calmness in the face of such monstrosity. At best, they give a mild twitch of the head, as if a gust of light wind gently tickled their necks. This in comparison to my seizure-like activity is simply a supplementary nail in my consultation-success coffin. And with this now a dawning realisation, plus the fact that Ryan's leg isn't about to fall off, I admit defeat and I show them to the door.

Now, silence fills my room. Momentarily at least. I stand and stare into the room.

'I can hear you, you little shit,' I announce bravely to the wasp. Now it's just me and him. David versus Goliath (though not sure which one I am yet). I work up some courage and resolve to catch it. I don't want to kill it, that contradicts the job description. Besides, I want to teach William that *all* life is important, even annoying little fuckers like this wasp. But before I formulate an actual plan, fate intervenes. My eyes track its final movements as it works its way noisily into the room's air vent, and off into the world.

Freedom. Liberty. Relief.

As I call in the next patient, now running late, I know it's for the best. I mean, I probably would've cocked it up anyway – and been stung.

So, good luck, old foe. Until next time. That, or I'm sure I'll meet your rural cousins later this year.

Wednesday, 6th March

Even without any hair, I recognise that infectious smile instantaneously. Mrs Collins is back in to see me – eight months on from her initial diagnosis of breast cancer. As she walks towards me, I smile warmly, suppressing my self-loathing that I didn't keep a closer eye on her progress – and jealousy that another GP probably did. I wrap my arms around her and unleash a hugely unprofessional hug. One I *really* mean. And I mean it to be unprofessional, I *want* to connect with her. Clearly a lot has happened. Breast-conserving surgery. Chemotherapy. A long battle. I listen intently, chin resting in my hand, elbow planted on the table. She tells me it's gone as well as the surgeons think it could have. The oncology team are optimistic too. She smiles. I can see hope in her eyes: she can see a life going forward. Beyond cancer.

I smile slowly, deep in thought and happiness for her, a relative stranger. She starts to cry tears of relief. Of happiness. Tears coalesce in the corner of my eyes as if magnetised and I blink them away. She can see. She places her hand on mine.

'Thank you.'

I lean back and laugh, *'Thank God you finally bloody well listened to me and went to that breast clinic appointment!'*

She slaps me on the hand as if to admit I was right. But I'm glad, so bloody glad. If she hadn't, she'd have lost a lot more than her hair. I'd be writing her death certificate instead of her medical sick note today. I cock my head, looking at her quizzically, *'I'm surprised you've not got more hair back yet?'* Again, with the same infectious smile she tells me there were some delays. She didn't want to do some of the treatments so there was some back and forth with the treating specialist team. And then she became quite unwell, ending up in hospital a few times with various infections, all delaying her cancer treatment further.

I nod. Taking it all in, she's lucky not to have had any spread of the cancer in that case. I glance at the clock as Mrs Collins folds up her sick note, placing it safely in her handbag. We're well past a ten-minute consultation now. It doesn't matter. It's these moments, these patient contacts, that reinforce my faith in the job, that make it worthwhile. And for that reason alone, I keep Mrs Collins with me for as long as I can. In the end, she leaves *me*! I want to bask in her positivity, and use it to galvanise the loss of strength and motivation in me.

What a heroine.

Friday, 8th March

Over a few beers and chicken fajitas (it's always *Fajita Friday* in the Skittle house), Alice and I have finally not only formalised *the* plan but already have its wheels in motion. Step one: our flat has been put on the market to sell. Step two: we're going to pull up our roots and move to the countryside in June *this year*, and as mentioned earlier, find somewhere to rent first before we settle on a place to buy. Step three: in order for steps one and two to be successful, I'll need to resign from my job at the surgery and find a new one in the countryside. Luckily, as Alice is freelance as a graphic designer, she can work from a home, wherever it is.

A simple but solid plan.

After finishing my beer, I lie outstretched on the sofa, full of fajita and excessive cheese. I extend my legs over Alice's and release a sigh of excited satisfaction.

'So when shall I do it? When shall I pull the plug on work, tell them?'

It's a rhetorical question more than anything. Alice turns to me from her equally over-satiated side of the sofa. I can see her worry for me: she knows quitting a job is never a nice process to go through. She also knows me well enough to understand that I'll worry about letting my colleagues down. As I'm about to reply – a reply admittedly laced with my worries – William stirs on the baby monitor behind us. No doubt having just flipped himself onto his stomach and now cuddling Bunny, his comforter that, although half-eaten and almost always with at least one ear soaked in saliva, has shared every nap time and bedtime with him for as long as we can remember. They are one and the same. To hear that noise, to look at Alice, to think about what adventures a life in the country will bring . . . I swallow the worry about to lace my answer to Alice and instead say, *'Don't worry, it'll be the easiest thing in the world, my love.'* I pause. *'I'll tell them at the end of this month. That way, they'll also have time to find my replacement.'*

And I mean it.

Really.

Monday, 11th March

Nothing's right today. My desk is an explosion of used ear thermometer caps, blood pressure cuffs of varying sizes, used clinical gloves (not yet migrated to the bin), and full urine sample bottles. A metaphor for this entire day. I can't think, my brain is saturated. Numbed by having to answer demand after demand after demand all day long. I try to take in the three unanswered instant messages from other GPs flashing on my screen. But I can't – I don't have the capacity to even consider them right now. The reception team try to call me for the third time in five minutes, no doubt with some other layer of shit for me to drown in. I choose to ignore it, just like their last two attempts.

My last patient has just left the room, having got their ten minutes' worth and unloaded the six chronically complex issues they've saved up for me. What do they realistically expect? Me to fix every one of them in the ten minutes we have? Respectfully, patient expectation is sometimes in the clouds. A dream world. And it's our fault, we let it happen.

I drag my eyeline up towards the clock. I'm now running forty minutes late. A little more energy escapes me as I sit hunched over, knowing this means the majority of my final five patients are going to come in pissed off – but naturally still expect me to resolve their multiple issues of today on the spot, like some performing monkey. The noise is louder than I expected. I take my clenched hands off the now singularly thumped desk.

Sorry, old friend.

I feel myself being totally overwhelmed by the stresses of today.

I'm losing.

I grit my teeth. My body tenses despite me not asking it to. I just want to scream. I really, truly, deeply do. It's all too much. More than all of that, I just want to burst into tears. My phone vibrates in my pocket: Alice. Even on shit days before this one, I'd try to put a little pep in my step on the phone so she doesn't worry. But I can't even do that for the first time in as long as I can remember. I let out a sigh as I realise that I'm not the only one having a tough time. William's been crying incessantly (we think he's teething) and Alice is exhausted and looking for support. So, what do I do? I see her tough day and raise it my tough day. I *over-moan* her moan. *What an insensitive dick.* Not only do I give her zero support but I then try to offload a few of my emotional bags of quick-dry cement onto her shoulders.

A fourth instant message arrives on my screen, just as unwelcome as its three predecessors. I flick to my jobs list while I continue venting, uncontrolled, to Alice. My heart sinks. I've such a painful number of referrals to write after clinic. I take a deep breath; I can't make this patient wait any longer. I tell Alice I have to go – blunt, unloving, and unlike the way I should be speaking to her.

A minute later, Francesca enters and sits down. She's twenty-one years old. *God, please be a simple contraceptive pill check.* I force an unbelievable smile and ask what I can do for her today. As I wait for her to respond, shuffling in her seat as if getting ready for her assault on me, I wonder if I should start saying, *what's the ONE thing I can do for you today?* Because something *has* to change. I can't – no GP can – manage a person's multiple issues in ten minutes safely, effectively, and properly. God, I'm ranting yet here it is: my emotional resilience dam burst. So, if you wonder why so many GPs are burnt out and quitting – well, here is, right now, me – a prime example. Because I'm a good GP. I hope so anyway. Yet somehow, here I am, so loathing of this fucking job and what it's done to me today, despite only ever trying to do the right thing for the person sitting in front of me – that I could get up right now and walk out.

Quitting. Done. Fuck you, job.

And, as I sit in front of Francesca, listening to her tell me the fourth problem she wants me to fix (including her four-year history of pelvic pain contrasted with her two-day history of a tingling in her right index finger), I know what's about to happen. And it does: I'm a dick. A total dick. I act completely out character for me, practically bullying her out of the room through my complete and utter personality failure. I mean, of course I can't fix your pelvic pain right now, and as for your little finger, who the fuck knows? It'll probably disappear in another two days, so why not just try to be a little more patient and wait more than just forty-eight hours of onset? Yet as I air this rant, I know too that Francesca's probably had to wait two weeks to get this appointment – and not even with her usual doctor. I can see how problems get saved up. It doesn't make it any easier though. Nor does the fact that we're trying to recruit more doctors into general practice, yet the numbers are declining. Sadly, I'm not surprised. Not with days like today part of most weeks for most GPs.

Francesca leaves the room, clearly on her way to ask for the complaints form from reception. But I don't care, not today. Because I just want to cry. I can feel it coming as I sit there, surrounded by my sea of warming urine bottles and a to-do list that laughs mockingly at my incompetence to keep on top of my workload every time I look at it. The sob escapes me. I stare at the floor, trying to swallow the next one down. But I can't. And so here, surrounded by medical detritus, crushed, I allow myself a little cry. A release of a tension that has, perhaps, been kept successfully at bay for the last eight months – held back I wonder, through the endless excitements of an evolving family life and holiday breaks. Still, here we are. I take a breath. Remember this, the bigger picture, and crack on. After all, what else can I do? Run out the room? The world keeps turning. So shall I.

Thirty minutes later, after the last patient leaves, I don't bother with any paperwork. I don't even bother to turn my computer off (again), I just leave. I want to go home – I can cry in privacy there. Perhaps I've just come face-to-face with my breaking point.

Nice to finally meet you.

Tuesday, 12th March

Walked in to find four full, warmed urine bottles lined up on my desk. Standing there, urinary toy soldiers, awaiting their orders. As I toss them in the bin, I can't help but hope this morning's patients have a penchant for that public urinal smell. Let's hope for a better day today; yesterday was not fun at all. Looking back, I definitely did break. Properly.

I never cry. Well, rarely. Yet I suppose we all meet our perfect storms from time to time. And that's what yesterday was really. If I analyse it, I can see a number of coalescing storm fronts. I was overworked with excess demand and running late in clinic; struggling with the complexity of the patients in front of me (and certainly in some cases, too complex to manage in ten minutes – or quicker, as I fought to make up time). Unfortunately, the last patient of the day (and therefore meeting me at my lowest ebb) turned out to be the most complex. Bring these factors together and you get your perfect storm. And they always, *always* feel like the end of the world when they come.

Yesterday was no different and I went home with my frustration at the clinic replaced by a guilt that I hadn't done enough, and had in some way punished the patients because I was stressed. The guilt then evolves into resentment for the job, spiriting away the joy of helping people. That's basically what I worked out last night when I sat down with a piece of paper and tried to analyse what the fuck happened. And it's a cathartic process. I feel better today. Now I'm not saying I'm not licking my wounds but I can see that I was perhaps a little overdramatic and the world really isn't going to end. I also expect that I'm not suddently going to quit my job in a hail of frenzied, wild emotion. I'll try to see out the rest of the day (and week) with a little more emotional balance, let's say.

Fingers crossed.

Wednesday, 13th March

Oh, come on, balance, where are you? I found you last summer, I'm sure. Seems somebody definitely wants me to fall out of love a little more with the job this week. I'm staring at Mr Kayll's set of blood test results through virgin eyes. While they work hard to visually process his results, my ears work even harder to collect and funnel the ferocity of words coming from him. My lips, I should add, after the howler of a start to my week, are working *even harder* than both to not say something that'll earn me a P45 in the post.

I've no idea who Mr Kayll is. Never met him. Based on this, our index conversation, I've no particular interest to either. This is another thorn in a GP's side – picking up another GP's patient and the tests they ordered for them. In this case, it was Dan, who I like, so can't be too pissed off with (though will be sure to return the favour next time Mrs Tally has a blood test). The thorn comes because it sometimes means you've got to interpret marginally abnormal results for a vaguely abnormal history and examination – all performed by someone else.

As I lean into the screen, scanning the results, I can't help but reason there's no bloody way I would have done some of these tests for a history of feeling tired. And to be honest, based on that history, I would have told Mr Kayll (very politely) to bugger off. That he is in fact tired because he's just getting over a cold, lives in a city, working a busy six-day-a-week job in consultancy, drinks anywhere between twenty-five and thirty-five units of alcohol a week, and goes to bed at 1am most nights after a session of Call of Duty on his PlayStation. *Man-child!* I could then tell him all this means he doesn't need a complex autoimmune profile and immunoglobulin blood test at the pointless expense of the NHS – common sense is free here. But of course, that's all annoyingly redundant information now. Because the results *are* a little funky. Only very marginally. Inconsequentially so in my opinion.

Sadly, Mr Kayll doesn't see them as inconsequential despite my reassurances. I peer at the phone's digital screen – nine minutes and thirty-two seconds and counting. I try to again explain that if a test result is only *just* outside of the normal range, it's not a huge call for concern (went down like a lead balloon, naturally), and that I would opt to repeat the blood tests in three months – and that he should aim to lose some weight, stop boozing, and get a decent night's sleep. When I explain the latter, in a slightly more buffered way, Mr Kayll shifts gear. From ten minutes and forty-one seconds to eleven minutes and two seconds, he *educates me* how, as a GP, I should know his entire history (since registering thirty-two years ago, I might add) and have had a detailed discussion with the GP who requested the tests.

Once Mr Kayll has finished living out his fantasy world, I pull him into my reality. He is one name, sandwiched between many others that I need to call in succession, seven minutes apart, before then starting to see patients in person (the first of whom is already keenly marked as *arrived* some twenty-three minutes before their actual appointment time). While I may have also softened this response (again, wanting to, at least for the foreseeable future, remain employed here), the point I try to illustrate is that I'm opening his clinical notes *as* I dial his phone number to speak to him. Simply put, there's no time built in to casually peruse my call list each clinic, digesting thirty-two years of clinical history over a well-brewed cup of tea.

I mean, it took me over five hours to wait to have a shit the other day, Mr Kayll (naturally, a sentence running through my mind rather than out of my mouth).

As we both pause for breath on the phone, I sense my stress levels climbing, Monday occurring all over again. The fight in me wains: I want to end this. I retreat from the frenzied debate and just book him in to speak with Dan (the GP who requested the tests) later this week. I explain how I'll be sure to have a long and thorough chat with him (I doubt I will, but will mention it quickly if I bump into Dan outside the toilet), and that I'm sure that he will be happy with this, wanting to follow up himself, ensuring good patient continuity.

'Something we strive for here at the surgery.'

Despite being true, a wave of nausea hits me at the thought of how strained we are to please absolutely everyone nowadays. And with that, the call ends. I exhale, forcing the stress back to a deeper, more dormant place in me. On the next breath, I click on the next notes as I dial another unknown patient. Still, I smile to myself. Because on the plus side, I haven't cried today.

Yet.

Friday, 15th March

After a week which nearly broke me, it's ended on a high. A thank-you card calling me *the kindest and best doctor they've ever met* from the family of a patient I helped look after in their last few months of life. I want to cry. Happy tears this time.

I know. Again.

Nothing but an emotional wreck this week.

Monday, 18th March

It's interesting, looking back at last week now With a more, let's call it, euthymic perspective. And what I realised was that there was something more to it, beyond just riding out the occasional perfect storm and the stresses that come with that. It was also about vulnerability – *my* vulnerability. Something I've always hated showing. Partly because it reveals my lack of confidence. Again, believe it or not, something which quietly plagued me over the years (and still does). An imposter syndrome of sorts. How, me, Max Skittle, couldn't possibly be good enough to be a doctor. Partly too because it makes me feel like I'm failing to meet the construct of what modern society expects of me, a strong and confident man. Not one who cries because he's overworked one day.

In the heat of the moment it made me feel like I was failing. Failing my patients. Failing to achieve all this and confirm that I am indeed an imposter. While I don't think the imposter syndrome will ever quickly disappear, I do realise that the latter – society's expectation of me – can go and fuck itself. Male or female, to express a spectrum of emotion, to be brave enough to show them as you face forward to society, isn't a vulnerability: it's a celebration.

Wednesday, 20th March

So far, so good. No dramas, no deaths. Nobody (new) hates me. I haven't even cried. As I walk towards the house of 89-year-old Mrs Kooyker, I can't help but smile internally about these small yet immensely powerful victories that keep me sane. This home visit – a review of Mrs Kooyker's constipation – should add to this. She's living with a very advanced dementia and suffers constipation quite badly – collateral damage of her long-term pain medication cocktail and, I suspect, an ageing bowel.

The phone call from the carers this morning flagged the concern: she hasn't had a poo in over a week, despite being given three different laxatives each day. The medical maths doesn't add up, so here I am, *rata-tat-tat-ing* on her front door. The carer opens it, and after brief pleasantries, I'm in the living room of Mr and Mrs Kooyker's family home – Mr Kooyker having passed away over a decade ago. I smile – you can see how he lives on through the few well-positioned smiling photos of married life. Tall, proud, and honoured, they stand next to her hospital bed, now occupying the centre space of the room.

Mrs Kooyker is fast asleep. I look back to a photo of her more than thirty years ago. She was very beautiful. Still is. Electric smile.

'*Been like that all day*,' the carer adds, breaking my train of thought. I never got her name but it seems too late now to backtrack to the detail. I make a mental note that I really need to be better with carer names. I look through her care-plan record and true to their call, she's not had a recorded poo for nine days now. Given the degree of dementia, a history from her probably isn't going to add too much – and to be honest, most likely it'll distress her even more. I leave her sleeping and check her observations. Gently lifting her arm up, I slip the blood pressure cuff on: normal. Pulse check: normal.

After putting the blood pressure cuff away in my bag (now an immediate habit as I hate leaving equipment at home visits – always embarrassing to have to go back and collect it), I pop the oxygen saturation probe on her finger. OK, 95 per cent. Not great but good enough (for her age, long ex-smoking history, and lying flat). Temperature: normal. Yet as I move to place my stethoscope over her heart – and now physically closer to the top of her chest in order to do this – I can't help but notice it's moving up and down pretty quickly *and* shallow. I move the stethoscope off. This isn't right. I time her breathing rate: thirty-three breaths a minute. I recheck to make sure I'm not just fucking the maths – I'm not.

It seems Mrs Kooyker's constipation is going to have to wait (although it's probably a contributory factor, if bad enough) as she's got bigger problems than that – I think she's in type 2 respiratory failure. Clinically, this means not only is she struggling to get oxygen into her body, she's likely finding it hard to get carbon dioxide out of her body.

I step back and look at her: *Shit. She's not sleeping, she's drowsy.* I suspect her carbon dioxide levels have built up and reduced her level of consciousness. As I end the call with her son, her next of kin, I now know that the family wishes (on Mrs Kooyker's behalf) are for her to have every level of treatment possible, including going to hospital. This makes my decision straightforward. I call for an ambulance. In the meantime, I do what I can, propping Mrs Kooyker up so she can breathe a little more easily and monitoring her observations. Sadly, I've no additional oxygen to give her.

Had we not called for an ambulance, I expect she'd be peacefully – and painlessly – dead within the next few hours. Yet, whether or not I think – for someone with this degree of advanced dementia – that this would be the kinder option, it really doesn't matter. I can only give the information and help the family make an informed decision in a situation when the patient can't do it for themselves (or, as in the case of Mrs Kooyker, hasn't stated their future treatment wishes before they became ill).

Twelve minutes later, the ambulance arrives. Fifteen minutes after that, Mrs Kooyker is carried out on a stretcher and on her way to hospital. I'd be very surprised if she sees life outside it again – a one-way trip.

Wouldn't she have preferred to die at home?

I warn the family of the poor prognosis. They almost ignore this. Their focus, solely on treatment. Walking back to the surgery, I feel a sense of calm. Don't ask me why, no idea. Maybe because it was straightforward? About the medicine and for once not everything in-between?

Perhaps.

I call Alice and have a chat about her morning with our increasingly energetic monster, William.

Calm turns to love.

Thursday, 21st March

I've greased the wheels now. I re-read the email one more time, making sure it sounds casual enough for our practice manager, Jasper, not to worry, but transparent enough to know there's something important I want to discuss. I hover the mouse icon over SEND. *Click!* And with that, the wheels are set in motion to request the meeting where I'll formally hand my notice in. For work to learn that I'm leaving them. Pretty important to follow through now, especially since we've already found a cottage to rent in June and got a buyer interested in our city flat.

I just need to keep all those proverbial plates spinning a little bit longer . . .

Saturday, 23rd March

Another weekend, another swimming lesson. I hold the water in my mouth as William once again bobs around in front of me – now just a slightly larger potato overboard from a shipping container. He's had to ditch the stripper hot pants, thanks to his thighs now precluding him from gaining entry despite Alice's best efforts. Instead, we now proudly sport matching palm-tree board shorts.

Subconsciously, I'm trying to be that cool dad. Reality however hits as I view my own gut, bobbing around in the clear water. Aspirations wane. A vertically stunted walrus in palm-tree board shorts hardly screams sex appeal after all. My attention turns to the water, warm on the inside of my cheeks. I take in the six other doubly incontinent infants as our familiar swim instructor, Hal, gets us to position our own child in front of us. As I stare into William's big brown eyes, him looking clueless as ever, I realise my predicament: this mouth's – *my* mouth's – contents is probably 75 per cent urine. My eyes burn into Hal.

Just give us the green light, mate, I think. Please.

A bit slips down my throat involuntarily. I hope, at the very least, it's William's urine. Finally, Hal gives us the nod.

Game time.

I turn to my darling boy. He gives me a big unsuspecting gummy smile. And with that, I spit my mouth, full of urine, into his.

It's called *water confidence* apparently.

Monday, 25th March

Jasper's confirmed our meeting for after my morning clinic this Wednesday.

I feel sick again.

Wednesday, 27th March

Lying on my examination couch, I feel like a goldfish. Out of water. Gulping for air. I shift my body to a more comfortable position and try to work out how many patients I've had on here. I do try. Briefly. Then give up. I can't focus. My hands sweaty, my legs fidgety. My heart knocks on my chest wall as if to check I'm still there.

It must be soon.

Leaning up to catch a glimpse of the clock, I see it's time. Time to break the news to Jasper that I'm leaving the surgery. It all feels so massive. More goldfish gulping. Still no water. I've never left a job before, nor, thankfully, been fired (yet). I realise this means I've no past experience to really know how to do it properly.

Is it like breaking up with a girlfriend? Shit, that's no help. I was always dumped.

Seems I'm heading in blind. *Shit.* No, really. *Shit.* I mean, maybe I shouldn't be doing this? Maybe it's not too late. Maybe I could just go in and tell Jasper that I wanted the meeting because I really want that big leather high-backed power chair I badgered him about last November. Maybe Alice, William, and I should just stay in the city. It's fine after all, we can make it work. There are tons of positives to city life.

Maybe. Maybe. Maybe.

I take a deep breath, aware I'm flapping.

Get a grip.

I look in the mirror: a different person from seven months ago glances back at me. More tired in the face, perhaps. I smile. Because behind the tiredness is a life far richer, far more motivating, far happier. I think of Alice and William. As if reading my faltering mind, a message from Alice pops up on my iPhone screen: a photo of her and William lying in bed with his favourite teddy – a dog – called *doglett* (*please, don't ask*) with the words: *GOOD LUCK. WE LOVE YOU. A&W X.*

Doubt blows away. I get up off the couch, I switch my mind from manual to automatic and select *drive*. I march to Jasper's office to give in my notice. Fast forward two minutes and Jasper is looking at me. Nervous. Him. No longer me. I smile. Calm. I roll out a few GP tricks used when breaking bad news. I tilt my head, I fire a warning shot, *'I've got some news you're probably not going to want to hear, mate.'* And then, as he leans in, stretching his hands out across the desk to mine, in a sort of *oh fuck, please don't do what you're about to do* way, I drop the guillotine: I tell him that I'm formally giving my notice to leave their employment at the start of June this year.

As the words finish, I hand him the letter which, if he'd chosen not to hear them, spell them out in black and white, letter by letter. He buries his head against the table. I fight not to say the word *sorry* because the first truth is I'm not. The second truth is that this surgery will very easily replace me. I am a good GP, but hopefully they'll find a *great* GP, someone who doesn't get so many complaints. I sit patiently, increasingly calm now that the fatal blow has been dealt. The guillotine resting idle, complete. I wait for Jasper to peel himself off the desk. When he finally does, he looks to me, *'Bloody hell, Max.'* I smile and shrug my shoulders innocently, telling him it's nothing personal. And it's not – he can blame William, I add.

Fifteen minutes later, I'm walking back to my consultation room. I sit in my chair and spin around unevenly (the broken wheel has remained broken since June now . . .). Mine for only another ten weeks. And after that, well, it's anyone's guess.

A blank canvas. It's been a while since I've seen one of those. How exciting!

Friday, 29th March

It's fair to say I'm exhausted. It's been forty-eight hours of fairly tricky conversations as I broke the news of my departure to the other GPs, nurses, and reception team at the surgery. It was also a fascinating insight into my place within it. A full spectrum of reactions, from total (and concerningly excessive) devastation to complete indifference (naming no names, Dr Phil). Which is why right now, I'm more than happy to sit back and relax for a few minutes as my Chinese translator chats away to my last patient of the day, Mr Li. I say *a few minutes* very deliberately. Take, for example, my last question – I asked the translator to ask Mr Li if he's got any pain in his chest. Mr Li's reply in Chinese is a hearty *twenty-two* seconds long (I timed it. Discreetly). The translator's translation after a brief pause, is simply, *'No.'* I raise an eyebrow.

Knowing nothing about the Chinese language, I'm chalking this temporal discrepancy down to my linguistic ignorance. That, or this translator doesn't even speak Chinese and is completely fleecing me by making up any old shit. Either way, I don't argue. It's the answer on a Friday afternoon that I'm looking for.

I sit back and listen to some more potentially made-up answers, slowly but surely relaxing into the weekend.

APRIL 2019

Wednesday, 3rd April

I'm sitting on the bus home after an uneventful first half to the week. It's packed, like it always is. And I'm tired, like I always am. The day should have been a seven out of ten on the patient-irritant scale (namely because the chair I was given to sit on during my home visit broke on first pressure, directing me onto a cat-shit ridden carpet). I should have been frustrated. Angry. Definitely stressed. But I wasn't. I'm still not, even now. Instead, I'm just feeling, well, pretty fucking Zen.

I budge over some more as four shopping bags attached to a tiny old lady tip onto the seat next to me. I smile. Nothing back. Just a dead stare ahead, the new societal *modus operandi* in this city, it feels. I hear it's different in the countryside. Well, that's what the TV show, *Countryfile,* suggests anyway. I shuffle at the thought of it all. Excited, despite the restriction of four shopping bags and a tiny old lady. I've been thinking a lot about ducks today. Mainly because 'Five Little Ducks' is the last song I sing to William before his bedtime. And of course, it's not the first time I've thought about them – if you remember, Alice and I at the wedding last September. I've realised if I were ever to turn into a duck, I'd currently be the top half, gliding serenely along surface water, navigating the chaos. Unflappable. Effortless.

It seems that perhaps gone are the days when I was more the bottom half of a duck, legs frantically kicking, a constant fight against the resistance of the water beneath. Against life. What changed? Who the hell knows. Maybe it was just the action of giving in my notice to work. Formalising the beginning of the end for one of life's chapters. Galvanising the start of the next. The new adventure. Maybe it would have happened anyway. Maybe this Zen-like state is all transient and tomorrow I'll return to being another stressed GP, another body to the endless homogeneity. Who knows? Who *ever* knows?

I try another smile at the four bags and the tiny old lady. Again, nothing. Well, maybe a hint of a smile from the bags. A crinkle perhaps. I suppose what I can say is right now, my life order has me in a good place. I'm a father, husband, and then a GP. I work to live, not live to work.

Greeting card clichés left, right, and centre.

Thursday, 4th April

Sometimes the cases I find hardest are the ones closest to home. Fran and Mike sit opposite me holding hands. I like them a lot. They're both in their late twenties, recently married, and people I'd imagine meeting through my own friendship groups. Well, I say *my* friendship groups, what I mean is *Alice's* friendship groups. She's the popular one with all the mates, I'm just her antisocial husband whose been adopted by them as part of the marriage contract they automatically entered into.

Fran has been trying to get pregnant with her husband, Mike, for eleven months now and it's just not happening for them. After a quick reminder of their past medical histories on the screen, I spin my chair around to face them and ask how they are. They wouldn't make it in television with the kind of fake, unrewarding smiles they flash at me. The *'yeah, you know, staying positive'* doesn't make it any more believable. I offer my own, equally artificial smile back: *'Sure.'* The elephant in the room is the huge unspoken pressures they're putting on themselves to get pregnant, sex no longer a pleasure but rather a functional task to be carried out for the seven days prior to ovulation and for the one day after. I know this is the elephant, by the way, as I've seen them both separately before in consultation. It's been raised separately by both of them. Of course, I can't tell them that (for confidentiality reasons, ironically).

Seeing them together in the one consultation, although a positive step, is still entry into uncharted waters. Our fake smiles run their course and I decide it's time to break the deadlock.

'How are you both doing?' I pause. *'And I mean,* really *doing.'*

A dangerously open question given the emotional swell that trying to have a baby brings. A glance is exchanged. I've seen it before. The couple signals, the pre-planned attack, the green light to *GO! GO! GO!* And, after a brief shuffle in their seats, that's exactly what they do: they tell me they'd like fertility testing. I nod in a way that I hope lets them know it's alright to ask for this, that I understand. Besides, I could also see it a mile off. What else would they want from me? And I should add, *I really do get it.* Alice and I didn't have a golden-paved road to William. It took time and we had our own detours. So, fuelled by my own experience, I naturally want to help. I get it.

I sit up, clear my throat, and explain how this works on the NHS. Since they're approaching the twelve-month marker of trying to conceive, yes, we can begin organising fertility testing. As an aside, because I know it's often a topic people think of with fertility, *in vitro fertilisation (IVF)* is offered to women and couples on the NHS – but this comes with a huge list of complex criteria – one which varies based on where you live (hence the IVF *postcode lottery*). This includes body mass index, age, and controversially that neither of the couple have a child from any previous relationships – something that's often bloody hard to discuss with any couples I see in my surgery exploring this option. I mean, you try telling someone their ineligible because their partner has an 18-year-old son or because of their age. It can only go down one way – badly. Back to Fran and Mike.Their shoulders start to relax and two separate puffs of exhaled air transit towards me.

'But,' the air is instantaneously reclaimed back into their lungs, *'your chances of* naturally *conceiving are still extremely good. Up to 90 per cent after two years.'*

Now sure, everyone wants to hear 100 per cent, but this is real life. As a GP, I've got a responsibility to deal in reality. Painting unrealistic expectations is a clear recipe for disaster. *Major disaster.* They nod, understanding of this. Still, I expect they will be blinded a little by the potential that having these tests will bring.

Answers. Reassurances. Results. A baby.

For Fran, it starts with a blood test to check one of her female hormones called progesterone. This needs to be taken seven days before her next period (used to help confirm that she's ovulating). As she has a regular menstrual cycle and no other health issues, she doesn't need any other more specialised blood tests for now. That's the better news. The less-good news is that she (and Mike) will also need a chlamydia test. Explaining this to a couple is always a bit like running nails down a chalkboard. I reassure them it's simply a necessary evil if they want any future fertility specialist referral to be accepted. They both again adjust in their seats, internally wincing at the thought of doing a test that they probably thought they'd left back in their teens. For Mike as well, he *is* going straight back to his teens. You see, for him, it's a little less about the *pain* of a blood test, and a little more about the *pleasure* of having to masturbate – albeit into a plastic sterile sample pot in a hospital outpatient department full of other men, all waiting to do the same. The semen sample is a simple way to check the quality and quantity of his sperm.

As I deliver the news to him, his eyes raise in an *oh, right* reaction. Clinical masturbation, you can't make this stuff up. The last poor bloke I saw in clinic who had to do this told me how he was ambushed by his wife back home afterwards with the question, *'Well, who did you think of?'* There is, I suspect, no safe way to answer this question. Unfortunately for him, his answer scored him *nil points* after he told her she didn't need to worry as they had porn there. Hard to claw back from that.

Ten minutes later, Fran and Mike move to get up, now armed with their test forms and a new (unhealthy) sense of urgency. Horses bolting the gates. I decide to sit them back down again for a minute and recap on the importance of having regular sex. To not make it into something on their to-do list that they tick off each fertile month – stress and pressure massively impact on sperm quality and fertility potential. So, I explain with a smile, *'Keep having fun.'* There ended my sex therapist soundbite to them (and thereby building upon my similarly themed success from when I helped Lea last November with her *big cock* problem). They leave, pretending to be calmer, me, knowing they're not.

To not know whether you can have a baby is one of the most emotionally draining roller coasters imaginable. People have a perception of what their life will be like. And for many it never enters their mind that the road to that life might be paved with detours, road blocks, and even dead ends. It tests a person – and a couple – physically, psychologically, emotionally in a way that's hard to quantify. So powerful, it can too, make or break even the strongest of relationships. At times, it rips you to pieces, from the inside out. Helpless.

I finishing typing my notes and can't help but hope that for Fran and Mike, it's a road they can avoid.

Sunday, 7th April

Lazy Sunday morning *fail.* Tried to feed William in bed with some pureed pear and yoghurt while Alice was at the gym. For a little fella, it's amazing how high up the wall he can flick it all. Newly painted, just to add to the pain of it all. I expect Alice will start speaking to me again sometime this afternoon – once I've cleaned the walls and thought of a way not to make it sound like a ridiculously ill-conceived idea. Which, in hindsight, it definitely was.

Tuesday, 9th April

I've never really been *embarrassed* before in a consultation. Until now. I also never thought, if the day should ever come, that it would be arriving in the heavily built form of Frank, a 44-year-old builder who I diagnosed with a compulsion to watch porn about six months ago. He's got a habit fierce enough to frighten off a well-seasoned Hugh Hefner. And one that's significantly impacting his quality of life – watching porn placed in importance above his family, work, and social life. It hints towards addiction (because that's what can happen, your life is taken over at the behest of all else you value and hold dear, no matter the cost) but as yet, porn addiction isn't a formally identified condition in the UK.

I shift, uneasy in my seat. I swallow a cup of cold coffee in an attempt to mask the lump cycling up and down in my throat. My cheeks flush with a glowing red. I trip over my words and I try to mask the awkward smile I want to release.

I mean, come on, seriously, what the fuck do I say to this?

He says it again, in case I didn't hear him the first time.

'Dr Max, you really are the best thing that's ever happened to me.' I nod. Although I think for Frank, that was probably superfast broadband. *'YOU . . . you are my medicine.'*

Dear God!

With little to come back with, I nod once more, and tell him that's it's my pleasure. I then ruin it by telling him that it's moments like these that get me up in the morning. I die a little inside at what's just come out of my mouth. This isn't some bloody Mills & Boon novel chapter finale, not to mention all the metaphorical erection connotations I've just unloaded. There we go again. I fight to stop talking – yet for once I really don't want silence – it giving even more space for Frank to serenade me further.

I sit back from him, allowing a physical space between us to grow and diffuse what's fast escalating into a patient – doctor *love-in.* And what a pair. The burley builder and the portly GP in a starched shirt with baby vomit on the cuff (discreetly hidden, I might add). I clear my throat and redirect the energy in the room towards what's next for him. More of the same, that's all he wants. I nod. What Frank's saying is that he just wants to keep seeing me. In his mind, I'm his medicine.

Quite the accolade. Alice would laugh her head off at the thought of this. Frank hasn't gone completely mad. He does, after all, acknowledge the psychological talking therapy has helped, as do the group meetings. Also, he has a good online support network (although I do find the idea of an *online* support group for a someone with a porn addiction desperately ironic). Despite that, he says it's talking to me every month or so about how he's been doing that has really helped him.

I look on, disbelieving. I mean, I'm clueless. For the majority of our consultations, I'm quite literally just chatting to him. Most of the time, I just say, *'Frank, don't look at porn,'* and ask if the fissures in his family are yet beginning to heal. You don't really need to be a GP to do that. Yet I can see in his face that he means it. This isn't the first time a patient has utilised me as their GP in this way; it won't be the last either. People see their GP, rightly or wrongly, as someone to not only get expert advice on their conditions from but as an impartial (and confidential) sounding board to check they're on the right path to recovery. Which makes sense to me, because being a GP isn't just about using drugs and tests to treat conditions. The spoken word and a sympathetic ear can be equally therapeutic in the right circumstances.

So, with this in mind, and with my new Zen mindset, now that my work notice has been handed in, I accept Frank's comments warmly. I smile. As part of the ongoing positive feedback loop for his progress, I also book a telephone call to speak to me in four weeks. Why fight it? Like I said, sometimes it's not about the drugs or the therapies or the specialist referrals, sometimes it's about sitting down for ten minutes and talking it out.

I'm basically a pub.

Wednesday, 10th April

I was right: Alice laughed. A lot. Last night, and then again this morning.

Thanks, my love.

Thursday, 11th April

I mean literally, quite literally, the moment after I'd taken off the *only* sodding pair of disposable gloves I've got with me, Mrs Abbeville tells me about the discharge oozing from somewhere deep between the toes on her left foot. Five minutes later, I walk back from her home visit with only one mantra intrinsically circulating my head – *don't touch your face, don't touch your face, don't touch your face* – full tubs of alcohol gel and medical industry strength soap being only a five-minute walk away.

Hands, you took a hit for me today. I owe you.

Friday, 12th April

Usually when I look through my pathology results late on a Friday afternoon, I do so with only one eye open – and a sense of impending doom. There's always the fear of coming across an absolute howler of a blood test result. *Waiting for you. Because it's Friday.* And shit things often take place as you're a finger-tip away from the weekend.

I take a sip of coffee, trying, as I have for most of the day, to ignore the curdled milk floating around in it. Forty-three results cleared. No dramas yet, three to go. The clock ticks on like my own personal metronomic cheerleader. One to go. *Fuck. Seriously?* When a haemoglobin (basically, your blood) result reads 71 grams per litre of blood (g/L) (the normal adult range is between 120 and 180 g/L) from a blood test taken this morning – and three months ago, it was 105 g/L – alarm bells should ring. And if they don't, someone needs to look for a new career (and a lawyer).

I click through to the patient notes. It's Jeffrey Wilkins. He's a lovely old boy who at eighty-nine years old has a medical history that makes for pretty sporty reading. He has an irregular heart rhythm (for which he's on a medication that thins his blood – perfect, just what you need when your results suggest you're losing blood), stage 4 chronic kidney disease (there are only five stages – and the higher the number the worse it is), recurrent falls, and previous bowel cancer. If you tried to think of the perfect clinical storm, you'd meet someone like Jeffrey. With all that history, it's also not surprising that his haemoglobin is lower than the normal range – when you have that much disease, it will inevitably be affected (we call it *anaemia of chronic disease*, rather unoriginally). It just shouldn't drop *that* low.

I dial. The phone rings, my feet tap impatiently.

God, I hope he's not already dead.

Jeffrey's clearly losing blood from somewhere. Question is, is he having any symptoms that could be due to so much blood loss, and perhaps more importantly, where's the blood being lost from? Oh yes, and thirdly, where the hell is it all going? The fact that he's on a medicine designed to make his blood extra-thin is just extra shit for Jeffrey.

I stand up: he's answered the phone. I breathe a sigh of relief that I've at least got through to him – and that he's not dead. Over the next few minutes I explain to him what his blood test shows and my concerns. Turns out he *has* been feeling more short of breath recently (that'll be because your haemoglobin is crushingly low and so not carrying enough oxygen around your body, Jeff, I explain in a more sensitive manner).

'Well, I'm just having my tea . . .' His response after I tell him I want to call an ambulance for him. I try to explain as clearly as I can that I'd like him to be alive to enjoy his tea *tomorrow* as well – and so to please just let me do this for him. Begrudgingly, he agrees. I sit back down, relieved. There have been times before when I've quite literally had to march around to a patient's house and convince them to go to hospital. Selfishly, I didn't want to have to do this today, not on a Friday night.

Not on Fajita Friday.

Once Jeffrey's finished his pudding, I've asked him to pack an overnight bag, all of his medicines, and to be ready to be picked up within the next hour. I also call his son for him and let him know what's going on. He takes the news like a son that's had to do this dance with his father before, and tells me he'll be over to join his father at home shortly. Three more phone calls later (the third to the medical team at the hospital, so they know to expect Jeffrey), and an ambulance is on its way.

I turn off the computer and can't help but glance to my once metronomic cheerleader, now reading 7:02pm. *Some fucking cheerleader you are now.* Alice will have put William down to sleep already, so there's no rush anymore. I'll give her some time to herself, a rare commodity nowadays. And with that, I stroll out of the surgery towards home, slowly. Putting work behind me for another week – although quietly keeping my fingers crossed for Jeffrey this weekend.

I hope he enjoyed his pudding.

Sunday, 14th April

Read an article this weekend about a hospital in London having a therapy cat. Wonder whether something similar would work at our GP surgery. I mean, we don't have a cat, but we could use William – hand him around for patients to cuddle. Therapy and free childcare for when Alice returns to work. What's not to love? Hang on, just realised – it's a bit late now, I'll be leaving in two months.

Oh, well!

Monday, 15th April

Back to work and as standard for a Monday, the world's gone totally fucking mad.

'Are you serious?'

It's the only question I have for Pippa and her mother (not surprisingly, Dad ducked out of this one).

'Yeah, they need a letter. And they said, you need to see your GP about it.'

That phrase, by the way, *see your GP about it*, is like a million untrimmed fingernails being dragged down a freshly glazed chalkboard to a GP – largely because it's code for *fuck off and let someone else deal with it*. And that is lazy. Somewhere in my top three of loathed attributes in any person.

As I take in what Pippa's asking me again – that the school are demanding a permission letter to excuse her from her lessons when needed, so she can go and change a sanitary towel for her heavy menstrual periods – I shake my head, in despair above anything else.

How anally retentive and insensitive can an institution be?

I stare at the computer, still disbelieving that this poor young girl has been forced to come in and vocalise this intimate issue with me. And then ask for a letter. I look to her and smile, releasing any anger that was building up (part of the Zen vibe I'm still on).

'Of course I will. And don't worry, I'll make it crystal clear.'

By that, I mean I'm going to tell her school what bloody idiots they are for making her do this and that they should be ashamed of themselves. Plus, if a letter from a GP is held in such high regard, then I'm really going to turn the screw. I add in the letter that Pippa is not to be asked why she needs to be excused – because this may cause embarrassment and further stigmatise (which is, by the way, *exactly* what their request has done) what is a completely natural physiological process.

As Pippa and her mother leave, two copies of the letter in hand, I add that if the school has any more archaic requests, they should be told to contact me *directly*. I sit back down after they leave and stare into nothing, turning over the last five minutes of lunacy in my mind.

Seriously, world, whatever happened to common sense?

Wednesday, 17th April

There's nothing quite like having a thank-you card on your shelf to give patients renewed confidence that you're not a total moron. And on an even more basic level, it just makes you feel great. I once fleetingly toyed with the idea of writing my own cards to put on my shelf, but realised my various professional governing bodies would most likely frown upon such creativity. Which is why to be sitting here before the start of my morning clinic, reading my thank-you card from Nick – the young lad I sent to hospital in January with a suspected new diagnosis of type 1 diabetes mellitus (later confirmed in hospital) – has me grinning from ear to ear.

He writes that he's adjusting to his new medicines, has got his energy back, and is now the vice-captain of the school rugby team. He thanks me for taking the time to care enough and show enough interest in him to work out what was wrong. I reach up and put the card on my shelf. Pride of place, next to Alice's latest dead pot plant.

Thanks, mate. You've made my day!

Friday, 19th April

A phoenix from the ashes . . . Mrs Kooyker *did* get discharged home after nearly a month in hospital. Surprised is an understatement, I'll have what she's having.

Indestructible.

Monday, 22nd April

A new week brings a new surprise: a good one this time. I give her a hug. A lot of water has clearly passed under Natalia's metaphorical bridge in the last seven months. When I last saw her in September last year, she was a very different woman. Unrecognisable. She was drowning. Drowning in an abusive marriage, and with her son, Ethan, who was in only a matter of time going to bear witness to it.

Natalia looks *so* well today. She beams a huge smile as she exits my hug and sits down. The first thing to notice is just how confident she is, holding herself tall and speaking with a gentle determination that only hid in the shadows of her life when I last saw her. She's getting a divorce (and happily so, having triggered the proceedings herself). She and Ethan are now renting a flat of their own. She's even started working again – and considering some further higher education study. She has independence. She sees a new path ahead. One without her scab of a husband (who, yes, I still have to treat as a patient from time to time).

I haven't stopped smiling. I haven't said a single word, I've just nodded. Smiled. Nodded. Smiled. Listening intently to the journey she's been on. It's clear it's not been one without challenge as anyone would expect when an abuser is involved. Seeing the charity worker really helped and Natalia got support, access to a lawyer for advice, and guidance on how to cleanly and safely extricate herself and Ethan with surgical precision from the toxic relationship. And she has – *they have.*

My biggest smile is reserved for when she tells me about Ethan: he's come out of his shell more and is doing well in school again. What more could I ask for? A thank-you card? Joking! I sit back and having hardly said anything, suddenly realise that Natalia may be here for a completely different reason – not at all related to the abuse she was victim of. It's funny, when people have massive life events like this, it's easy to get so blinded by them that you don't see that the other grumbling, day-to-day health issues still exist – life keeps turning – even in the face of trauma.

I raise my eyebrows in surprise. Natalia's here for no other reason, she just wanted to come and see me. And to thank me. Another smile breaks across my face. I sit here in a genuine state of happiness for her and Ethan. It makes all of the countless consultations where I'm told I'm *not doing enough*, I'm *not fixing their* (impossible-to-fix) *problems*, and my personal favourite, that I clearly *don't care,* all totally worthwhile and fully palatable.

After Natalia leaves, I'm left staring at her clinical notes screen. Once again. How do I put her strength into words? First, I just type *Thriving.* Then delete it for something fuller that might make a little more sense if another doctor were ever to read her notes. *A previous victim of domestic violence, now a survivor. And thriving in life.*

I hope others can take optimism from her story and see that it is never *impossible* to break away.

Tuesday, 23rd April

Eyes, I bloody hate eyes. By this, I mean it's the one part of the body that I don't think I'll really ever be confident in treating – at all really. In fact, I'm positively convinced that I was asleep during all eye-related lectures throughout medical school. Beyond a simple and common eye infection (called conjunctivitis), anyone with an eye problem will be unknowingly joining me in deep, murky, and uncharted waters.

Remember, a GP is a General Practitioner. Hence *Jack of all trades, master of none.* Although as patient problems become increasingly complicated, and more of the subsequent long-term management redirected back to the GPs from hospitals (who are, I should add, also overwhelmed with demand), this phrase doesn't ring as true as it once did. And this should therefore be very bad news for Graham, currently sitting opposite me – in dark sunglasses. At 9:10am. On a not particularly sunny morning.

Graham's sunglasses are naturally therefore a bit of a red flag. But what he doesn't realise is that it is, in fact, his unbelievably luckiest of days. Because I, for reasons unbeknown to me, attended a one-day conference on ophthalmological medicine (that's the name of the eye medicine and surgery speciality) last weekend. This means that I'm currently a total wizard on eye conditions. Graham sits here with me, glasses still on despite both of us being in the dark now the strip lighting's off and the blinds drawn, as I overenthusiastically unload a systematic set of eye history questions at him. Sudden onset, red and painful eye with sensitivity to light (hence the shades) and blurred vision.

I nod with more passion than I've ever had for an eye-problem patient before. *Shit.* I sit back, amazed. *I've got it.* Graham has acute anterior uveitis – a serious inflammatory condition affecting the front part of the eye. I've genuinely never seen it before and so am (unsubtly) thrilled. I explain to him that he needs to go to the local hospital, where the ophthalmology (*remember that word, pub quizzers*) team are. They'll be able to examine him with specialist equipment, confirm the diagnosis, and start treatment (eye drops).

He nods in my general direction, but looking like Stevie Wonder, I can only assume he's actually looking *at* me. With that, I send him off to the hospital, referral letter in hand, before I make a quick call to the ophthalmology team to let them know that he's on his way to them.

Hopefully . . . If he can see where he's going.

I make a mental note to play some Stevie later tonight to William, continuing his music greats education.

Wednesday, 24th April

Well, well . . . perhaps miracles aren't just the reserve of children's stories after all. Standing here, I can't quite believe my eyes. Patsy (all 142.6kg/22.4 stone of her). Alive. In her own home. And still wearing her same legendary smile across her face. No wonder. It looks to me like she's been spoiled on the NHS – now lying on a new large-framed hospital bed (I assume there *is* a bed underneath Patsy, anyway) and with a shiny and rather unsubtle ceiling-mounted mechanical hoist glistening over her.

I close my eyes for a brief second and picture the front of her house as I walked in. Nope. No Patsy-sized hole outlined, *in memoriam*, by fresh bricks and mortar. Patsy gathers steam to reposition herself using the various hoist pullies dangling from the steelworks now bolted to her ceiling. As I wait, I glance over some more of her disastrously long hospital discharge summary, a clinical version of Tolstoy's *War and Peace.* Not surprising if you've been a hospital patient since November the year before.

I look up to a now more upright Patsy. *'You had quite the lengthy hospital stay, didn't you, Patsy?'* She laughs out loud, telling me she thought she'd never leave.

No shit. Me too. Then again, I didn't think she'd even *get in*, forever entombed in her home. The purpose of my visit is administrative more than anything else. Nobody from the surgery has seen her in a while (partly because she's been enjoying hospital sponge-baths courtesy of some unsuspecting locum-agency healthcare assistant), so we needed to check in on her. I jumped at the chance, seeing as she's in my top five favourite patients of all time. Realising as I say this, that I'm making a complete rookie error, I let, *'So can I help make things any better for you?'* escape my mouth. I hold my breath, knowing the fuse is lit.

Patsy's not looking at me, instead currently doing what I can only describe as knocking her arm fat and watching it swing from side to side.

'I'm fine, thanks.' She pauses before adding, *'Do you think I've lost weight?'*

The fuse goes out. I stare, unbelieving, at both remarks. The reality is I sadly doubt Patsy will ever shift a huge amount of weight, but still, I want to encourage her every step of the way. So, I lie. Again. And tell her I do think she looks slimmer around the face. And Patsy's *fine*, tells me she's happy. And so, having given her a big hug and kiss on the cheek, telling her to stay out of trouble – *and* hospital – I escape for an early lunch, aware of my own expanding tummy (especially since William's arrival).

Patsy's final impression on me is to buy a salad . . .

Friday, 26th April

Turns out it was acute anterior uveitis! If it wasn't on the computer, I could kiss Graham's discharge summary right now.

Sunday, 28th April

Alice has just returned to find William in an inflatable rubber ring. Rigged up to a rope. Being pulled across the kitchen floor. While The Rolling Stones' '(I Can't Get No) Satisfaction' blares out of all the speakers. Currently some way from explaining how this constitutes this Sunday's *nap time*.

Tuesday, 30th April

Lkxsd[wd skew]

I was going to write something profound (well, *semi*-profound) about this month as it's been a nice one, but William's currently sitting on my lap. It seems he's beaten me to it with this, his cack-handed contribution on the keyboard.

P.S. Still feeling Zen, team!

MAY 2019

Wednesday, 1st May

My final month at this surgery and it starts with the news that Mrs Kooyker died. It seems whatever she was having to give her that *Phoenix rising* status ran out. I run my finger back and forth over the mouse wheel as I stare, deep in thought, at the notification of death letter on my screen. I take a breath in. Hold it. Let my thoughts turn over a little more in my head. Then release it.

I nod to myself, a sort of processed acceptance. I think – *I hope* – she had a good death. After all, she died at home surrounded by her surviving family. She was comfortable. Pain-free. Distress-free. No more back and forth to the hospital. No more uncertainty.

Just peace in finality.

Friday, 3rd May

Seems Mrs Kooyker isn't the only one who ran out of a supply of magic. Mr South sits here, barking at me like some angry little pit bull from his chair in reception. I feel last month's Zen status slipping. He points at me. In high-definition slow motion, I see tiny flecks of frothy spit fly from the mouth I'd love to shut.

Readjustment on my Zen status. It's not slipping, there's been a fucking landslide. Much like when I was accused of murder in the waiting area last year (*so many happy memories here*), today's waiting-room occupants watch with a blend of abject horror and unplanned pleasure. I stand here, acutely aware that holding a bright pink mug with hearts on it (*I lost my mug last week*) is doing nothing for my overall defence – or attack – right now.

Mr South's problem, apart from intrinsically being a bit of a knob, is that he's been waiting to see me for nearly two weeks for a review of his chronic obstructive pulmonary disease (COPD, a breathing condition largely the result of cigarette smoking). As an aside, if my waiting times are creeping up, maybe this means I'm finally gaining in popularity? That, or we've got a lot of staff on annual leave. In any case, this is no-man's-land territory. I can't walk off towards the kitchen, that would look weak. But it's also so early in the morning that I'm not sure I can be arsed to really get into this right now.

My eyes flick to the other waiting-room patients. *Annoying.* I see some regulars of mine. This means I really should work to save face, avoiding the ensuing public humiliation by patient. Patients talk after all – and if I don't react, my ratings in the *Popular GP polls* could plummet. I shore up my posture and decide to commit to the fight. Mr South continues to bark, doing that thing knobs do in public when they feel they've got the momentum and upper hand – looking to other people for mutual support. He looks the wrong way, as I know Mr Peters on his left is seeing me for a rectal exam after a recently raised prostate blood test – so unless he wants me to choose my biggest, roughest finger, he'll not be supporting him.

I open my mouth to try to reason with him. *Barking.* I raise my hands in a way that says *calm down*, sadly further showcasing the pink heart mug to the wider waiting-area audience. More barking.

Goodbye, Zen.

I shout for the first time ever at work: *'STOP. Just STOP. Mr South, this is unacceptable! If you wish to see me, I will see you. But if you think this behaviour will be tolerated here, you are very, very* (I think I even growl at this point) *wrong.'* I inhale for my next chapter and verse: *'So have some manners – and* (I'm really on a roll now), *extend some courtesy to everyone else around you in this waiting room – people who may have come for any number of sensitive issues – and who do not need you shouting the place down as a prelude!'*

He stares at me. I can't quite tell if I've just kicked a pit bull in the balls – or tamed him. More staring. It would be an awkward silence if I wasn't distracted by the thought that he may well be about to stab me. He doesn't. Instead, in a last-ditch attempt to show dominance, he tells me how *we GPs are all the bloody same.* I look at him, pink heart mug held proudly: *'You're right, we are the same. Because we* all *bloody care!'*

A few nervous smiles evolve from the spectators. Like they've just seen the naughty schoolboy told off in class. And with the victory now surely mine, I go to get the coffee so desperately needed – especially if I'm going to have to sit through ten minutes of one-on-one time with this plonker.

Saturday, 4th May

It's been nearly a month and a half, yet I still can't get used to the fact that, at eight months old now, William's shit is looking more and more like an adult's: pasty, but, yes, definitely a little *log*-like.

I've seen a lot of weird stuff, but this is up there with some of the weirdest.

Tuesday, 7th May

After a quiet weekend, I'm back in work. Now, medication reviews in clinic are meant to be relatively straightforward. The patient comes in. You check what medications they're on. Find out how compliant they are. Ask if there are any side effects. And – most importantly for the patient – if they're working. It should be a sort of pharmacological celebration of previous efforts to get a health condition under control. And if it's not, then it's an opportunity to change or adjust medications, moving closer to that goal. Simple.

Unless you're Mrs Wojcik, a long-term UK resident, originally from Poland. Clearly here today to test me. Like a well-rehearsed drill, my body develops a sinking feeling. Mrs Wojcik rummages deep into her bag and hands me a thick (as in so thick, it has serious weight to it) brown A4 envelope – and a compact disc. Now this CD is another one of those red warning flags: it usually means someone's had radiological images, such as a CT scan (which combines multiple X-rays to make a detailed image of the area of the body scanned), which have been copied onto it. Through no fault of their own, a patient then thinks I can just pop the CD in my computer and review the images, like it's as easy as opening an email.

I've never once done this. Namely for two reasons. The first is that I'm no longer in medical school and so don't have to waste my time trying to interpret grainy black radiology images with some psychopathic surgeon barking at me. Instead I can just read the radiology report. Infinitely easier. The second is that the software needed to read a CD packed with complex radiological image data is not universal – and certainly not loaded onto my geriatric NHS computer with barely enough power and memory capacity to manage a Microsoft Word document before crashing. Yet, being the soft touch I am, I wander into the eye of the storm and take the A4 envelope and CD with a smile and an *'Oh, brilliant!'* Which I don't mean. At all.

It turns out Mrs Wojcik became bored of waiting for her regular six-monthly respiratory reviews with her long-term respiratory consultant on the NHS for her chronic lung condition – which has been brilliantly managed by them up to this point, I should add – and so decided, while visiting family in Poland, to pop in and see a respiratory specialist privately. Naturally, they changed every single bloody medication. And then prescribed it all in Polish.

I look up from a page of the report, not understanding a word of it, and glance at her quizzically. Mrs Wojcik tells me what it *roughly* translates as. I smile. That's sweet. I explain *roughly* doesn't quite cut it. Here we go . . . The air temperature drops with the same beat as her smile does. She straightens up – the universal patient sign for disapproval.

It's post-lunch. Caffeine has tickled my brain's neuroreceptors. I'm fired up, let's war! I explain that I cannot just alter all of her medications that have been meticulously titrated and monitored by her long-term NHS respiratory consultant just because she got bored of waiting.

It's the NHS, waiting should be its middle bloody name for Christ's sake!

I look at her more intently. It's hard to hide my annoyance. I don't agree with erratic private or overseas clinical input (especially when I can't even read the clinical letters) that then has the patient whipping the NHS with some leather-studded belt and expecting her to ask *how high?* And all because another one-off clinician in another country tells her to *please jump.* She looks pissed off. That's fine, it's important not to please every single patient. If I do that, it means I'm giving everyone what they *want.* Not what they *need.*

I neatly file away the letters and CD into the brown A4 envelope, tapping them down into it, to break the silence if for anything else. I then hand it back. She's furious. Luckily for me, she's also polite, and I can tell although she may have thought she would, she's not going to cause a fuss. I want to keep her on side – but need her to see *my side.* I explain I'll need this specialist to provide English translations of all these clinical letters. That I'll then share these with her long-term NHS respiratory consultant to see if these are sensible (and even available on the NHS) medications to prescribe. And that of course, if she's unhappy with any of this, she's always welcome to see another GP.

There, my cards on the table.

She leaves, much less smiley than when she arrived. Still, we can't have everything we want – I'm not bloody Father Christmas!

Wednesday, 8th May

Broken. Dishevelled. Unsure if it's day or night. Unsure if that even matters anymore. Unmistakably, Darren and Jenna are back. This time, as new parents. I stand at the door smiling as they peel around the corner, now transporting their precious cargo in a tank of a pram – yet to be stained irreparably with vomit, milk, and of course, shit. I remember how much Alice and I looked after our pram at the start with William, wiping it down every time it got a little city dirt on it. Now, it's a seasoned rally car for William.

Scratches. Mud. Blood. All badges of honour now worn on it.

Both reply with tired smiles. As they enter, I peer into the pram. Pink. Tons of it.

'Well, hello, Nancy, nice to meet you,' I whisper as she sleeps soundly. Wrapped. Protected. Loved. All of it very special – although – I lean back up and look at them both, *'Bloody exhausting, isn't it?'* They nod. Even the nod is tired. This is Nancy's eight-week check-up, a chance to look her over from head to toe and chat about any worries Mum and Dad may have. I love these sessions since it's a really rewarding part of my job, finally meeting the baby after caring for the mother during her pregnancy. Being an albeit small part of their journey to parenthood. And this is, after all, *very* new territory. One which little prepares you for. Like someone trying to describe what it's like to freefall without a parachute and then actually doing it.

Darren and Jenna give me the same response to my question that 99 per cent of lying new parents do – a sort of *yeah, but you know, it's just so great.* What they're actually saying is that it can, at times, be the most fucking horrendous thing in the world. No sleep. Constant fear of breaking your newborn child. Endless laundry. Nappy changes (that despite best efforts, still end up getting shit everywhere – like the fiddly metal bit of my watchstrap that today acted like a fork, carving neat lines into William's). Endless demand feeding. And all that's just the baby. Then there's the adult relationship. Sex is now just a noun rather than its more enjoyable verb. Your other half becomes something else. A teammate, a shift partner. But sure, apart from all that, bloody fabulous!

After we sit chatting for a few minutes (thankfully, everything's going well for them, making my job today a lot easier), I explain we need to get her out of the pram and onto the examination couch. There, she needs to be stripped down completely (including the nappy), so I can check her over. Their hearts break. I can hear it, no words required. After all, I'm asking them to wake their baby. Their current low-demand, sleeping, quiet baby.

What sort of person would do that? Me.

Not only that, over the next five minutes I'm going to shine lights in her eyes, fake drop her backwards (to test her Moro reflex – the one where their arms extend out like Jesus), poke her in the mouth, and push her hips in and out. And that's the highlight reel. There's a lot more. Then, after comprehensively pissing her off with all this, I'm going to just hand her back over, naked and screaming, for Darren and Jenna to deal with.

Five minutes later, that's exactly what I did. And exactly what happened. I turn to the new parents as they get Nancy dressed, simultaneously trying to soothe their now tiny pink beast, and reassure them that she's doing great. From her ten fingers and toes to the two perfectly beating femoral blood vessel pulses in her groins (this is to make sure there's no indication of an abnormal blood vessel exiting the heart, called a coarctation of the aorta). They smile at the news, though clearly pissed off that I couldn't have come to this conclusion via my initial peer over into her pram. I also tell them that they, as parents, are doing great – an important message as these early stages can fill any new parent with self-doubt.

After filling out Nancy's red book (every baby gets one – it's their personal health record that contains information about their growth and vaccinations status, for example), I send them packing. Quickly. As I open the door, I comment with a smile how healthy her lungs sound. More tired nods, more tired smiles. With just a hint of hatred this time. I give the door a gentle push and click it firmly shut. The screaming blunts slightly. I smile. I remember William's eight-week check – it seems so long ago now. He's already *eight months* old. Blink of an eye.

As I sit here in my chair, listening to the screams grow ever quieter as the distance between us matures, I think how much Darren and Jenna have changed. Three months ago, when I met them for the first time, they were at the doorstep of their new chapter. They were fresh, excited about the unknown. Now, this second time around, they're well and truly into it. Deep in this next eighteen-year long (and then some) chapter of their lives. It's because of this that the window into their lives I see today looks so very different. Rearranged. Upside down and turned around. And for what it's worth, from the sidelines, it looks like they're doing a brilliant job, even if they don't realise it.

Parenthood. I'm beginning to see is a wood for the trees type of situation that goes on for the rest of your life.

Friday, 10th May

It's not just me, right? It *would* be creepy if a patient books a phone consultation with you – and then, when you call them – they tell you that they're standing outside your consulting room.

Thought so.

Sunday, 12th May

This weekend is leaving me far too much space to think. I must have picked up four picture frames in a row now. William coming home for the first time. Alice nervously walking towards the church on our wedding day. My late grandparents smiling together. Our first wedding dance (to Stevie Wonder's 'Signed, Sealed, Delivered', if you're wondering). I look around our living room.

Shit, I'm in dangerous territory. Three beers in. On my own (Alice is out seeing some girlfriends and William's snoring face down in his nursery, one ear of his bunny rabbit comforter safely inserted into the corner of his mouth). Worst of all, I'm listening to Ed Sheeran's 'Perfect' (I know, tragic). I'm reminiscing. Snuck up on me after that first beer. I smile to myself: why fight it? I know I secretly love a reminiscing session. For all the hot air, I'm a softie deep down. I decide to escalate. I get out a photo album. As I turn the pages, I smile more and more. I pause. Sip my beer. For all of life's attempts at generating chaos over the last twelve months, I think I can now see *that* wood through the trees at last. I can see the bigger picture. *Our* bigger picture.

Out of the corner of my eye I catch a glimpse of the single sheet of paper on the kitchen table. That's the plan that Alice and I made only two months ago. Already it's got lots of now ticked boxes. Put this flat up for sale. *Tick.* Find a place to rent in the countryside. *Tick.* Join a locum GP agency there to get temporary work. *Tick.* Arrange for a removal van. *Tick.* Look for a nursery for William. *Tick.* Leaving drinks with work and friends. *Tick.* The list goes on and on . . . It fills the page in two columns, in fact. But ultimately, as I stare at it, I realise we're ready.

Ready for the move.

Just as well given the only boxes that remain unticked are *last day of work* (now agreed as Friday, 7th June) and *leave the city for good.* Not long now, not long at all. Just four weeks.

I return to the photo of our first wedding dance. Alice has her arms wrapped around me. We both look so excited. I know I still feel that way when I put my arms around her. And I'm pretty sure she feels the same. My eyes glaze.

For fuck's sake. Again, Max?

Really, I shake my head at the ridiculousness of my own internal monologue. Time to snap out of this. I put on the television and find the Rugby World Cup 2003 documentary I was part-way through – and attempt to quash this solo love-in, fast spiralling out of control.

Tuesday, 14th May

If you served it on a plate, it might look like a delicious strawberry flavoured fondant with an escaping ooze of freshly infused Madagascan vanilla custard. Instead, it's under Mr Littman's left armpit. And it's fucking massive. I gently poke it with a gloved index finger. It's so soft and squidgy, my finger almost sinks into it. At the same time as I press, a few bubbles of yellow cheesy, foul-smelling pus trickle out of its straining punctum (which is a bit like the mouth of a volcano).

'You said it was a small *lump?'*

I don't take my eyes off Mr Littman's monster of an abscess as I speak. It's fascinating for many reasons. First, just the indulgent thought that one big squeeze would burst this bad-boy wide-open, sending infected pus everywhere. Second, how on earth can Mr Littman even begin to think this is a *small* lump?

He looks down at me from behind bespectacled eyes and explains it's only been like this for few weeks.

'Right.'

It's the only response I have for someone who thinks a 10- × 10-centimetre volcanic abscess under one of his armpits isn't worth being seen sooner than after a few weeks. Transfixed, I continue to stare at it. Like it's about to give birth to something at any point and I can't miss the miracle moment. I poke it again, partly out of clinical interest. Partly just because it's so grim. Mr Littman also needs this sorted out quickly. As in *this afternoon, quickly.* With a past medical history that includes type 2 diabetes mellitus (albeit with excellent control of his blood sugars on his last tests), he's at higher risk not only of this abscess getting even bigger, but of developing sepsis (a life-threatening blood infection) – and then dying. All bad things.

He nods solemnly as I explain these facts to him.

'So, I should have come sooner?'

Wow, I'd hate to see what medical problems he has when he really panics.

The phone rings. I wait impatiently for the surgical registrar to answer. A very happy doctor answers the phone. I explain to Sophie, the surgical registrar, that I've got

Mr Littman with me here, who is going to bring her team an unbelievable amount of carnal pleasure with a ginormous abscess that needs to be incised (that is, sliced open with a scalpel) and drained. We share a rather one-sided exchange of just how pleasurable doing this incision is going to be, namely as I'm aware Mr Littman is sitting right next to me – who finally, I should add, is looking more appropriately anxious.

I place the phone receiver down. Referral accepted, plan made. And with that, I send Mr Littman and his abscess out the door and off to the hospital. I really hope nobody bangs into the side of him on his way there. If they do – *POP!* It'll all be over before the surgeons get to have their fun.

Wednesday, 15th May

Alice made me poached eggs this morning as a midweek treat. As I passed the knife across the perfectly domed egg-yolk roof, yellow, rich, gooey yolk free-flowed out and onto the toast.

It'll take a while, I expect, not to think of Mr Littman every time I do this.

Thursday, 16th May

The march towards my departure from work draws ever closer. Which means this day was always going to come. And, pathetically, if I could do *this* breakup by text message, I definitely would. Luckily for Mrs Tally, she's about to get one last phone call. The, *I think we need to talk* call. And, in light of her increasing dependency on me, I have – like some former teenage self, had I ever actually had to do the breaking up part – rehearsed what I'm going to say.

I sigh as I dial her number, knowing full well just how much shit she's going to give me for this. The phone rings. And it rings. And it rings. Hope rises in me. She's not going to answer. I've tried my best (a lie) to let her know I'm leaving. I could just hang u—

'Hello?'

A bit of wee escapes me, I'm sure. I try to respond with as much professional enthusiasm as I can muster, but Mrs Tally is a savvy old girl. She knows something's up – mainly since I'm calling her. Something she knows I try actively to avoid. What happens next is somewhat challenging. Questions are raised. Awkward questions.

'How can you leave me?' and *'But the carers are still so terrible!'* – a rhetorical question I've grown to understand. Finally, there's my favourite, *'Well, I can just register where you are.'* I bounce on the balls of my feet, painfully uncomfortable energy coursing through me. I say I'm sorry. That it's not her, it's me.

Another lie.

She circles around and asks the same questions again. I bounce some more, awkwardly answering the same as before. I glance down at my table. On the notepad, I've written a few inspirational statements in preparation for this point of the conversation – the point when I feel myself wavering. Buckling under the verbal might and omnipotent presence of Mrs Tally.

BE FIRM. BE STRONG. BASICALLY – DON'T BOTTLE IT. I read.

I let my forehead hit the desk. My words sound like some advertisement for an erectile dysfunction medication. She starts to sob. *Fuck, give me a dumping from a girlfriend any day.* I lift my now-aching head and with one final deep breath, blurt out, *'So sorry, Mrs Tally. Take care, goodbye.'* I put the phone down. And just like that, a memorable chapter of my clinical life closes. Ironically, one that had very little to do with medicine.

Still, I'll double-padlock this one.

Saturday, 18th May

This weekend is all about hiding. It was my work leaving drinks last night. Turned out to be that fatal combination of too much booze and the kind of deep and meaningful conversations that need to be locked away in a suitcase. Which is then weighted with rocks. Put in the trunk of a car. A car doused in petrol. And set alight. Before finally jacking the handbrake of its burnt-out smoking shell in the dead of night and rolling it into a stagnant lake. Forevermore.

So, let's all move on. It was lovely, that's the party line.

Tuesday, 21st May

Seven months on, they still haven't sold those singing garden gnomes. Mind you, totally believable when you think about it. I sit next to them once more, déjà vu blissfully sweeping over me. Mr and Mrs Leigh, legends of my patient top-five list. I glance around to check for any other new updates.

No new dreamcatchers. No new photos of perhaps, say, the more contemporary Trump administration. I don't think

Will Smith has done any new films either, so his Fresh Prince of Bel-Air photograph is still doing time on the Leigh's wall.

Clinically, I'm here to check on a rash that Mr Leigh's developed. He called me earlier about it. But of course, no GP can properly assess a rash over the phone and so, since it was a rare quiet day for home visits – and I wanted to tell them in person that I'm leaving the surgery – here I am. Turns out, on close inspection, he's got ringworm, a common fungal infection easily cleared up with some anti-fungal cream. Still, I do wish it didn't have to be in the creases of his groin.

Not a region of Mr Leigh I need to see before lunch.

Reassuringly, he tells me he'd sprayed some Lynx *down there, 'so, it wasn't too smelly for you, Max.'* I nod. They say it's the thought that counts. Sadly, it then gets a little awkward. Not a *keys in a bowl party* kind of awkward but a *we'd love to invite you and your family to Sunday lunch* awkward. I get that this might sound like a harmless invitation, but there are lines you don't cross as a GP. Boundaries can be blurred, perspective easily lost. So, I respectfully decline. They insist. I decline again. They insist some more. I sit there, thinking why the fuck couldn't they have just given me a singing garden gnome and be done with it?

Back to the wall. I look at my shoes, swallow, and decide to be cruel to be kind. I give them a *shit sandwich.* I explain that while incredibly flattered (*the first slice of bread*), we sadly won't be able to do that because it wouldn't be professional to do so in the capacity as their doctor (*the shit*), but will of course tell my wife how incredibly thoughtful you both are (*the second slice*). *Sandwich made.* I smile and shake my head gently from side to side as they begin to counterargue once again. They concede. Finally.

An awkward silence fills the room. Like a date that's going great, before you then kill it off by asking some uninspired shit question like, *what's your favourite song?* (I did that to Alice on our first date . . .). And so, on this rather sour note of rejection, I leave. I walk away resigned that I'll never see the inside of their fantastically unique world ever again. Yet I do smile. I smile at the fact that if ever I were to, I'd bet my life those bloody singing garden gnomes will still be there, batteries not included.

Friday, 24th May

I've come to realise that planning a move is pretty stressful. Throw in a move to an entire new part of the country with more trees than front doors, and the need to juggle multiple life issues for your little family when you get there, and it all becomes pretty time-consuming too. As a result, the bedroom ceiling has had the whites of my eyes burning into it, through the dark of night, for weeks and weeks now.

Which is why, after taking the last two days off to try to keep on top of it all with Alice, I'm genuinely relieved to be in work. Coffee consumed. Another one of William's vomit stains cleaned from my shoulder. And I'm ready. *Inhale.* Pause. *Exhale.* I quietly pray for an uncomplicated, easy day. The first patient enters. They ask me if I'm their postman. Genuine question. An acutely delirious elderly patient is not the start to my requested uncomplicated, easy day.

Time to pray to a new God perhaps.

Monday, 27th May

Hippocrates was spot on when he said *if we could give every individual the right amount of nourishment and exercise, not too little and not too much, we would have found the safest way to health.* Now that was around 2,319 years ago (give or take a few decades) yet it seems many of us, judging by the obesity crisis that we continue to sleepwalk deeper into, are resistant to this idea – or, at least Harry is.

I look at him. Then away. Pausing. Shifting the mouse marker around the results screen aimlessly. Working out the best way to tackle the now very apparent issue.

'So why am I so tired?' Harry's question breaks my preparation to deliver a softer entry into the topic. So, I go in blunt: *'You're really unfit. That's the first issue.'* He looks up, visibly injured by my statement, not even comprehending there's more to come. *'And your lifestyle is terrible.'* His head and neck cock back, the way someone does when the unexpected punch isn't pulled. Even just a little.

At forty-seven years old, Harry has been to the GP for a few niggling health issues, but nothing exciting. What is major, however, is his gross lack of self-care. He does no exercise. Sits at a desk all day. Lives off snack food. Smokes half a pack of Benson & Hedges each week. Washes this down with around ten pints a week on average (that's about double the recommended limit), and sleeps about six hours a night – *because he loves Netflix.* The man's a living example of how to self-destruct. And not the first one I've encountered (my mind drifts back to Mr Kayll last March). I won't bore you with the details (you can go onto Instagram, where there'll be a dentally well-enamelled doctor who can neatly summarise it all for you), but basically, it's all shit for your body and mind. And *very* anti-Hippocrates.

Over the next ten minutes, I walk a slightly shell-shocked Harry through all the reasons why he might die because of these things. He nods, trance-like, and I suspect a little overwhelmed.

'So, the blood tests were OK?'

Fact is, every single test poor Harry has had – from a chest X-ray, lung function test (called spirometry), and electrocardiogram of his heart to the blood tests looking for a myriad of causes for tiredness (from anaemia and vitamin D deficiency to thyroid disease and heart failure) – all demonstrated one thing: *Normality.* And so, when faced with these facts and marrying them with his lifestyle, the answer is simple: *He* is the problem. He lacks cardiovascular fitness, adequate rest, adequate nutrition, and is taking on too many toxins through smoking and alcohol excess.

'Most likely why you're tired, Harry.'

After a period of cerebral digestion, he leaves armed with a plan. But I'm pessimistic, jaded through past experience. Because it lacks the one thing he really needs, the one thing that I *really can't* give him: *Motivation.* Sure, I can dole out advice on how to live more healthily and make his lifestyle less likely to kill him, but without motivation, it's not worth the paper it's printed on. The words spoken. Motivation is everything. And there's no pill for it. Whoever makes one, well, they'll be saving humanity from being crushed under its own expanding weight.

Now there's a Hollywood movie plot for you.

Tuesday, 28th May

Better late than never. I've developed a new strategy for managing the distinct lack of time to have lunch at this surgery. *Finally.* It's all about the timing when working through my phone call list of patients. I phone the patient, food in hand. Then once the call is over, I shovel as much as I can into my face. I type the clinical notes up while frantically masticating (no, that's a *c*, not a *b*) the food. Once chewed, I finally swallow as I dial the next patient on the list. The process is then repeated until the indigestion gets too much.

That's lunch – a GP's lunch at least.

Thursday, 30th May

I'm reaching for the words but find none. I scrunch my toes hard into my shoes to distract me.

Distract my eyes from filling with tears.

As I do so, Diane sits in front of me, gently holding her tissue. Calm. Poised. Serene. I would be tearing down walls. Screaming. Angry. Hating the world. In the moment I'm hit with a complicated flood of admiration. Respect. Awe.

How is she so calm? Her brother committed suicide five days ago. He was only twenty-eight years old. She, only thirty-one.

The room turns the silence over and over and over, like a kneaded dough, heavy and raw. And Diane and I just sit here, letting it be. A couple of minutes pass. As if exiting a deeper accessed memory of her and her brother from a happier time, she looks up and smiles. I smile back, nod invitingly. I'm here to listen. Nothing I can say will make any of this better.

She smiles some more as she tells how she has been looking through photographs of their adventures together. She's been reading exchanged jokey text messages. Emails. Digging out old homemade family videos. Smelling the old and oversized jumper she borrowed from him but then pretended she'd lost so as not to have to give it back.

She catches a few tears running away from her eye to her cheek with the tissue. I swallow down another lump in my throat and look to her clinical notes on the screen briefly. I'm not looking for anything, I just need to look away. This is heartbreaking.

Diane has her own history, her own battles. Depression. Deliberate self-harm. Anorexia nervosa. Drug and alcohol misuse. She smiles some more and tells me how she's spent years looking for love, but doing it wrong. And not just, she adds, in the wrong places but for the wrong kind of love. A synthetic, instant, and never-lasting love.

In her body image. In cocaine. In alcohol. In toxic relationships.

Only now, in the last five days, having poured over with fresh, forever changed eyes the photographs, text messages, emails, and pieced together the tiny and, at the time, seemingly insignificant life-interactions with her brother, does she realise just how much she was loved *by* him. And how much she loved him. I say nothing, sit back in my chair and nod slowly. There's heartbreak to that realisation: to the realisation of what you didn't necessarily see right in front of you.

Real love. True love.

I suppose that can be the problem with life. The chaos of it. It pulls you away from truer, deeper priorities. And while we can all love our families and friends on a superficial level, do we really give them the time, justice, and effort that *they* and *love* really deserve? It's hard sometimes, this modern life.

Before she leaves, Diane tells me although it's hard to realise she's found that true love with her brother, in and after his death, she's glad, all the same that she found it. We both agree that's something to hold on to and celebrate. Because after all, it was there all along. His name was Samuel.

I will always remember this consultation with crystal clarity.

Friday, 31st May

Not that I should ever need to be reminded, but after yesterday's case, I squeeze Alice and William that little bit harder as we say goodnight to each other.

JUNE 2019

Friday, 7th June

5:21pm, my last day of work after a week of patient goodbyes in clinic.

This is weird. The chaos is about to stop, the off-switch flicked. Well that, or just relocate it a few hundred miles. I stare at the screen: my last patient is a gift, surely? The GP Gods have looked down at me and said, *Max, here is a parting gift from us – to you.*

It's Benny, the man who walked into my clinic room almost twelve months to the day and asked me what the meaning of life was. My 5:30pm patient. My *last* patient. And the very same man who once held top spot on my list of all-time patient greats. Yet, like anyone at the top of their game, it's finite. The Leighs stepped up, dethroning him. Perhaps that's life, a cycle of endlessly trying to climb some form of mountain.

Physical. Mental. Emotional. Some peak to reach.

A quick glance at the clock also tells me that time too is on my side. Largely thanks to my penultimate patient being a simple contraceptive pill check. Another gift from the GP Gods, I suspect.

Quick. Easy. Minimal brain power required. Welcomed. Since I mentally checked out of work a week ago.

It gives me time to think. To reflect on this last week of my life as a GP in the city and what you've seen of it, or is that what I've chosen to show you? Have I been selective? shown you the best bits? The worse bits? Believe it or not, there are even bits I didn't feel could go into this book – no matter the anonymity – consigned to me and only me. Ultimately, it's my story. My life as a GP. It might not be like other GPs'. In fact, I'm sure it isn't. And that's not because they don't see the same societal cross-section of patients and clinical issues as I do in clinic, but more because of the way I see those patients and those clinical issues. How I choose to *be* in those moments. That's unique to me.

Every GP will have their own story, their own *The Secret Doctor* book within them. I don't know, perhaps I'm talking complete bollocks. Perhaps it's the melancholy and nostalgia of the moment that's leading me to look at this past year through warped self-perception. Now some of you may be celebrating the fact that this is the final chapter, having loathed my book, my story, and my interpretation of others on their health journeys. Maybe adjectives like *arrogant*, *angry*, and *inconsiderate* will fill the review pages. Yet, I've made peace with that. First, because there'll always be people out there who you can't please. That's life, nothing I can do about this. Second, I hope there'll still be enough of you who *do* find a connection with some of the patient stories. Finding them interesting. Resonating. And third, well, I just wanted to share what life as a GP is like. Unfiltered. Getting it all out my head. The good times. The bad times. Everything in-between. A cathartic process for me personally.

Writing this book has made me realise every contact, every experience, has the potential to chip away for the worse, or reinforce for the better. It just depends on how you look at them. And what you choose to look away from.

Woods for the trees.

Friday, 7th June

5:23pm

Benny still isn't due for five minutes or so. The last appointment. I stand up, stretch, pace. Nervous excitement. I can't believe this is it. Unsure how to kill the time, I plant myself in the *patient* chair opposite my own, well-saddled, one. I look out into my consultation room to see what they see: another dead pot plant. I've lost count now this year. Alice won't be pleased. Yet, besides my inability to keep a £4.99 (apparently) indestructible supermarket plant alive, it strikes me how all they can see are clinical instruments, clinical waste bins, clinical notices, clinical books.

Clinical. Clinical. Clinical.

I slump deeper in the chair. That's really not great, I didn't realise this. After all, everybody who walks into my room needs to be seen as people, first and foremost. Not patients. And yet the way this room, *my room*, is set up for them, they are almost instantly swallowed up in a foreign, medicalised environment.

Unfamiliar. Clinical. Sterile.

I make a mental note that wherever I end up working, my next consultation room will be a trick of the eye, making the patient question if they're even in a GP surgery. Maybe every patient will leave like Suzie, the sweet 6-year-old girl that I saw last week, declaring, *'But he doesn't act like the other doctors do, Dad!'* on her way out.

Every GP needs to sit in their patient chair. See what they see.

Patients . . . I migrate back to the safety of the old and familiar consultation chair, buttocks settling into it like two old friends meeting for one final embrace. I click through previous clinic lists. So many people, so many patients – all of whom I'll never see again. All now handed over to other GPs at the surgery to continue their care. In that new GP's way, not mine. I try to do the maths and work out how many I've seen over the last year. But I can't, my mental arithmetic skills turning out, as I expected, to be incredibly shit. Plus, my iPhone battery's dead. And who last used a calculator on a computer? I wouldn't even know where to find it. I abandon.

Click and *scroll*. *Click* and *scroll* . . . Some patient names trigger nothing. No recollection. Some trigger joy and amusement, others sadness and disappointment. What I've realised is, nobody really *wants* to see me. To see a GP is to say, more often than not, that something isn't right. I say that, as of course, happy news like pregnancies and the need for exciting travel vaccinations do cross my path as well but ultimately, it's about a declaration of fallibility.

Open to illness. Injury. Vulnerability. People don't like that. They are the people that I meet. And of course, we shouldn't forget those who I don't meet, who actually need the most help. They may just never ask for it, even realise it's needed. We all know them. Suffering silently. Hidden – often behind the British stiff upper lip – its owner's tacitally suffering. Sometimes I do get lucky, picking them up by chance on a home visit – as with Mr Cheema and his chronic loneliness last December. Or perhaps I'll be seeing them for something else innocuous and benign when another, more critical issue emerges. This was definitely the case, *in extremis*, with the late Mrs Kooyker, who, if you recall, I was asked to see for constipation – and it turned out she was in respiratory (breathing) failure and about to die.

The reverse is also true: the frequent flyers who see their GP as a daily engagement, whether there's something wrong or not. Some are lovely, harmless, and fun. Others, like Mrs Tally, well, less so. *The Pick'n' Mix of life.* One that I've no doubt echoes across every GP surgery and community the length and breadth of this country.

There's a poem by Robert Hastings called *The Station.* My uncle introduced me to it a few years ago. On the surface, it's about a simple train journey. Moving from station to station. But then, as the poem progresses, the reader – and, I expect, the passengers – realise there's no endpoint, no final destination. In fact, come to think of it, there aren't even any stations. You see beneath the black and white of the words is the poem's true meaning: that life is one continuous journey with no final destination (even death, it can be argued here), and it too has no stations leading up to it. Because for every goal we have in our life – falling in love, buying a home, having financial security, or even just being happy or safe – the station we think we'll arrive at when we achieve them just fades away into nothing, an illusion in our minds. Instead, the goal's realisation simply gives way to yet more tracks leading to more stations. And this will of course be stations that once again fade into nothing on approach.

Goal after goal.

And while it's true, I'm not an illusion, the poem did get me thinking about the health journey a patient goes on. A lifelong journey, in fact. Perhaps being a GP is a bit like being a station on their journey. Just a stop on their constantly evolving life, filled with blind corners and endless straights. It's with this geographical unpredictability that endpoints and goals constantly outgrow. Evolve. Change. As a GP, when I look back at the patients I've seen this year, I realise that it's about being this station *when they need one.* Occasionally making repairs on the tracks, or perhaps changing the direction of travel. Whatever it is, it's usually transient. All in the hope that I've sent them in a better direction than from whence they came. But don't get me wrong, I know all GPs aren't the same. You may have had very bad experiences. Terrible, in fact. And not all adjustments made at these station health stops are well received, wanted, or, dare I say, sometimes even suitable or helpful. Because GPs are human as well. We make mistakes, and we will – the job just commands us not to. Which is simply impossible. I know in my career I'll miss cancers and make clinical mistakes causing pain, distress, and suffering. They may even result in death. It's something I live in accepted fear of. Why so sure? Because we'll never escape the fallibility of being human. No matter the barriers and safety checks put in place, you can never truly beat the unpredictability of the mind.

Expectation . . . The last patient I saw got me thinking about this: she wanted a year-long prescription for her contraceptive pill. Fair enough. She was a last-minute add-on to my clinic because it was *URGENT*. Why so urgent? Despite her last prescription also being year-long, meaning she had three hundred and sixty-five days to prepare herself to get a new prescription in time, she didn't. To me, this is less fair. That is a failed responsibility that rests with her, not me. Yet ultimately, she was an unhappy customer. *Annoyed* at having to come in to see a GP (despite kindly being given an appointment as a clinic extra). *Annoyed* at being asked questions about migraines, blood clots, and cancers in her and her family's history. *Annoyed* at having a physical review of her blood pressure, height, and weight. All, I might add, questions and steps designed to make sure the medication remains safe to prescribe and that her risk of having a stroke or blood clot hasn't become unacceptable. *Annoyed* at me because I don't want her to have a stroke. That, I can live with. What I couldn't live with is learning that she had a stroke because I didn't want to offend her – and so didn't do my job properly.

This, I realise, is another lesson learned over the last year of keeping this diary: you simply cannot, and critically, *should not* aim to please every patient. I'm lucky, I've had the most fantastic mentor at this surgery – a very respected senior GP with a sharp (but fair) tongue and wise head, the kind of GP I can only aspire to be one day. I'll dearly miss the support of them since this job can be incredibly lonely and isolating at times. My mentor told me that if, on my patient feedback, I don't have a percentage of patients saying they would *not* recommend me, then I'm *not* doing my job properly. A penny-dropping moment for me. What they're saying is exactly what this seemingly simple request for medication case highlights – that expectation has to be met with what's clinically proportionate, acceptable, and safe. An entrance with a demanding *I want* or worse, *I expect*, therefore has no place in my clinics. And, as I've talked about before, to me, this felt infinitely worse in a life as a private GP. Because of this, I can say with great happiness that I'll aim to keep my percentage of patients that would *not* recommend me as an ever-growing number. In fact, I check on my percentages monthly. What a target. I think it'll keep me on the straight and narrow, guiding my moral compass in the workplace to try to do what's right for the person sitting in front of me. Not to be intimidated, bullied, or coerced instead into what they *perceive* to be the right thing for them. Sometimes, that truth, brutal as it may be, is to say *there's nothing else that can be done.* False promises have no place in general practice.

Still sitting in my chair, waiting idly for Benny, I continue to turn all these thoughts over in my head. Some year-long post-match analysis. A hollow knock brings my dormant door to life. I sit up.

Benny, early? Impressive.

With an overzealous wrench of the door handle, my eye-line scans the doorway's vista – finding nothing but the wall opposite. Peering down, I am, however, met by someone. A five-foot-nothing elderly lady so bent over, I expect she's permanently staring at her tiny feet. This definitely *isn't* Benny – unless a lot's happened since I saw him last year.

'Room twelve?' a voice croaks from well below me.

'Sadly not,' I explain with a smile.

Impressed she even made it up the flight of stairs, I guide her back towards her true destination before returning to my room. I sit. Resume my thoughts about Benny's possible question for today. I smile. Isolated moments like the one just now always make me love this job even more. Pure interaction, unscripted, unpredictable, unrehearsed. Plus, all with people from every single walk of life. People you might never normally come into contact with. Bloody hell, maybe even actively avoid, crossing the proverbial road if you had the chance. And it means an almost chameleon-like approach is required for every single consultation, something I mentioned right back at the beginning in the prologue to this book. Working out how to best engage with the person in front of me, how to build rapport with them, understand their wants and needs, all before then steering towards some shared agreement. Always for the betterment of the patient. That often means *me* moulding myself to *them*. Where GPs struggle, is when they can't do that, or they force it. Patients see that, they're no fools.

All of this is about putting the patient at the heart of everything I do. Of patient-centred care. And though not always easy, it will forever remain the goal.

My goal. *An illustrious, yet intangible station. On their journey.*

Of course, it's not all sunshine and roses with this approach. And if this is at all ever a hindrance rather than a help, then it's because I'm sometimes too keen to be a people-pleaser. Too moulded, and so lose sight of independent thought and impartiality. This makes what I mentioned earlier about *not* giving in to patient demand and expectation, well, somewhat of a personal challenge. Something my mentor taught me isn't always needed. Something I see now, more than ever. And it's true sometimes it can get me in trouble. After all, speaking to my patients in the same way as I'd speak to my (*fine, Alice's*) friends in the pub can sometimes come as a shock, yet I remain undeterred, happy to assume the risk that comes with it. Because it means they're getting *all of me*. Not just some stiff, polystyrene professional GP-version of me – *the real me*. Something I hope breaks down barriers and creates more open conversations about their health. And that must only be a good thing, right? Over the past year, I've tried to do this with every patient – even the Mr O'Keefes of this world.

A text from Alice: she's wishing me good luck for my last ever city patient. I reply with a list of emojis, including a dinosaur by mistake.

Benny, honestly!

Impatient restlessness fills me once again, so I begin to clear out some more desk drawers. *Shit*. Discovered are pile upon pile of old discharge summaries, discarded prescriptions, GP letters, and my drawings of obscure bits of anatomy (all very shit, and thoroughly reinforcing such decisions as last June's not to illustrate the impact of a butt-truncheon on Leigh's bowels). I hold the wedges of paper in both hands, definitely a year's worth at least. I look at my tiny waste paper bin – filled with the last-ever dead pot plant to grace this room. Hardly a safe, confidential way of throwing this all away. But then it *is* my last day. I look around as though someone might be lurking in the corner to wag a finger at me, then stuff them all back into the drawer – my replacement can sort that out for me.

A leaving gift.

Besides, it could be far worse. It might have been Mrs Chambers' dead mouse, still wrapped up in clingfilm from last November. I sit back. Exhale. Smile to myself. When you've mentally checked out, you've checked out. Plus, I'm tired. Physically tired. Mentally tired. Motivation has left me. The surgery having taken its pound of flesh. You see, the days here are a constant cycle of processing. Always questioning your decisions. Are they right? Are they wrong? What might I have missed? Is there something else this could be? Do I know enough to be making the right decision? This last one's massive – and the one that keeps me awake at night.

Now, I don't want to bore you with a psychology lecture but there's a model called the Hierarchy of Competence developed by Noel Burch, in the 1970s. It's a four-stage model about what you understand about your task or duty. For me, as a GP, that duty is to know about medicine. And this feeds into all those daily decisions. It starts with the scariest stage, called *unconscious incompetence.* Basically, you don't know what you don't know. You're clueless. And you don't even realise it. Terrifying. Then, as you learn more, you become aware of the gaps in your knowledge. This is the second stage, called *conscious incompetence.* So, you go away and you learn stuff (like medicine) and then successfully apply it – but with thinking effort. This is the third stage, called *conscious competence.* Finally, it all becomes second nature and you can do it without really thinking. This is stage four, called *unconscious competence.* Every day I ask myself if I'm being *unconsciously incompetent.* Because that is a seriously sobering thought. *Fear* . . . what a motivator. Still, I've made peace with that now (I didn't always feel that way). Today, I'm happy to walk through the work, hand in hand with fear. It makes me better at my job, it levels me. A rationalising gyroscope in my head.

And that can only be good for the person sitting opposite me.

Friday, 7th June

5:29pm

Any minute now . . . the final act. I stretch out my legs, letting myself slide down the chair a little more. I clasp my hands on my lap. Relaxed, staring at the ceiling. Waiting. Musing. You know I've been thinking. Thinking a lot today about what I wanted *you* to get out of this book, what lesson to impart to you. What's my message? But I'm hesitant. I mean, does there really need to be one? *Should* there even be one? The problem is, I'm just a GP. I'm not a politician. Not an academic. Definitely not some irritating influencer. My career focus is simply the person in front of me – all I've ever been professionally interested in. And that's never changing. Besides, I find the whole notion of preaching some lesson incredibly patronising to you. So, all this means I've concluded that I only have one simple suggestion. It's not profound, it's not going to change your life – it's just something that might be nice to carry with you. And it's this:

> *To always consider the* ***knowing – doing gap*** *in your life's actions.*

Essentially, this is about recognising the size of the gap between ***knowing*** what you should do – and whether or not you're actually ***doing*** **it**. In health, this concept is simple: if you want the surest way to maintain your health, just think back to the Hippocrates quote I mentioned when I met Harry last month (see page 316): *if we could give every individual the right amount of nourishment and exercise, not too little and not too much, we would have found the safest way to health.* It's about positively building a good health base and then keeping ill health at bay. Proactive, not reactive. And sure, there are some extra bits you can throw in – sleep, socialising, support, and so on – but all in all, the old boy's hit the nail on the proverbial head. And critically, you *know* all of this already. The question is, are you *doing* it? Plus, we've also now managed to summarise all the endless bullshit online about how to be healthy. In one vulnerable sentence. Stripped back. Basic. Bare. No tricks. And definitely not dressed up as yet another health trend. Because if you look really closely, all these trends collapse back to the same principles – *be active, eat sensibly, rest, look after your mental health.* So, I can happily announce, with immediate effect, all online social media health influencers can retire. Of course, this *knowing – doing gap* extends far beyond just our health.

Being kind. Being supportive. Being inspirational. Basically all the Clinton Card expressions you can think of.

If we can all do that, maybe the world will end up in a little better place. I know, *deep.* But it is my last day, so I'm allowed to say this shit.

Friday, 7th June

5:31pm
For fuck's sake, Benny! You're late, hurry up.

I love this job but sometimes I do hate the person it makes me. Those days where my brain feels like it's about to explode from my skull and I can't think straight – but *have to.* Because the person sitting in front of me has been waiting for their ten minutes. They want me, and all of me. And why should they care anyway, if my day's been hard? They've got a health worry and they need their GP. At their best. Focused on their problem.

For me, if I'm honest, it's the self-frustration that grates at me most. I almost wish I was less caring. Colder. Perhaps I'd sleep better then. You see, I have this inner battle. One part of me wants to ignore their third health issue (typically, something you know you can't, like a breast lump), and palm them off for another day, for another GP. But then there's the stronger part of me that knows this isn't right (this goes back to that *knowing – doing gap*). The result? I'm left feeling frustrated at myself for choosing to do the right thing. But that *is* the feeling. Frustration. Because I realise that *I'm choosing* to run late, *choosing* to get home late, *choosing* to miss William's bathtime. And the person in front of me won't ever see that – they *shouldn't* see that. Yet what spills over into their consultation as collateral damage is a blunter, ruder, harsher side of me as their GP. Unlocked. A side that before I became a doctor, I didn't really appreciate that I had.

Emotional veneers scratched away.

I slash through concerns with little empathy – getting to the heart of their issues yes, but giving them short, blunt, unvarnished (even cruel) answers – not sugar-coated or digestible in a way that encourages a patient to come back to me or even feel part of the decision-making process. I always feel shit afterwards once I realise that it's happened. Again. The guilt. The resentment for the job. And the resentment that I couldn't stop it. It's the brutality of a service totally overwhelmed with demand, the days of the *single-problem consultation* long dead. Why? Lots of reasons really. People can't get appointments nearly as easily now and so naturally, they *have to* save up their problems, dropping them at my feet all in one go. People have more access to information online and so self-diagnose (usually the worst conditions imaginable) more. People are more health-anxious for similar reasons. And despite these changes, the expectation has never changed – it's all to be sorted in a ten-minute consultation. This sounds self-pitying, I realise. It's really not meant to be. I don't blame patients. At. All. Also, I'll always serve them as best I can. It's just a self-reflection that it really fucks me off sometimes that I'm diligent. Because it damages the life outside of work – a far more important part of my life. With my family. With Alice and William. I hate that so much. I feel like I've failed them. Failed my family. And that's not just by being late. That's by coming home stressed, grumpy, snappy, frustrated. Like a new cohort of Snow White's seven dwarfs. Thankfully, it happens less often nowadays. I'd like to think I've learned how to recognise and manage it much earlier. That is, however, *reactive.* And so, I continue to strive for a longer-term *proactive* approach – a Zen – much like the one I transiently stumbled across in April. Besides, I have the most incredible wife – she gets me.

All of me. My inner, complicated, irrational inner clock. My horologist.

It brings a lump to my throat at even the thought of just how much she means to me – a book in itself. And through that understanding, she knows how to deal with me when I come home like some angry bear with a sore head. It's not rocket science either. She simply asks for my index finger and then pulls it, like it's some stress-release valve. At the same time, she asks me to blow out through my mouth. And then she hugs me. And it's never failed.

What a woman!

I look at my iPhone screensaver: Alice and William laughing, eyes smiling. I take in every detail. The creases of William's mouth. The gumminess of it. The way Alice has her arms safely around him. The way he leans into her. All those rolls of baby fat. So many. Safe. Secure. Happy.

Midway through this year, I changed as a person. And that changed me as a GP. Life, before William, viewed through a different set of eyes. And in that instant, when he was born, that all changed. Nothing prepares you for it. People sometimes talk about getting ready for big milestones in life as a process. Take becoming a doctor . . . You work through medical school for years before then being introduced into the job of doctoring. There, as a junior doctor, you're given a pretty strong guide rope, a safety net, and a team around you. A slow process. Organic. Gradual. Becoming a parent isn't like that one bit. Sure, you can talk about having a baby. You buy all the gear that comes with having a baby (most of which is never used). Then you wait. And then one day, out of nowhere, there they are: a baby. *Your* baby, now your immediate and constant responsibility. The totality of it. Forever. How can that not change how you see life?

For me, having William enter my life did two key things to my viewpoint. The first is that it shifted my empathy at work immeasurably. Now, when I see children who are ill, I imagine William. I imagine how I'd feel. The worry. The fear. The unknowing. The helplessness. Even how *he'd* feel. It brings a much more visceral emotion to me than before, when William wasn't in existence. Before, yes, of course it was sad. But it didn't knife me in the chest and twist like it does now, it was more an abstract concept. I tread carefully here. This is how *I* feel, this isn't to say that not having children means a person cannot care for and treat them with sincere love, compassion, and professionalism. Again, I'm just telling my story, I don't want to offend.

The second change to my viewpoint on William's arrival was much more unexpected. Now, when I hear news about children's suffering, or watch a film in which a child is at risk, hurt, killed, it *really, really* gets to me. Cuts deeper. Finding the artery. I think of our boy asleep, safe and sound, in his cot. I think of how the mother and father of that child suffering must be feeling. It's so weird. And to be brutally honest, I don't think I have the writing skills to do it justice on this page.

Sorry!

Friday, 7th June

5:35pm

Benny has five minutes to turn up. After that, he's officially missed his appointment.

*

Stepping back from my story, it might seem simple to see why Alice, William, and I are escaping the city life for the country-side. After all, it'll probably be safer. Quieter. Cheaper. More friendly. Right? I mean sure, maybe. And sure, that's probably what I had in my head when William first turned up – a yearning to rush him to a better place to grow up. And when I think about life as a GP in the city, again, sure, the knee-jerk reaction is to think that it'll be easier in the countryside. Less stress. Less complexity. Less pressure. The many months where I've talked about the struggles I've felt in my surgery, and the impact it's had on my family life – well, yes, they should only galvanise this idea. True. And yet, despite all of this, I realise none of that is the underlying catalyst for leaving. I understand now that we could have happily continued to make an amazing life for the three of us (and who knows, maybe one day, four or five) here in the city. There's so much opportunity here for William, for all of us. So many things to see and do. Friends to make. Adventures to have. So too could I have worked up the ladder in my surgery and maybe one day become a GP Partner – effecting the change where I think it's needed, from the top down. And anyway, despite my rants, I actually love the surgery I work in. It could *all* have worked. Because city life *does* work, I realise that now so clearly. Which has left me for some time then wondering, why *are* we leaving it all? In the end, the answer was a laughably simple one – for a new chapter. For the pursuit of a new adventure. Not a better one. Not a safer one. Not a cheaper one. Just a *different* one.

So, in less than a month I'll be living in the countryside with Alice and William – who will, incredibly, be nearly ten months old by then. Life will be very different, the next step of the Skittle family journey. We'll probably all be wearing wellingtons and doing non-city things, like saying *hello* to complete strangers passing us by.

What a headfuck that's going to be.

I'm nervous, I think we all are. Well, except William. He'll remain clueless for a while, I expect. Will the pace of life and work be too slow? I'm expecting countryside life to be quieter, and I hope, calmer. The city's frantic personality has worn me out over the past twelve months, of that I'm certain. I just hope we're not too overwhelmed by it all, that it's not too much of a swing in the other direction towards isolation. I'm sure it won't. Yet, it's such an unknown. I don't know, I just can't gauge it. Still, we love the idea of becoming part of a community again. Of having the time and the space as a family to grow together. Of finding time to have a healthier lifestyle with less stress (all of which seeps into how I perform as a GP). Who knows, maybe I'll even join the local rugby club's veterans side (now being the wrong side of thirty)? And then perhaps one day, if my body holds up (and Alice allows me), William and I could even play a match together. What a laugh that would be!

Professionally, I expect my clinics won't be too dissimilar to how they are now. But what I'm expecting is more home visits and more of them for geographically isolated patients (you can, of course, be surrounded by people and buildings in a city and still be very much isolated). I have a feeling there'll be more of an expectation for me to assume risk even that little bit more when making clinical decisions, without the safety net of a state-of-the-art hospital just down the road.

This is the remote countryside after all. If Mrs Gray's car accident taught me anything last October, it's that nothing's ever that simple when you live remotely. Whatever happens, I just hope we're safe, healthy, and happy. That's all that matters, all any of us want. And as for work, well, the goal remains the same: don't be a good GP, try to be a great GP. Look into people's windows and just help them. That's it, no change to the plan here. It remains that simple. Even if I'm swapping gang affiliations for farmers' union affiliations. I really hope, as an aside, that when you finally close this book, you'll have seen how seriously easy it is to be a bad GP. But my God, bloody hard to be a good one. And it's the latter I choose.

Every day. Even on the worst ones.

Friday, 7 June

5:39pm

I stand, smoothing out my trousers. Getting ready to wander down to reception and see if Benny's around. See if the muppet's forgotten to register his arrival. Yet here I am, stopped in my tracks as life repeats itself, roughly twelve months on. I stare at my crotch.

You're fucking kidding me?

Violated again with yet another white stain. Not yoghurt this time. That was a life *before* William. This is a post-William world. This, is baby formula milk. Which looks even more like cum than the Greek yoghurt did.

Great. Crusted. Conspicuous. Suspicious.

I pause, weigh up my options. And I smile. So much water has flown under my bridge since that yoghurt first hit my crotch. I almost feel like a wise old owl now. I give it a rub. It makes it look even worse. Flakier somehow. More smeared. More suspect. I look up and sigh. It doesn't matter. Besides this time I know water's definitively out of the question. No need to look as though I've pissed myself for the last patient of my career at this surgery. So, I do nothing. I just let it be. As I go to move once more, taking a step towards my door, my computer screen flashes an update to my appointment list:

5:30pm FRAY, Benjamin: DID NOT ATTEND (DNA).

Oh, Benny.

My last patient, a bloody DNA.

Well, what did I tell you? No Hollywood endings in this life. More's the pity really as I had *my* final answer to Benny's question on the meaning of life:

The pursuit of ongoing happiness.

Right, time to go home. We're done here. This is how my story as a city GP ends. I put in my earphones, turn up the volume on Elton John's 'I'm Still Standing', and close my consultation-room door for the last time.

MY TOP FIVE PATIENTS OF ALL TIME

Like children, I know you're not supposed to have your favourites but still, I wanted to give a shout-out to my final top five patients of the past twelve or so months. And to say, thanks for not only letting me be part of your health journey but for teaching me a few lessons along the way too . . .

First place:	Mr and Mrs Leigh, for just blowing my mind in every single way possible
Second place:	Natalia, for showing what is possible in seemingly impossible adversity
Third place:	Benny, for having the courage to voice a question we all surely wonder
Fourth place:	Patsy, for showing the power of endless optimism (and a simple smile)
Fifth place:	Mrs Tally, for teaching me a new level of patience!

END NOTE

January 2020

Until death meets us, health journey's on without pause. Always evolving, for better or worse, as the days, months, and years tick over. I thought about sharing where all my patients are now – what stage of their health journey they're at. Are they better, or are they more ill? Do they have a new diagnosis? Did they complain about me? Did the treatment fail?

Are they even still alive?

But then I realised that it would be completely redundant to do that. Now I know this will annoy some of you, but as ever, I'm not too sorry. You see, by the time this book has been read, those patient journeys will have moved on in some way, shape or form.

No arrival. No final destination. The journeys instead march alongside the sliding sands of time.

The joy is in life's journey. And perhaps being a GP is ultimately about helping everyone take that journey for as long as they possibly can. Now, what's not to love about that?

EPILOGUE: THE CORONAVIRUS

Tuesday, 1st June 2021

In June 2019, where my last chapter ends, we were all navigating our own ebbs and flows of modern-day living. All with our individual goals, worries, ambitions, and expectations. And like the patients I shared with you in this book, health journeys that were very personal to each of us.

Today, after the past year, we perhaps look at the world a little differently. Cautious of the unknown. The, what *can* happen, seasoned in our collective experience of the coronavirus pandemic. Even now, so many months on, it can feel like we are, on a daily basis, watching the dust settle and rise, and settle and rise again, as the pandemic continues to write events that many of us thought never would happen.

As the pandemic stands right now, we can all hope that the worst is behind us (here on our small island at least). We have all stumbled through the unknown path of a pandemic and seem to be emerging on the other side as the country gradually re-opens. And while we have seen vast successes in the NHS vaccination programme (the most successful in its history), Covid-related hospital care, extraordinary volunteering efforts, and sheer bloody-mindedness to not give up, everything still feels somewhat unpredictable and we all rightly remain a little edgy. I certainly know I am, especially now Alice and I have another baby on the way to join the loveable wrecking ball that William has become.

And while it's completely understandable to feel this sense of unease, I want to use the rest of this epilogue to pull your minds back to the time when we were all just taking those early stumbling steps on this path: entering the first lockdown, confined to our houses except for essential shopping and an hour's worth of exercise a day, not knowing that a vaccine would even be a possibility. It also goes some way to showing my thoughts, emotions and concerns about being – and how to be – a GP during this time, as the Covid crisis was only just beginning. It may seem like a lifetime ago, particularly as life (currently) shows signs of normalising. Yet, of course, it really wasn't, was it . . .

Friday, 3rd April 2020

Don't worry, it's likely a self-limiting viral illness. A sentence that's rolled off my tongue – and I guarantee all other GPs' – hundreds, if not thousands of times. It is, after all, an incredibly common clinical scenario, seen every single day by GPs: the cold-or-flu-like illness. One you've all experienced to varying degrees. The cough; feeling a bit hot; the fatigue; the muscle ache; the sore throat. You get dispatched from your GP consultation within ten minutes, reassured by that most reassuring of statements – *don't worry, it's likely a self-limiting viral illness* – accompanied with benign advice to drink fluids, take some regular paracetamol, and rest. And, as sometimes needs to be the case, a comment thrown in about how *no, you don't require any antibiotics – we're waging war against global antibiotic resistance, don't you know.*

But then, in December 2019, the world began to turn on its head. Slowly at first. The novel coronavirus, a severe acute respiratory syndrome virus (which causes the disease called COVID-19) emerges in China. And then the world *really* starts to spin. The coronavirus spreads rapidly across the world. Fast forward to the 28th February 2020, and the first case has already been identified in the UK. By 11th March 2020, a global pandemic is declared by the World Health Organization (WHO). And today, just over a month later, on the 3rd April 2020, we sit in expectation of the peak of COVID-19 cases that will devastate our country (and especially the national epicentre of cases, London). With it, many lives will be lost. We all know this now. The Government has been preparing us for this for weeks. The fact that we are constructing multiple makeshift 4,000-bed Nightingale hospitals (all with ventilator capacity) is a pretty big red flag. Today the death toll of patients who have died with COVID-19 in the UK is 3,605. This number is estimated to be upwards of 250,000 by the end of the crisis – with no action taken. A number impossible to comprehend.

It's no surprise, therefore, that this country has echoes of being on a war-footing right now. Something many of us have never experienced, nor thought we would in our lifetime. I certainly didn't. And if I did, I didn't think it would be over a bloody 120 nanometer-wide virus. Yet here we are, facing up to what is unmistakably the greatest threat to our collective health and way of life for decades. The good news, though, is that that we are British. And we do not get taken over a barrel by anyone. By anything. And certainly, not by a virus who shares its bloody name with a beer that requires a lime. Instead, we are doing what we all naturally and inherently do in times of British national crises – putting aside differences, pulling together (but at a distance), drinking lots of tea, clapping a lot – and fighting back hard. Very hard.

And it's this fight back that's seen the way we live change so irrevocably in the last month. Early measures of social distancing evolving into household isolation and shielding for the extremely vulnerable. Hand-washing techniques married up with birthday songs. Everyone knowing who on earth Professor Chris Whitty is (the Chief Medical Officer for England, in case, well . . . there really is no excuse by now). What two metres *really* looks like. Rainbows in windows. How to best utilise your permitted one hour of daily outside exercise (and not get into trouble with the Police). Clapping. Lots and lots of wonderful clapping. Toilet roll as a tradable commodity. The definition of a key worker (and how much we bloody love them). And, of course, how to work from home. And although these may vary from the extreme and draconian, to the perceptibly light and fluffy, each step and action here has immense value. They are stock in the fight. They either suppress the spread of the coronavirus, or they boost our collective morale and determination to stop the spread. To say, 'fuck you' to the virus. All underpinned by the simple and unambiguous Government message:

Stay Home. Protect The NHS. Save Lives.

But it's hard. We are forced to accept the devastatingly real and visceral impact measured by the loss of life that we have seen, and will continue to see in the coming weeks. And then there's the never-ending, yet-to-be fully realised collateral damage. If you are anything like me, it is a slow and gradual drip of realisation at the true impact of this virus.

Our families and friends. Our health. Our society. Our liberties. Our economy. Our future. A day that punctuated such realisa- tion for me – and I expect many of you – was Mothering Sunday. This year, a day to be celebrated at distance, with a phone call, or wave to a sash-curtained window. Ironically, I was less upset that I couldn't see *my* mother – but upset that my mother couldn't see *her* 90-year-old mother. Because, being frank, at that stage of life, you never know when *that* year, is the *last* year.

Now, I have tried. But to summarise the health implications feels an insurmountable task. Yet even in these early stages, concerns are being vocalised: the rise in reported mental health problems – new and exacerbated – through instructed isolation, for instance. Ironically, this was already a problem in our pre-coronavirus congested world, which I talked about earlier in the book. The lack of NHS non-emergency services provision on patients awaiting care to help improve their quality of life. Most of all, the worrying realisation that many patients with non-coronavirus (yet still acute and serious) conditions are reluctant to access emergency services or speak to their GP. Perhaps they're worried about being infected (or infecting others) with the coronavirus, or they don't want to bother such services at a time of national crisis. I have heard all of these reasons, and more, from my patients. I tell them all, the NHS remains open. For all. It just feels a little different.

Then, of course, there's even the way in which I go about my job. In *The Secret Doctor*, you read about my life working in the city. You learned how my working day was predominantly framed by face-to-face patient consultations in the morning and afternoon – separated only by the inevitable rushed lunchtime home visit and endless paperwork. In that life, telephone consultations formed only a small part of my day. In that life, having some viral-cold and flu-like symptoms did not breed unfiltered fear, or require full personal protective equipment (PPE) – or periods of complete quarantined isolation, for that matter. At times, this instruction to self-isolate feels like something out of *The Handmaid's Tale* (if you haven't read it, now's *really* not the time to start). One to add to this book's already long list of things that medical school didn't prepare me for. Mind you, I can't judge them too harshly for that . . .

Over as little as four weeks, life as a GP has changed considerably. I can't remember the last patient I saw face to face. It must be nearly three weeks now. I spend my entire working day on the telephone (or occasionally, via video link) to patients. I do all this work remotely, at home. Our GP surgery doors, for now, essentially shut to all but essential nursing care such as administering regular anti-psychotic injections, wound dressings or urgent bloods (that are safer to have in surgery rather than in hospital). Every single clinical decision is now an intensified *risk – benefit* equation. *Risk,* being if they take this action, is their chance of catching or spreading the coronavirus higher? *Benefit,* being if they take this action, is there a chance they will stay healthier, and as a corollary, reduce their chance of being admitted to hospital or overwhelm already overwhelmed hospital services, like A&E departments?

To me, during this coronavirus crisis, the function of any GP is clear:

- To identify clinically unstable possible COVID-19 patients and refer them to COVID-19 teams
- To support more clinically stable possible COVID-19 patients in their homes
- To maintain the ongoing health of patients, despite severely restricted access to services
- To manage acute and chronic conditions in the community setting where possible
- To protect A&E departments from being overwhelmed by doing all the above
- To provide a focus for the local community if they need advice or reassurance
- To galvanise our Government message: STAY HOME. PROTECT THE NHS. SAVE LIVES

By galvanise, I mean that at times, I need, in no uncertain terms, to tell people they are being ignorant and reckless to ignore this critical message – putting the lives of others at risk – simply because they think the rules don't apply to them. We are a nation of over 66 million people. If even just 1per cent had this mind-set, it's a problem. Otherwise the coronavirus can ruthlessly spread with ease.

At least for now, due to family and health reasons, my part in the coronavirus crisis battle is confined to the telephone. There are, however, countless GPs working across multiple sites and treating COVID-19 (suspected or confirmed) patients face to face. Up and down the country, dedicated

COVID-19 *hot clinics* are being set up. At these, unwell patients with possible COVID-19 can be assessed. Any local GP can refer a patient they have already remotely assessed (by telephone or video) and suspect has COVID-19 – and importantly, *is clinically deteriorating from it.* This deterioration means that they need a face-to-face review. These clinics are staffed with allocated and volunteered GPs, nurses and other healthcare professionals who have (we hope) adequate PPE to safely perform a physical examination, take clinical observations (including oxygen saturation levels, respiratory rate, and temperature) and if needed, perform blood tests or other investigations on a potentially highly infectious patient. They do all this at selfless and conscionable risk to themselves. And not just because it's their job. But because they care. Of course, there is a natural limit to the level of care available at these clinics. If critically unwell, these patients can then be referred into hospital for further specialist care, which can, in many cases, include support on an Intensive Care Unit (ICU).

I'm conscious to avoid letting this epilogue become too *American*, with overstated outpourings of admiration – but my role as a GP needs some context in this crisis. We GPs, are just one cog in the wheel of the NHS – a cog with specific roles I've already discussed. But oh boy, there is so much more (the NHS is, after all, the fifth biggest employer in the world). There are the endless community teams from district nurses, paramedics, social workers, palliative care, and hospice teams, to all the staff keeping the social care system going from cradle to grave. In the hospitals, the list goes on. The rock stars are of course the incredible and inspiring

ICU teams, who are giving those most acutely unwell with COVID-19 the greatest chance of survival. There are the A&E department teams who are dealing both with potential COVID-19 patients, and yet still all the other routine A&E department footfall (albeit lighter in present climes). In-between these two departments are multiple medical teams running the hospital wards. There are the cancer teams, ensuring cancer care continues as best it can in such challenging times. To make all this function, there are all the other invaluable healthcare assistants, porters, catering staff, cleaning staff, administrators, receptionists, security staff, and management teams. Thousands of retired healthcare workers are also returning to the front line. And finally, let's not forget, since its inception on the 24th March 2020, the NHS volunteer scheme, that already has hundreds of thousands of people stepping up to give their time. Inspiring stuff, for even the stoniest of stony hearts. I'm sure I will have missed people and teams off – but look, you get the idea: many, many cogs, all with a shared vision of saving lives. A vision, I should add, that is shared in – and out – of this crisis. We should be very proud of our NHS. It is a national treasure.

This crisis requires me to be more critical of all my clinical decisions. Largely because I am basing them on the clinical history alone – that is, what the patient tells me – and, what I ask them. Gone are the days (for now at least) when I could physically see my patients in front of me, examine them, and take a full set of observations. Now I'm sitting with a pair of Apple iPhone earphones jammed into each ear, hunched over a NHS laptop at my kitchen table (and, more often than not, with William trying to ascend my leg). Here, I'm trying to extract as much information from the patient as possible, knowing this is going to be as good as it gets. Because as I say, I can't just get everyone to come in and see me anymore. I can't just send everyone to A&E. I can't even just send everyone to the COVID-19 hot hubs. I need to assume a higher level of clinical risk (and therefore both responsibility and culpability) to protect those services and their capacity. A risk level that goes far beyond what many GPs, I suspect, were comfortable with before this crisis. Then again, we are in exceptional times. And part of our role in them is to do just that: to absorb the risk and therefore protect the NHS.

Let's take this morning's telephone clinic. It was full of patients who suspect they have the coronavirus. Consultations like these have evolved to fall into two distinct parts. The first part is establishing the probability that they may have the coronavirus. In a way, that's been made pretty easy, with the current criteria for a suspected coronavirus infection as black and white as having a fever above 37.8 degrees and/or a new, continuous cough. There is, however, a gaping caveat to this. People with the coronavirus can have *no* symptoms, misdirecting gastrointestinal symptoms (such as diarrhoea), myalgia (muscle ache), or a sore throat, to name but a few. Reading between the lines, this all means you may have the coronavirus without even realising it. Which comes full circle to why we're all, very appropriately, instructed to stay at home. To stop the spread, and save lives.

The second part is evaluating just how unwell someone is. This is the trickier part. I need to ask the right questions. This is essential to understand, for example, how healthy their respiratory system is (which is the primary system that the coronavirus damages). *How would you describe your breathing today? Is it different from normal? Are you able to complete daily tasks as normal? Are you more breathless than normal when you exert yourself? Can you speak in full sentences? Would you say your breathing has changed? Shallower? Faster? Is there a cough? Productive? Dry? Continuous? Constant?* Then there is either the description or, via video consulting, a visualisation of the patient. *Are your lips paler or blue? Does your skin feel cool or clammy? If you place your hand on your chest, does it feel like it's moving more/faster/shallower?* These questions are endless – but all have purpose. Principally, because it's all I have. I don't have a breathing rate (there's no large scale proven, reproducible, effective, or validated way to do this remotely), oxygen saturations or heart rate. Once the information is gathered, I make a simple decision: can I manage this patient at home? And to what risk, if I misjudge it?

All this is difficult, and draining. But there are still moments of lightness, moments where I can still smile at the marvellous ridiculousness of humanity. This starts with one of my patients on this morning's telephone consultation list. Mr Green – who, like many of this morning's clinic, suspects he has mild symptoms of the coronavirus – called up with an important pharmacological question. *Will this coronavirus crisis affect the supply of my Viagra?* He is asking for a three-month supply (I suppose there are only so many puzzles you can do in isolation). I reassured him that, at present (because some medicines are indeed encountering temporary supply issues), his Viagra distribution network is not in imminent danger. I ended the call with a stark warning not to have sex if he begins feeling more breathless than usual – especially if it's before he starts.

Then there was the consultation last week from Jonny, a lovely 80-year-old chap, who called me up because he was told by his hospital specialist to get his corona care package from his GP. I checked my work emails to make sure I hadn't missed anything about corona care packages. *Ok, Jonny.* I pause, trying to find the right words. *So, did your specialist tell you what was in these care packages?* Without missing a beat, Jonny informed me that he was to get a face mask, gloves and antibacterial soap from me, his GP. Five minutes later the call ends with Jonny sadly thinking a little less of his specialist and their pipe-dream packages. This call then swiftly followed another patient's personal verruca crisis, followed by one with concerns surrounding online rumours that the 5G telecommunications networks are in fact the real cause of COVID-19. And so, just as in the rest of the book, the glorious insanity of life continues.

Because that's the reality. The wheel of life really does keep turning. Our health keeps changing. Evolving. Even the coronavirus can't stop that. Patients keep travelling on their journeys. On those journeys still appear health issues from the mundane and inconsequential, to the devastating and life threatening. It's just that now it feels slightly different. And no, I don't just mean the giant fuck-off corona-sized elephant in the corner. It's that it's a kinder wheel. Patients still call. They still share the same problems that existed in our pre-coronavirus crisis world. But now, more and more, these calls start with an apology. With an *I'm sorry to bother you at such a busy time* statement that I am quick to correct. Nobody needs to apologise. Not even my verruca man from last week. The NHS is here for everyone, all the time. That was the case before the coronavirus arrived on our shores. It will also be the case during – and after – it leaves them. There, that's my Clinton Card moment. We all just need to be prepared to take a few heavyweight punches and be knocked down the priority order for care, that's all.

There's also all the well-wishes. The *thank you for all that you're doing for us* comments that are increasingly passed to me by patients on the phone. It is so lovely. But you're speaking to a man with full-on imposter syndrome which is why my automatic response will always be that I'm just doing the same job I always did. Nothing special. There are scores of keyworkers doing so much more. That is where the praise should be directed. So that's what I tell my patients.

It feels difficult to find a note to end on. There have been so many unspoken critical and defining actions already taken during this crisis, so many incredible people (inside and outside of the NHS) who deserve recognition and praise, and so many things for us to talk – and worry – about, as we wade deeper into this crisis. None of these I can do any real justice to in the epilogue of a book about my life as a GP, some ten months before coronavirus even entered our lives. It would be rude and disrespectful to even try. The books about the coronavirus will come, and come from people who have experienced far more of it than I. But what I will not do is moan. Nor will I lament others' purported failings of our Government to act hastily enough, to choose the less effective herd immunity approach before switching to a suppression approach, or to provide enough personal protective equipment to healthcare workers. There are enough ongoing column inches in the newspapers for you to learn about that. Instead I chose to remain positive and optimistic. That we will overcome this crisis. And besides, who gets everything right? I simply don't see the need here to add my criticism when every single person is working towards the shared common national goal. PROTECT THE NHS. SAVE LIVES. In fact, I really wish at least one reporter at the daily press briefings with the Government would stand up, and at least start with a *thank you for all you are doing*, before taking their pound of editorial flesh.

I want to close by talking about *care*. Right now, we're showing each other in this country – and the rest of the world – just how much we can, and do care. It's a stripped-back, exposed, vulnerable kind of care, no longer hidden by the noise of fast-paced modern living. The coronavirus has eradicated all that noise for now. It's readjusted our focus and perspective of what's truly important in life. We are a nation that cares. Care for our family and friends. Care for our communities. Care for our keyworkers. Care for complete strangers. Care for everyone. Because we're being unified – unified to decline being taken over a barrel by the coronavirus. And all of us have a part to play in this. A positive feedback loop in which the more we all individually act, the more we all collectively want to act. Our collective health journey. A shared window for us all to peek through into the life of our society. It's a journey that has, without a doubt, injected a sense of togetherness that hasn't been seen for decades. Since War. Just like Bob Marley sang: *One Love.*

One heart. Let's get together and feel alright. Well, once social restrictions are lifted.

And besides, if there's anything that we Brits do well – it's to find light in the darkness. And right now, that's precisely what we're doing. . .

Tuesday, 1st June 2021

Even as I re-read my words, it seems strange – another lifetime even – with so much water already under the bridge. It has been an incredibly tough year, with too many lives lost too soon, as well as plenty of others whose lives have been blighted by financial instability, long Covid, or the loss of loved ones. It has been a time of collective national trauma, which we will all be recovering from for years to come.

However, there are encouraging signs. I am not only back in the GP's surgery, but am now seeing more and more patients face to face (in full PPE, but a victory nonetheless) which is fantastic. All of them – as will you – feeling like pandemic veterans. PPE, Covid-secure, Pfizer, Oxford-AstraZeneca, Anti-Vaxxers, Track and Trace, socially distancing, vaccine priority groups: all part our everyday conversation and vocabulary now. Covid-19, part of our new way of living.

Right now, there is hope. A lot of it, actually. Normality – or something close to it – appears to be fast approaching, thanks to our three lockdowns, social distancing measures and British and global vaccine programmes, which are now very much in full swing. Yes, they are by no means perfect and with clear inequalities between countries yet to be anywhere near reconciled, but still, at least it *is* swinging: not bad for a little over 12 months of work. Work that would normally take many, many years. Most importantly, Covid-related death rates and hospitalisations are significantly down. Just today, we hit zero Covid-19 deaths across the country, for the first time since the pandemic began.

But nothing is perfect and clouds intermittently seem to drift over this hope, such as new and emerging variants like the B.1.617.2 (rebranded as the *Delta* variant – and yes, even a virus gets branding nowadays) which threatens the vaccine programme's success. And if the past year has taught us anything, it's that certainty of safety is not guaranteed. This is to be expected and accepted. After all, when has it ever been guaranteed in life?

Over a year ago, I finished by saying that if there's anything we Brits do well, it's to find light in the darkness. Well, despite it all, I think we have. As a collective. And moreover, with the strength and resolve we have earned through shared hardship, I believe we will continue to brighten our futures against this virus – and any others that may decide to come for a fight.

Max.

Acknowledgements

There's a phrase by American industrialist Henry Ford that goes, *whether you think you can or you think you can't – you're right.* Basically, he's telling us all to believe in ourselves. And while I agree with him to a degree, I don't think his phrase tells us the whole story. You see, the truth is that there's often a lot of people behind that belief. Any belief for that matter.

That's what writing this book felt a little like. Sometimes, it felt like a possible process. Sometimes, entirely impossible. What has you reading *The Secret Doctor* right now, are the people behind me. They are the people who showed me to *think I can* more than to *think I can't.* They showed me belief. So, it's with great delight that I want to thank them.

To my wife, Alice, and son, William. You are the best team in the world. Even if I can't ever actually use your real names! You never failed to support my late night writing sessions – particularly when I'd come home grumpy after a particularly horrendous day in clinic and then moan about having to write that evening. You also always forgave me when I would wake you both up at 2am as I crashed into the bedroom, tripping over one of William's particularly loud toys (I'm sure left there deliberately by Alice – or William). Alice, you let me live out my bucket-list dream of writing a book. Thank you, my love. To Mum (sorry for all the swearing in it), Dad, my brother, and my wider family – many of whom don't even know about this book – thank you for always being there for me. No matter the issue, you always give me uncompromising love and support. I am very, very lucky. I can't wait to surprise you with the anonymous excitement of this book one day! As long as you don't say *I just read this really shit book* . . . and unknowingly show me mine.

To my patients. You are the true unsung heroes of this book. Never to be known. Never to be named. Never to be aware. But still, thank you. Thank you for all that you've given me. My life is richer for knowing each one of you. Even those of you who drive me fucking mad. (You know who you are.) I just hope that I give back to you in an equal measure. It's been a pleasure and privilege to be part of your health journey.

To my publisher, Bonnier. There are so many people to recognise and thank here. But let me start with Oliver Holden-Rea, my first editor and the man who opened the door to this writing opportunity. I say first editor as he decided to bugger off to another exciting publishing job opportunity right before the final copy! Oli, you took me right up to the try line (I love rugby, sorry) with your vision, passion, and belief. I am so grateful, pal. But this meant I was therefore lucky to have a second incredible editor take me under their wing. This was Susannah Otter. With inspiring experience, passion, and attention to detail, Susannah, you got *The Secret Doctor* over the try line. I couldn't have done it without you. Thank you for showing me ways that I didn't think possible to make the book as enjoyable as it could be for anyone reading it.

Behind the more public heroes of Oli and Susannah are the unsung members of Bonnier. From the incredible graphic design and illustration team who designed the brilliant book cover and jacket, to my copyeditor Jane who made me laugh out loud with her eagle-eye comments to some of the less savoury statements in this book, and who did a lot of fact checking against some of the medical language I used. To Nikki Mander, my publicist at Bonnier, thanks for getting this book to as many people as possible and always being so enthusiastic over email! And to the assistant editors, Madiya and Sophie – and the sales teams – a heartfelt *thank you all.* Finally, to the legal team (*cough, who I hope not to need again),* thank you. Writing this book sometimes felt like a tightrope between humour and being struck off as a doctor. I hope, with your help that I landed on the right side . . .

Henry Ford was right in his phrase – belief is powerful. It was belief that imagined this book. But it was all these wonderful people who made that imagination, a reality.

Thank you.

Max